A SENSE OF PURPOSE

A Sense
of Purpose
Recollections

Suzy Eban

Maps by Martin Gilbert

HALBAN
LONDON

First published in Great Britain by
Halban Publishers Ltd
22 Golden Square
London W1F 9JW
2008
www.halbanpublishers.com

ISBN 978 1 905559 11 4

Three chapters, *An Ismailia childhood, Cairo* and *Ismailia revisited*
appeared in an earlier form in *The New Yorker.*

Typeset by Spectra Titles, Norfolk
Printed in Great Britain by
MPG Books Ltd., Bodmin, Cornwall

Contents

Acknowledgements

I am grateful to my family and friends who surrounded me with their encouragement, and especial thanks go to Gina Fromer for her support in the publishing of *A Sense of Purpose*. Particular mention must also be made of my niece Michèle Klein. My children, Eli and Gila, followed my work with total filial interest.

My warm thanks to Ellen Hashiloni, my bilingual secretary, who worked devotedly with me for many years according to my pace and time possibilities. Also thanks to Geeta Gariby for her close association with my writing.

I owe particular gratitude to my publisher, Peter Halban, who took on my story as an informal saga of my life and the fifty-seven years I shared with my husband, Abba Eban. It was a pleasure to work with my very caring and able editor, Judy Gough, who had a sense of participation in my work.

I am moved and deeply grateful for the two special maps created by Sir Martin Gilbert which is a most generous token of his friendship for my late husband and an honour for me.

Foreword

Born in Egypt, I was brought up in the spirit of Hebrew Palestine. I lived in the Middle East but was given a French education. I married an Englishman and we both became Israelis. Perhaps such drastic extremes need no explanation in a portrayal of an Israeli life, a life where one encounters people who still speak more languages than anywhere else in the region.

The Israeli, before and after Independence, was in the majority a bicultural person although Hebrew pervaded our society. For the masses of newcomers, Israel was not only a home of their own, a humble shelter, it was also the space where their past lingered, was rejected or utilized for the purpose of inspiring new social creation

None of us can ever forget that for hundreds of thousands of displaced people, Israel was a refuge from haunting memories, a place to savour the taste of liberty even within hardship. For others, driven by ideals and not necessity, Israel was a renewed historical space for their own values and potential.

Everyone has his or her story in this Land. This one is my own.

Suzy Eban
Herzlia, September 2008

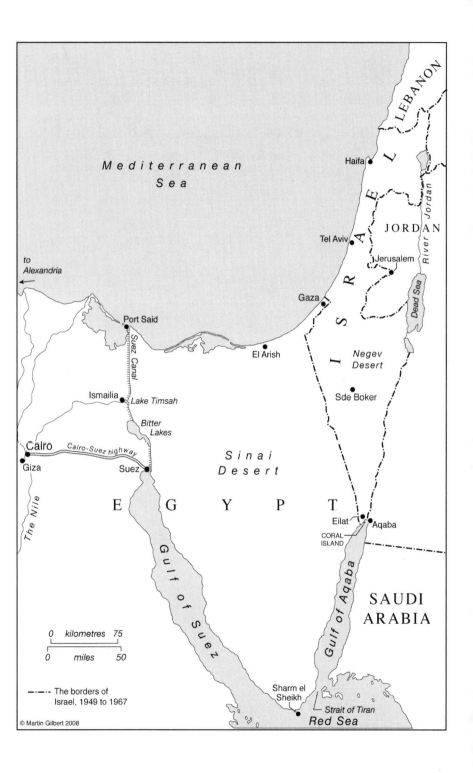

LEBANON

Mediterranean
Sea

to
Alexandria

Haifa

ISRAEL

JORDAN

Port Said

Suez Canal

Tel Aviv

Jerusalem

River Jordan

Dead Sea

Gaza

El Arish

Negev
Desert

Ismailia

Lake Timsah

Sde Boker

Bitter
Lakes

Cairo

Cairo-Suez highway

Sinai
Desert

Giza

Suez

The Nile

E   G   Y   P   T

Eilat

Aqaba

CORAL
ISLAND

Gulf of Suez

Gulf of Aqaba

SAUDI
ARABIA

0   kilometres   75

0   miles   50

—·—·— The borders of
Israel, 1949 to 1967

© Martin Gilbert 2008

Sharm el
Sheikh

Strait of Tiran

Red Sea

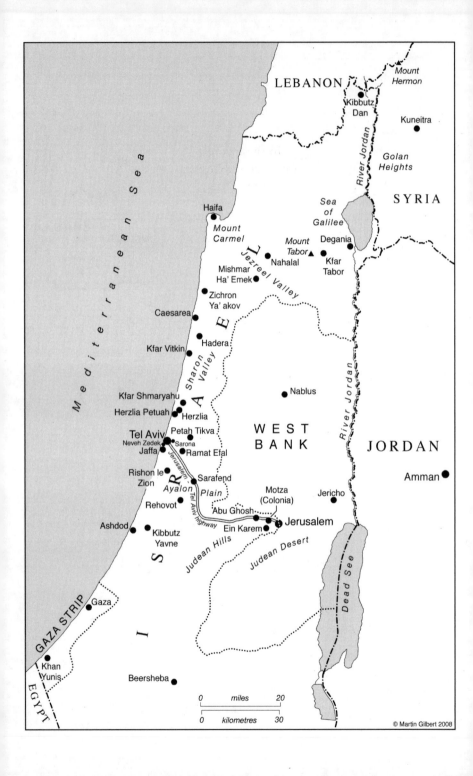

© Martin Gilbert 2008

To the memory
of my beloved husband
Abba Eban

I

An Ismailia childhood

Ismailia, an Egyptian town once called "The Emerald of the Desert", is located halfway along the western bank of the Suez Canal where it enters Lake Timsah. My family left Ismailia for Cairo when I was still a teenager and the next time I set eyes on the place of my birth, just after the Six Day War, I was looking at it through field glasses from across the water. Standing with my husband and a group of Israeli soldiers on the eastern bank of the Canal, Ismailia appeared dusty and utterly abandoned. An ominous silence had settled over the place, and the buildings on the empty beach stood with shutters closed. Dark dredgers and cranes floated idle in the port with no workers in sight.

Behind the old Suez Canal Company houses – all with red-tiled roofs, off-white walls and balconies with terracotta-painted slats – were untidy grey blocks, buildings that had been built since we had left to accommodate the population increase. Just about the only moving object was a black and white buoy trembling gently, midway across the Canal, like the machinery of an old clock. I began to tell the group something about the town, pointing out various features. Straight ahead was a steep road climbing up to a hospital once run by an order of nuns. To the right, a statue of the Virgin Mary, precariously standing on the edge of a roof, looked down on overgrown gardens.

Before long, I realized that my memories of Ismailia belonged to another era and were comprised of moments that had no particular relevance to these young men. These were soldiers who guarded fortifications and patrolled night and day, waiting, listening and staring through their glasses far inland – searching the flat plain for the black dots of Egyptian fellahin, or peasants, moving across the sands. Among Israelis, the Canal was known merely as a boundary on the maps of battles between Arabs and Jews. Aside from my own family, it seemed that no one remembered the Canal in its days of serenity and prosperity…

I was born at home. Home births were customary for the small European community of Ismailia. My mother's younger sister Rachel came over from Palestine for my birth, but it was my father who was actually present, as he was at each of our births.

I was often told that my parents were very pleased with my arrival. My brother Nachman preceded me by four years and two girls, Tsilla and Aura followed me – all three girls born in the 1920s. But I was the new experience after a boy. My parents called me Shoshana. A while later my name became Suzy both within the family circle and outside, as if it were a snappier way to call me to order.

One of my earliest memories is of someone placing my doll's cot, a charmingly crafted object of light wood, on the floor directly in front of me. There were white tulle curtains falling to the sides and a blue satin bow perched on top. Inside this creation were frilly pillows, a lace-edged bedcover and, of course, my doll. I can't remember her name for it was the staging that was by far the most exciting part of her, but I remember training the doll into the functionality of daily life, tenderly feeding her, caring for her and rocking her to sleep as Tsilla, my chief playmate, stood by.

In another memory, Tsilla and I are standing in front of what seemed at the time to be a huge curtain – as if meant for actors on a stage. We are playing with those toys that children pull along by a cord, under the patronizing gaze of grown-ups. We play in a one dimensional way: back and forth. I was a year older than Tsilla and the boredom this engendered rendered me semi-conscious.

How far back can childhood memory go? One summer day, while swimming, I kicked my leg against the pool's wall in a long, underwater slide and, coming up, for air I had the sudden sense that I was sliding out of my mother. I was staggered by this bewildering click of the mind, and attained what seemed to me to be an equivalent of the primeval cry. Could this, then, be my first, indeed my very first, sensation-memory?

My childhood was uneventful, save for having all the usual diseases at the proper times, except for mumps, which of course I had to contract right after my honeymoon. I did have trachoma at a tender age, a common disease amongst the people of Egypt that was not meant to reach the hygiene-conscious Europeans. My mother thought that the nursemaid must have removed the net over the perambulator during some of the nonchalant hours we spent in the verdant gardens of the green oasis that was Ismailia.

We lived on the Place Champollion, Ismailia's central square, named after the nineteenth-century French Egyptologist who decoded ancient hieroglyphics. Two identical houses, the doctor's and ours, both belonging to the Compagnie Universelle du Canal Maritime de Suez, dominated the block. My father was not directly employed by the Canal Company, rather he managed one of its suppliers, the Electricity and Ice Supply Company, whose headquarters were located in Alexandria. He had been appointed to this position at the age of twenty-two after finishing his engineering studies in Nancy, France, and our house came with the job.

What a house it was! It had balconies running the whole length of the second floor, supported by narrow wooden pillars that forked at the top, like upturned rakes. The pillars accentuated the exceptional height of the rooms which had been so designed to best suit the climate. There was parquet flooring throughout, including the bedrooms, and after a waxing the house smelled of turpentine for days. It was only as an adult, looking through one of my mother's old recipe books, that I discovered how this waxing was done. Two kilos of yellow wax added to two litres of turpentine and one litre of benzine were melted over steam and left to cool. The mixture was then spread thinly on the floors and allowed to dry for an entire day, during which we were sternly warned to step around the floor edges only. After twenty-four hours, our servant Ibrahim would take a stick weighted down by a big, padded square of lead, and push it back and forth, polishing every inch of the floors. It was a tremendous feat for one man. Ibrahim lived in what was known as the Arab Village in Ismailia and came to our home each day, staying until after dinner.

My father was a great buyer of oriental carpets. Every now and then a cartful of these carpets would be brought to the house and he would examine them out on the terrace. The whole process was laborious and time-consuming. All of the home's furnishings, later discarded as unsuitable when my parents moved back to Palestine in 1947, were quite remarkable. My mother's *petit salon* featured a sofa that had been ordered specially from the French Alliance School in Palestine. It was covered with thick, hand-woven, red cotton with a central pattern in gold thread, and the walls of the *petit salon* were decorated in a thin red-and-gold striped fabric to match. It was hard to tell whether the decor was a product of the European idea of the East or vice versa. Most of the furniture in the room had been carved in Damascus with countless intricate wood cuts set in lacy geometrical patterns. Then there were some small oriental chairs inlaid with mother-of-pearl that were dreadfully uncomfortable and on which nobody ever sat, and a large, wall mirror. It was an awful lot of orientalism for one small room.

Across the entrance hall stood the *grand salon*, which had a different character altogether. There was an elaborate cornice and the salon was overlooked by a crystal chandelier. There were copies of Louis XVI armchairs with down-stuffed seats and ormolu ornaments flanked the mantelpiece. The fireplace, a copy of the Paris original, was never used, since the only wood in Ismailia available for chopping was in the Bois de Boulogne. It was into this room that my parents brought their guests of all nationalities: Ali Bey Leheta, who was the Member of Parliament for Port Said; various Swiss businessmen connected with my father's company; a Greek banker; British officers; French *sous-chefs* whose wives used to leave cards in advance of their calling and, of course, a number of family and friends from Palestine.

The terrace floor outside our windows creaked at night and we children would tell each other that somebody was hiding there – most likely Zamaluti, the lovable thief of Egyptian stories, who was so clever at fooling the police. Every night, the eerie sounds brought with them a renewed certainty of his presence and when we were told to undress and go to bed, my sisters and I stood transfixed, listening for evidence of his presence.

Our fascination with Egyptian folklore was unusual, for everything in the little town – the population was about 15,000 then – bore the authority and taste of the Canal Company. We lived in Egypt and yet apart from it. In the administration, all senior personnel were French, although in lower echelons there were Italians and Greeks. My best friend was the daughter of a Dutch pilot named Boon.

There seemed to be no socializing between the Arabs of Ismailia and the Europeans who were brought there, in one way or another, by the Canal Company. French bureaucrats nostalgically recreated a Club Hippique and promenaded in the Bois de Boulogne. British officers and soldiers from the nearby Moascar Army Camp sailed down Lake Timsah from their Yacht Club. An Italian colony with its own school for girls run by the Franciscan Order, a Greek colony with its own church, and even a lone White Russian princess (from whom Mother took painting lessons, copying languid scenes that looked like faded Watteaus) all lived their independent lives. But for the French enterprise, we all believed, there would have been nothing worthwhile in the eastern part of Egypt. It would have remained another of those vast expanses which had existed in the country across the centuries: roamed by jackals and trekked by occasional caravans.

We were never ever left alone, be it outside or at home. It seemed that there were always too many dangers. We would often see Bedouins riding through Ismailia on their camels and were warned to stay away, because Bedouins were known to catch little girls with lassos. Once, when they were in town, I hit on the idea of walking backwards so as to be able to see any potential lasso and avoid it. The house was always scrupulously locked at night, with Ibrahim closing all the heavy French shutters on both floors. He was as anxious to have the house locked up as we were, for he believed with uncompromising certainty in afrits, powerful demons from Islamic mythology, which he had apparently discovered once at the bottom of our staircase. Some years later, he was dismissed for over-indulging in hashish.

My siblings and I all went to French schools: my brother Nachman, until the age of twelve when he was sent to boarding school in England, went to the Order of Friars of Ploermel across the street and my two sisters and I went to the nuns of the Order of St Vincent de Paul. The schools were run in the colonial spirit, with little relevance to their country of residence, and not one word of Arabic was ever taught. We studied Ronsard, Boileau, Montaigne, the history of France and the glories of Romanesque and Gothic architecture with European nuns. We learned all the *départements*, *sous-départements*, and *préfectures* of France, along with the French rivers and the French colonies.

In the beginning, making the transition to French from Hebrew (which we spoke at home at the insistence of our parents) had not been easy. When Tsilla began school, she was seized by such exasperation at not being able to understand anyone, that she opened all twelve taps in the lavatories, causing complete havoc. I was called in by the Mother Superior to translate her castigations into Hebrew for my sister.

It must have been no less traumatic for me to enter a French school at the age of five, not knowing the language. Perhaps this explains why I can't remember what happened to me in those first weeks, or how I felt about it. All I remember is that at one point, I expressed my own frustration by running away from school. As I ran, an Arab man on a bicycle pulled up next to me and began to ask irrelevant questions that frightened me. When I got home, my mother was quite astounded to see me turn up so soon after I'd left. All I could say was that I had simply found the school door open.

Once a year, the President of the Canal Company would visit and the school would undergo a thorough overhaul in preparation. I distinctly remember one such visit by the Marquis de Vogüé, a white-haired gentleman who wore spats and carried a stick with a gold knob. He was accompanied by the Canal's *agent superieur*, the Baron de Benoît, who also wore spats. As they entered each classroom, the students rose for inspection, and the two looked us over as though we were well-bred pets kept by the Canal Company at a perfect standard of conventional upbringing. This girl or that would be pointed out as "The daughter of so-and-so" and of course we would step forward and curtsy, only to be dismissed after a few questions.

There were other special visits, as when General Maxime Weygand or former President Gaston Doumergue came with his wife, the novelist Delly. There was great excitement: her books could be found in the school library and were much sought after during the time allotted to us for the reading of novels. They contained stories of love, pure and romantic, shared by people so favoured by nature that they seemed unreal, but when we finally saw Delly we almost collapsed. This dumpy little *bourgeoise*, with her dumpy little husband – no matter if he *had* been President of France – could this truly be the author of tales brimming with such beauty and passion?

The school was built in the shape of a large quadrangle and contained a broad inner courtyard, where we played *la marelle* (hopscotch) with a broken piece of terrazzo tile. There were classrooms along three sides of the courtyard, the fourth containing the nuns' quarters, with a garden and a passageway leading to the chapel. The school gardener was an Arab called François whom we assumed was a Christian. At any rate, the nuns and the lay teachers spoke to him in French. In the courtyard stood a few old eucalyptus trees – one with such a vast circumference it must have been there in 1869 on the day the Empress Eugènie, sailing nearby in a great convoy of celebrities and crowned heads from Port Said to Suez, inaugurated the canal that her subject, Ferdinand de Lesseps, had built.

My sisters and I were allowed to miss chapel, coming to school every morning at ten past eight, but we stayed in class for the hour of catechism without participating. Catholicism was the Canal Company's official religion. There was chapel every morning, prayers before going home for lunch at twelve and on starting again at two, and more after we had gone home at four. Once a week, an abbé with a thick Marseillais accent heard mid-morning confessions of tardy homework from the less conscientious pupils.

Academic excellence was emphasized at the Order, and its message instilled through fear. Every day after lunch, without fail, I recited the lessons for that afternoon to my mother, the emphasis being not that I comprehended them but that I could rattle whatever it was off by heart as rapidly as possible. Our social behaviour mattered no less than our academic records and everything was divided between *bien élevé* and *mal élevé*. And then, of course, there was sewing. We learned to do the tiniest of *coutures anglaises* (what the English ironically call "French seams") as well as embroidery. In our later years at school, we were also given an "ethics" class by the Mother Superior, her handsome face hidden under a white, starched, wing-like cornette. As a tiny girl, I was once consoled and kissed under that cornette after I had fallen down, and I remember feeling as if I might suffocate in the midst of a glowing, white light.

One pretty nun who taught us English seemed to take a special dislike to me. One day, as we were preparing banners for a religious procession, she dipped a brush in a bucket of glue and, with a brisk up and down movement of her wrist, spread the glue over part of my face, getting some of it in my eye. This sudden and harsh attack took me by surprise and I can still feel the hurt today. There was a tap in the classroom and I ran over to wash off the glue, trying all the while not to cry but rather to seem as amused as the others were. I did not report the incident at home, of course; children in those days accepted public humiliation in a way they never would today, and I doubt my mother would have confronted the teacher to demand an explanation had I told her about it. Years later, I met one of the nuns from my school at the Hospice of St Vincent in Jerusalem. She told me that the pretty nun had been shot during the trouble in 1956 after the Canal was nationalized but that the Mother Superior had made her way safely to Beirut.

Near our school was a park whose sweet-water canal provided the city's drinking water. A charming little ferry, really just a large wooden box pulled by a clanking chain, ran across this narrow canal and the chain splashed back into the cool water as we pulled to get to the other side, where palm trees nodded over flower beds and wide green lawns. The verdure was an enchanting deception, for all around the city and its lake, which provided some consolation for the landscape, was nothing but desert. Dunes, sensually curved by the wind, ran right down to the water. Their sand was fine and pale, a superb balance of ochres and white, and it was a joy to slide from the top to the water's edge. Our antics spoiled the dunes and then we went away, but when we came back every grain seemed to have been put back into place.

Beyond the sweet-water canal, at the end of a main artery called Muhammad Ali Street, stretched the Arab Village. It was a dirty place where plaster flaked off the walls of the houses. Arabs went about in *ghallabiyehs* (we children were surprised they were wearing pyjamas in the daytime), as they attended to the small commerce of such places. Within the Village were to be found revolting apparitions, such as toothless beggars with pus-ridden eyes, blotches, scabs and fly-covered faces. The men we saw pulling barges of cement or building materials along the canal, wearing thick harnesses to protect their skin from the ropes, came from this part of town, as did Ibrahim.

Every May, on the Egyptian holiday of Sham-el-Nessim, the shops would fill up with garishly decorated sugar dolls, and Ibrahim would always bring us one. The doll had red cheeks and phenomenally generous breasts on top of a body made out of a large sugar cone. Barren Arab women would visit the small mausoleum of Sheikh Ennedek – a saintly Frenchman who converted to Islam in the time of Napoleon's conquest of Egypt – because it was believed that their fertility could be restored there. Resting on a sand ridge that seemed rather high above ground for such a flat landscape, the shrine overlooked Lake Timsah. Chickens strutted among people and litter, and ibis, perched on the backs of emaciated cows and water buffaloes, pecked flies off the beasts. Little Arab girls, the rims of their eyes blackened by kohl and the palms of their hands reddened with henna, ran about in shiny long dresses, many of them in a bright colour known today as shocking pink, by French Ismailia as *rose arabe* and which should be found unacceptable in any time or place.

My sisters and I, in contrast, were required to wear uniforms: pleated blue serge in the winter – heavy, cumbersome and itchy – and yellow-edged blue and white checked cotton in spring and summer, the latter with elbow-length sleeves and white piqué collars and cuffs that were most impractical in the heat. We also wore broad-brimmed straw hats, over which Mother insisted that we wear a pale green veil to protect our skin from freckles. I don't remember the other girls setting out like that – or getting freckles, for that matter – but Mother's authority was such that we never questioned anything she said.

As I look through the family albums I see how stereotypical the pictures of us are. We were always out-of-doors, often with some antiquity to be found behind us, left over from the time of the construction of the Suez Canal in the nineteenth century. Sometimes the photographer had us all standing in a straight line or grouped together; sometimes we are sitting one at a time in the rattan armchair that had been sent up through the Canal from China. Taking a picture then was an act and not a happening, and we look like a still-life that has been placed there to be painted. We are summed up by our disparities: the tall parents and the small children, the old and the young, the family and the guests.

Oh, how these pictures remind me of the fun details in clothes and the customs of dressing at the time! How amusing it is today, when clothes are stripped of all such workmanship, to think of the trouble taken over soldier-like rows of buttons, each sewn on by hand, not to mention the hand-stitched button-holes. I could almost count them on my aunt Rachel's dress all the way from the side of her neck down to her hip, and a similar number on Mother's dark dress, some in front and a whole line of them round her waistband. I wore handmade lace collars and bows in my hair as big as my face. Even now I can hear the crisp swish of taffeta ribbon curled smoothly round a thick wisp of hair, then plumped up over my head whilst I stood absolutely still. Mother's tea-party hat was made of a delicate, stiffened lace, with a halo-like brim through which the light filtered gently over her face. There were hats skimming the eyes, high button shoes, scalloped pinafores and more.

There is one picture taken by my father of my mother and the four children: the three of us girls with apple-cheeks and straight, short haircuts and Nachman in a white sailor suit (I don't know whther it is because the Canal Company was called the "Maritime Company" that he was always nautically outfitted). My mother is in one of the low-waisted dresses of the 1920s, her black hair pulled back. My baby sister Aura sits on her lap and stares perkily ahead whilst holding on to Mother's big rope of oval ivory beads with her little hand, as if clinging on to a lifeline; you can sense their tactility – an echo of our childhood.

In another picture taken in Paris, we girls not only have identical short haircuts, but we also have the same knee-high silk stockings with the same intricate band of design at the top. How I used to resent my family's way of shopping! As clothing choices in Ismailia were almost non-existent, we always bought during our trips abroad and always in threes. We would march into a place and come out with the same item sized to fit each one of us. My parents beamed with pride whenever we were lumped together as "*les petites*" or later "*les trois petites Ambaches*", the latter being my maiden name. We three sisters seemed eternally locked into one unit known as "*les enfants*", and it appeared to me to be almost impossible to escape it, or to be, on occasion, known as an individual.

My first attempt to venture out of the "system" was in Milan, when my sisters and I were to choose our own individual, party-dress. My parents came with us to what I remember as a large, empty room with a parquet floor, decorated in the traditional European drawing-room style. Surrounded by mirrored walls, some youthful styles were modelled for us. Tsilla, always very good at clothes, chose with immediate decisiveness a real "little angel's" dress made of petrol-blue silk with a handmade lace collar. I realized she had pre-empted everybody else's selection by choosing the nicest, dreamiest dress there, so I said in defeat that I would design my own. It turned out to be a graceless creation, as if the dissent was due to serve me right.

Sometimes, if we had visitors from other cities, my father would ask the company for its motor launch, *La Fauvette* (The Warbler). It was festively outfitted with white scalloped awnings and furniture covered in white, and the brass in the cabin was very shiny. We would travel up and down the Canal, timing our trip between ships. Even in winter, we children preferred to stay out on deck, drinking hot, sweet, milky tea, our eyes stinging from winds that seemed cold by our semi-tropical standards, and the white-lettered, navy-blue pennant of the Canal Company flapping above us.

On our more usual outings, my father would take us for a drive along the Canal. He owned the first private car in Ismailia – a Chevrolet – which he learned to drive by reading a manual and practising in the empty streets. There was not much choice of route. One could either go south towards Suez, along a road sporadically lined with eucalyptus trees, or north towards Port Said (where once a year our Italian music teacher used to exhibit his students' talents to a mixed assortment of parents both from the Canal Company and the world of commerce). We used to stop at the monument of Djebel Mariam, built in the mid-twenties to honour those who had fallen in the desert during the First World War. Out of nowhere rose two huge, tapering walls of stone and concrete, representing the continents of Africa and Asia with the sky seen between them symbolizing the Canal. My sisters and I would run between these walls, fascinated by the cavernous echoes of our shrieks. On windy days I would cling to the walls as the clouds sped across the corridor of blueness above and made me dizzy.

The roads all along the Canal were mere ribbons of asphalt laid atop the sand. After windstorms, the sand would so entirely cover sections of the roads that they seemed to disappear. At the end of our rides, towards sunset, we often bought bouri, a Mediterranean fish, from men in feluccas, after shouting to them across the water, "*Fi samak?*" (Do you have fish?) In winter, when it got dark early, we could only see their lanterns, and we would have to yell and yell just to get the men out from under the tarpaulins. In the dark, big ships beamed their harsh lights across the whole width of the Canal and ahead of their passage. It was better to be driving in the same direction, otherwise their oncoming lights would blind us and my father would have to stop and wait until the ships had passed.

Arriving home from a drive, my father would withdraw to his study and spend the rest of the evening with his stamp collection. He sometimes rewarded us children with a glimpse of his extraordinary Middle Eastern stamps, our favourites those from Egypt. He was very proud of the King Fuad stamps, with the King depicted three-quarter length and with his moustache waxed *à la turque*, commemorating the opening of Port Fuad in 1926. My father had attended the ceremony which was held in a tent and where, he reported to his wide-eyed children, the men wore top hats. There were also stamps commemorating the Graf Zeppelin's flight over Egypt in 1931. Airmail had been inaugurated in Egypt only a short while before, part of the new "air consciousness" of the 1930s.

One summer, we took a cabin on Lake Timsah, near the city's beach. This was one of the few places where Europeans and Arabs mixed. The water near the shoreline became very dirty at times, making it impossible for us to swim there even in the despair of the sultriest days. (The Canal Company eventually decided to build its own beach, with asbestos huts that could be manoeuvered to block the sun, and when it was finished a luminous cleanliness reigned everywhere.) From the beach, we would wave at people on the decks of ships sailing through the Canal, and as they waved back to us, I remember feeling left behind somehow. After each ship passed, the water drawing away simultaneously from the two shores created a powerful swoosh that was just about the only authoritative sound one ever heard from Nature in that place.

Both Lake Timsah and the Bitter Lakes, further south, were waiting stations for ships, since there, unlike in the Canal, they could pass each other freely. Small convoys of ships proceeding in one direction would wait on the lakes for convoys going in the opposite direction to leave the rest of the Canal clear. Ismailia had no international commerce or trade, only a great deal of maritime traffic. According to Ferdinand de Lesseps's original plan, it was meant to be the equal of Suez and Port Said, but in fact it has remained administrative and residential into the twenty-first century. No passengers ever came ashore and no cargo was ever unloaded, even from ships moored in the Lake. All the children in Ismailia had little albums cataloguing the flags of maritime nations, and we would scan the horizons for signs of rare ones. Bored by the frequency with which the P&O (Peninsular and Oriental) line plied our waters, we all relished the appearance of some South American flag, and our eyes would follow it eagerly over the trail of foam.

My mother and father had both been born in Ottoman Palestine, their parents having immigrated in the 1880s, when the first Jewish quarters were being built around Jaffa and outside the walls of Jerusalem. We were living in Egypt because of my father's work, but our roots and culture lay north of Sinai, and the language of that world was Hebrew. In fact, I knew no other language until I went to school and, just as the knowledge of Hebrew drew me closer to the people around me in later years, it separated me from the other children when I started school. At home, we had private teachers brought in from Palestine who lived with us and whose main qualifications were that they did not know a word of any other language, thus assuring that only Hebrew would be spoken. Every day, my father received his Hebrew newspaper from Palestine. We children learned Chaim Bialik's poems in Hebrew and Sh. L. Gordon's (known as Shalag) commentaries on the Bible, just as they did in Palestine, and we sang Hebrew songs that were sung in Palestine, such as "*Hapilu*" and "*Kinneret*".

There is an old photograph of one such tutor named Shlomit, who came to us when I was five and stayed a good number of years. She drilled us so well that at Passover I recited the *Had Gadya* (one of the songs in the Passover Haggadah), in Aramaic in one faultless go and my father rewarded me with a pound. I promptly told him I would buy Shlomit a car with it. In the picture I have, she looks amused as she strikes a kind of self-hugging pose. It is a gesture of coquetry and fun that I like because I remember everybody else around as being so serious – especially my mother who was dedicated to the graceful fulfilment of daily life and the organization of a large household. We had three tutors over the years but when I was fourteen the tutoring stopped since my siblings and I could no longer cope with Hebrew studies on top of all the work they gave us in school. By then we were speaking in French among ourselves most of the time. It could not be helped – after all, it was the language in which we studied and that which we heard everywhere outside our home.

The greatest complication in our household was trying to run the kitchen according to Jewish dietary laws and in teaching new cooks the rules. Every bit of meat, in order to be kosher, had to be shipped in from Cairo and in the summer, it often arrived in an unsuitable condition. Nevertheless my mother held fast to her religious beliefs, and my father went along with her. We had two sets of cutlery and china, one for dairy and one for meat meals, and even two kitchens for the cooking. There was a small synagogue in the village, with just about enough men to form a *minyan* (ten adult men), but we never went, for it was not within walking distance of our home and driving on the Sabbath was forbidden. My mother kept the Sabbath as rigorously as it had been kept during her pious upbringing in Palestine: candles at sunset on Friday, no travelling, no writing and no handling of money. She observed important religious holidays for one day, as in Palestine, not for two, as in the Diaspora. This distinction was very important to her.

She missed her family terribly and relatives from Palestine often came to stay with us. Sometimes we went to Palestine to visit my grandparents and the first time for me was when I was six or seven years old. These trips were great adventures. My maternal grandparents lived near Jerusalem in Motza, a tiny settlement in the Judean hills that they had helped to found, and my father's parents lived near Jaffa, in Neveh Zedek (the Jewish quarter established by Ezrat Yisrael – a welfare society – in 1887). We would set out in the dark to catch the midnight train leaving from Kantarah, north of Ismailia on the western side of the Canal.

Tucked into my berth, I could barely sleep for excitement as the train swayed across Sinai. Through the night the train made a number of stops, but they were only checkpoints from which crews were sent out to maintain the track, clearing off the ever-invading sands. Then, early the next morning, there would be shouts of "El Arish!" at the first sighting of that port on the Sinai Mediterranean coast, and like a miracle we were speeding along in the early sunlight past clusters of palm trees on a sandy shore and looking out on to a broad, cerulean sea. People don't know of this journey now. The railway has not been in operation since Israel's War of Independence in 1948, and with each succeeding outburst of fighting in Sinai, more and more of the old tracks have been dismantled by one army or the other.

2

In old Palestine

Bleary-eyed and excited from the dusty train ride through Sinai, on arrival I was always immediately ordered to a grey, galvanized bathtub on the stark cement terrace at the back of the house. Sliding into the water, I would gaze at the green parasol above me, formed by the criss-crossing of a squat olive tree's small, blunt, silvery leaves. The delicious smell of burning wood drifted out from under bricks supporting the large tank full of boiling water next to me.

No contrast could have been greater than the one between the pampered life of Ismailia and that "other world" of Palestine. A donkey, prodded by an Arab with a stick, went back and forth between a five-metre deep pump on the steep hillside of the house and the kitchen, carrying a pair of carefully balanced jute sacks containing shiny four-gallon cans of water for our baths and household use. For our drinking water, Maazuza, our faithful Arab servant, brought us a daily *jara* of crystal water from a nearby well in the valley. Making her way through dry, unkempt vegetation, she carried her head taut and straight under the large earthenware container which she rested with masterful balance on a cloth folded thickly over the white veil covering her head and shoulders.

I can see myself today, looking out through the iron bars of my grandparents' bedroom window and across to the hill opposite Motza where the Arab village of Colonia, so named by the

Romans, still stood.* The vine terraces across the valley were bordered by long, stone walls formed by interlocking chips of rock. Soft light filtered in through the window screens. Beyond them was violent sunshine, the hum of crickets, and the weight of summer aromas emanating from the heated secretions of pine bark, wild sage, and other tough little bushes whose leaves would scent your skin with a fresh fragrance when crushed between your fingers. A bowl of Mediterranean fruit always stood cooling on the window sill: figs and plums from the family grove and grapes covered with a thin white dust, a distillation of that landscape.

Plain oil lamps hung on the whitewashed walls of the stone house. There were no pictures, due to the strict Orthodox Jewish tradition that forbids the depiction of human likenesses. The arid whiteness of terrazzo tiled floors was everywhere until you came into the family room, where a floor of black and ochre arabesques formed an oasis of colour with the translucent green of the domed oil lamp above the dining table. It was within this radius of illumination and under its halo of intimate protection that family news was discussed and letters read and re-read during the long, quiet evenings. Colourless schnapps from my great-uncle Yerachmiel's winery was on the table, and warm tints of brown cognac and golden torte would fill the room with soft, welcoming shadows. It was always exceptionally dark outside, and in such an isolated place visitors would call out to identify themselves before stepping through the door.

There were only a few families in this valley, no more than a total of fifty people, from the Makleffs near the bend in the main road with its small stone bridge, to our family higher up the hill where my grandfather Mikhel and his brother Yerachmiel lived. Yerachmiel was the village *Mukhtar*, or chief, and the Arabs called him *Hawaja Rahamim*, *Hawaja* being the Arabic equivalent of

---

* 800 Roman soldiers established a settlement called Colonia around Motza after the destruction the Second Temple in 70 AD.

"Mister", and *rahamim* the Hebrew word for "compassion". It was a lovably, indigenous and bilingual tribute. Next door to our family estate was the home of farmer Broza, who had studied botany and agriculture in Russia and who played the violin, an instrument rarely seen during the immigration of the early twentieth century. In an old faded portrait, Mr Broza looks uncannily like a Chagall fiddler. In addition to no running water, there was no electricity, radio or telephone in those days and so, after dinner, the grown-ups would continue to sit around the table and chat, concluding the meal with glasses of tea so hot they had to be held in embossed metal holders brought over from Eastern Europe. Finally, their prayer of giving thanks after the meal rose from the table in faint unison.

My great-uncle Yerachmiel had complete faith in the story in the Book of Zechariah that forecast the Messiah would enter Jerusalem from the west while riding a white donkey. Since the only road serving Jerusalem from the west was our own Motza thoroughfare, Yerachmiel would seat himself on a rock at the roadside whenever an inner voice told him that the Messiah might be coming. It was neither pretence nor act, but simply part of his strong, sustaining faith.

One day Yerachmiel saw six men wrapped in white prayer shawls coming around the curve of the main road. He gasped at the vision, thinking them to be the men who would precede the Messiah, but when they greeted him, he learned that they had come all the way from Safed – one of the four religious centres in the Holy Land – to meet him, "the Saint from Motza", of whose many good deeds they had heard a great deal.

My grandfather Mikhel had his own earnest beliefs, though his centred around the dream of a Jewish State. With full commitment, Mikhel and his wife, my grandmother Gittel, had established themselves in Palestine solely by their own efforts. Mikhel had led the way, identifying with the aspiration to renew the Jewish homeland, and his family followed later. When Theodor

Herzl proclaimed his vision of a Jewish State in 1897, Mikhel and Gittel had already been part of the "Return to the Land" for twelve years. I can hear my grandfather now, telling the story of Herzl's visit to Motza in 1898. He described how the founder of Zionism had walked on the soil of Palestine as if he were its uncrowned king and had planted a cedar upon the hill at Arza to commemorate his visit. Although the tree turned out not to be a cedar, and all that remains of it today is a mere stump, it became one of the many symbols of the Jewish State. Every President of Israel has since climbed that same hill after his election to plant his own tree, following Herzl's example.

I last saw Gittel in Motza in 1946. I was a young bride and she was eighty, sitting sideways at the table in the family room like a life-size reproduction of a Whistler portrait and exuding her awesome presence. Dressed in her small, unadorned, dark prints, with delicate features, limpid blue eyes and finely grained skin, she looked like a woman who had endured a lifetime of asceticism. She was never a particularly effusive grandmother but on those evenings we spent together in the flickering light of her oil lamps, as she told of the many journeys she and my grandfather had made across the barren landscape of Palestine, moving from one place to another until they settled finally in Motza and made it their permanent home, I felt a particular closeness to her. It seemed, out of all her grandchildren, that she had chosen to tell her story to me. The memory of those quiet evenings has remained with me, softening her more puritanical side in my mind. Sometimes we seemed to reverse our roles and I, finding her so touching and brave, would unabashedly kiss her in the midst of whatever she was doing, causing her to blush like a child at my impetuosity.

Throughout the years, our conversations consisted chiefly of my listening and her talking, but on our final visit I sensed that for the first time she considered me a woman in my own right. About to embark on my own pioneering adventures in the early years of Israel to come, I believe that she saw in me a continuation of her own story and hoped that I would carry the torch she and my grandfather had lit.

Gittel had lived in the Holy Land throughout three major eras: the last years of the Ottoman period, when the country still lay ravaged after four centuries of Turkish rule; the following British Mandate and, finally, the beginning of the independent Jewish State. In 1948, our old family property in Motza still stood, dominant in the Judean landscape, commemorating a proud pioneering effort that dated back to the years 1901, when the land was bought, and 1904, when it was settled. For half a century it stood alone, an unexpected splash of coral red on the side of what became the Jerusalem-Tel Aviv Highway, with no competition anywhere in sight. Induced by my eager curiosity, Gittel brought her early days in Palestine in the mid-1880s and - 90s alive, enlarging my lifetime experience vicariously to a full century. I revelled with an almost sensuous delight in my own ancientness, and tried to understand the scenes of my early childhood as if I had experienced them from an adult perspective. I found her stories to be intensely gripping, and even now I remember them as if they were my own.

Gittel once nostalgically remarked that her husband had not come to Palestine as part of an organized movement. "There was no such thing then," she said modestly. The Zionists had not yet formed themselves into a mass labour movement with the men identifiable by their khaki trousers and Russian-style shirts, and the girls by their bouffant, bright-blue cotton bloomers. "We were here long before," she said in her humble voice. Gittel would never have been able to consider such provocative extremes of dress as girls' bloomers and was quite pleased that Mikhel, the *mitnaged* (anti-Hasidic rationalist), was demonstrably progressive enough in his modern garb. To our amusement, a family picture from 1902 shows Mikhel and Yerachmiel wearing western suits, bowler hats, starched wing-collars and ties, looking totally incongruous in the Palestine of those years as they prepared for a business venture in South Africa and the Congo. During that period, Palestine was miserably primitive and poor, and the brothers had heard that after the Boer War there were great opportunities in various African countries, so they journeyed to South Africa in the hopes of earning money for their growing families.

Mikhel was the first of the family to settle in Palestine after he witnessed the fatal beating of a friend by Russian anti-Semites. It was a common occurrence in those days, and he realized that even if he were to escape such a fate, he would, in any case, be drafted for twenty-five years of compulsory military service and be forced to defend a country where Jews were for the most part not allowed to own or work land and were denied access to schools, universities and most professions. Hundreds of Jews had already been killed. Remaining both Jewish and alive became one's chief preoccupation, and this was not how Mikhel wanted to live. As a young man of nineteen he announced to his family and beloved Gittel that he was leaving for Palestine and, several months later, crossed Europe by foot to Constanza, here he boarded a ship for Palestine, prepared to sleep on deck.

Grandfather Mikhel's original surname was Sacile, after a small town in the Udine region of northern Italy where Jews from Spain had fled after the Inquisition. Two hundred years later, in the eighteenth century, they went to Poland to build a new town called Jamosh, a replica of an Italian town of beautiful medieval architecture, still in existence today. Wanting a new name, in the period before the revival of Hebrew as a spoken language, my grandfather took that of the man whose passport he had bought in his village before coming to Palestine: Steinberg. When, on a Friday night in 1884, Mikhel's father received the news that his son had arrived safely in the Holy Land, he went to tell his neighbours the good news, sang the thanksgiving prayers with relief and ecstasy, and died of a heart attack.

Grandmother Gittel would not join Mikhel until two years later, in 1886. In the meantime, her eleven brothers and sisters had left for America as part of the wave of Jewish emigration from Russia and Eastern Europe in the 1880s, fleeing the pogroms. After their arrival, they sent her the fare to Detroit where they had settled, having matter-of-factly betrothed her in advance. Defiantly, she turned all this down and exchanged her prized Atlantic-crossing ticket for one to what was called "P-o-lestine", so upsetting her family that for the rest of her life only one of her half-sisters, Rose, would write to her.

Travelling a different route than Mikhel's, Gittel embarked in Odessa on the Black Sea and sailed via Constantinople. Since her unwed status meant she had to be chaperoned for the duration of her trip, she travelled with an elderly couple from Sohovole, her native village, sleeping between these two guardians every night of the ten days' passage, to secure unequivocal protection. "No young people came to Palestine then," Gittel used to say of those early days of immigration. People came only to die in the Holy Land and be buried on the Mount of Olives, the ultimate privilege of the pious. Young Gittel, a naive country girl, was an anomaly amid a group of sick, weary people in their waning years, and the sea and the star-studded nights were her only consolation.

After a journey of two weeks, her ship finally anchored in Jaffa and she was able to set eyes upon the man she loved as he stood there amidst the chaotic scene of Jaffa's port, proudly sporting a red fez. She stared in disbelief at the completely altered man; her once strikingly handsome Mikhel was now sallow and emaciated and, as she later confessed to me, if she could have gone back then and there, she would have done so.

Jaffa seemed a primitive port after Odessa. Because of a barrier of rocks, ships were forced to anchor at a distance from the quay, and rowing boats, manned by strong, tanned Arab porters, ferried the passengers to the shore. Stripped to the waist and wearing black Turkish ballooning pantaloons cut to just below the knee, they rushed on board and swarmed throughout the ship, snatching the travellers' plump bundles. If the sea was too rough for the small boats to dock, they stood in the water and carried the passengers, piggyback, to shore, dumping them on the floor of the Customs House like so many sacks of merchandise. There on the quayside, people were shoving and pushing, begging for business. Salesmen, dragomans and money-changers shouted out their wares in the local Turkish currency: *bishliks, kabaks* and half-*kabaks*, as well as the smallest coin of those days, which Arabs and Turks alike called by its Yiddish diminutive: *tsenerel,* meaning "a tenth".

As soon as the port and the din of the customs shed was left behind, my grandmother told me, she encountered unbelievable filth and the shocking reality of oriental street life: beggars, naked or ragged children with skin sores and runny noses, Arab pedlars, brutal light and huge horse flies that stung like needles. Storekeepers would hang long strips of paper covered with fresh glue to trap the zooming insects. Soon she would have the problem of the merciless heat to deal with, and how to keep cool while wearing the long-sleeved dresses and opaque, dark stockings dictated by Orthodox tradition.

After her arrival, Gittel stayed with distant members of her family called the Danins; the head of this family, romantically believing in the cultivation of the land, would later find the arid Motza terrain that in 1904 was to become Gittel's home. It was Danin and his wife, in the absence of her parents, who married her off a few days after her arrival, as was only proper.

The wedding took place in the Danins' tall, Turkish house at 15 Butrus Street. Due to her family's disapproval of her journey to Palestine, Gittel had arrived without a wedding dress. Buying one was impossible in those days when all clothing was homemade, so her head was encircled with a white garland and her body wrapped in a length of white cloth that served as a makeshift gown. The local orchestra – no more than a woman rattling a beribboned tambourine – performed, as my grandmother wept at the oddity of it all. She circled her bridegroom seven times and he stamped on a glass, according to Orthodox ritual.

After the wedding, the women made Gittel wear a *yasma*, a coloured cotton kerchief, to make her part of the local scene, and initiated her into the custom of covering herself Muslim-style when she went out into the street – a length of cloth running from head to mid-calf and fastened beneath the chin. Without this cloak, they warned her, the Turks were sure to misinterpret things, and pinch her in the most inappropriate of places.

On Butrus Street the oriental women, who always stayed at home, sat all afternoon watching the street life from their wooden balconies, their heads just visible from down below. Groups of Turkish and Arab men would sit for hours on low stools in some shady spot, leisurely smoking their bubbly *narghile*, and Gittel recalled how puzzled she was at first at how strikingly different the rhythm of life was here – where she had come from, the men worked all day long.

The courtyards were filled with exotic pomegranate and palm trees, and on the outskirts of the town lay groves of the renowned Jaffa oranges, large and heavy with thick, wrinkled skins. In the market there were masses of a red fruit she had never seen before, surprising in its lack of sweetness. The vendors called it a *pomador*, which today we know as the common tomato.

The weight measures at that time were the *rotel* and the *okia*, and lengths of cloth were sold by the *ama*. Even in my own youth, I remember merchants measuring cloth by holding it taut from their chin to their outstretched arm, a remnant from those early market days.

Not only were the sights and tastes of Jaffa foreign, the sounds were exotic as well, and set the tone for the religious saturation of this new land. The first Muslim call to prayer rang out at dawn every day, and on Sundays there were church bells as well. In later times, when she visited Neveh Zedek, the precursor of Tel Aviv, Gittel remembered that in the days preceding Rosh Hashanah, the

Jewish New Year, the synagogue's beadle would make his rounds before dawn, knocking on the shutters of his sleepy congregants' homes to summon the men to *slichot*, the annual prayers of repentance. On the second day of Rosh Hashanah, whole families would go to the seashore and empty their pockets into the waves as *tashlich*, a symbolic act of discarding the previous year's misdeeds.

Mikhel and Gittel stayed in Jaffa for only a short while, and soon moved on to their true, spiritual destination: Jerusalem. Travel to the Holy City was by diligence, the only public transport in those days: a wagon drawn by two horses, with three benches that could seat up to four per bench. Riding over the hills was rough; the Turks paved the road between Jaffa and Jerusalem only in the 1890s, and until then a journey that would eventually take just one hour took all night and half the next day.

The journey included two stops: Motza and the Khan. Motza, the smallest of the twelve original settlements (called the "colonies" at the time), was where the Steinbergs would eventually settle. The Khan, at the edge of the Ayalon plain, was a Turkish inn that had existed since long before anyone could remember. Traders accompanied by their livestock would rest there overnight before their climb over the Judean hills at dawn. (Night travel wasn't safe in those days with marauders occupying the road. Such men once accosted my great-uncle Yerachmiel, taking not only his money, but also the very clothes off his back! Yerachmiel, family lore has it, was forced to hide until nightfall and then return to Motza on foot, naked.) The Khan today remains a neglected stone ruin, its significance likely lost to the thousands of people passing it each day as they speed along the Tel Aviv–Jerusalem Highway.

Despite the obvious hardships of settlement in a new and difficult land, my grandparents believed it was a privilege to live in Jerusalem, and despite the city's austere appearance and difficult living conditions, they felt graced by a transcendent spirituality. I recall how, as a child, I was led by my grandfather through the narrow alleys and up to the Western Wall of the ancient Jewish Temple. Afterwards, he would take me to the Tower of David to hear the English Police Band play, which he hoped might compensate for all the numbing stone structures, but although young, I instinctively understood and perhaps shared in some of his reverence for that place.

In the 1880s, the Turks bolted the Old City gates at night and it was so frightening and dangerous to stay outside that no one dared leave their homes. The Old City was comprised of different communities, each with its own customs; its only Jewish inhabitants were elderly people living in great poverty, occupied with studying the Holy Scriptures, and living off the *halukah* – charity money collected by Jewish communities abroad eager to support the continuity of Jewish life in the Holy Land. These were times of great trial and tribulation: Grandmother remembered there once being a plague of locusts and the sky suddenly darkened as hordes of them descended on everything in sight, denuding the land of its plants and grasses. The Yemenites, a fine community of desert Jews who lived in their own quarter, grilled the swarming locusts to crispness over a makeshift fire and ate them, as was the custom in Yemen.

In 1896, my grandparents moved from Jerusalem to Jaffa where Mikhel had become the contractor for the first Jewish hospital. Gittel had already borne four of her six children in Jerusalem: Zvi, Le'a (my mother), Rivka and David. They lived in the same courtyard as an Arab family and waited for the new Jewish suburb of Neveh Zedek to be ready. Neveh Zedek consisted of little flat-roofed houses set one against the other to protect its inhabitants against brigands and marauders, three main streets and a few transversal ones.

My paternal grandparents, Zalman Ambache from Bialystok and Beila (*neé* Klatzkine from Lithuania), also went to live in Neveh Zedek, a few years after my father was born in 1892 in nearby Jaffa. Our family name went back five generations, beginning with Aharon, my father's great-grandfather. The lineage then continues with: Aharon's son Nachman, Zalman my grandfather, and then my father Simcha and his son, my brother Nachman (named after *his* great-grandfather Nachman, and known in the family as Nachman II). The family name, Ambache, is a Hebrew acronym for the thirteen Articles of Faith of Maimonides (translated: "I believe with complete faith"). Of the generation before Aharon, my father's great-grandfather who, sick with cancer, came to die in the Holy Land and be buried on the Mount of Olives, we know nothing.

It would have been unlikely for the two families to meet since the Steinbergs were quite Orthodox while the Ambaches were secular. Even later, because of the unequivocal orthodoxy of my mother's family, the two families never became close.

Neveh Zedek was a little fortress of East European life, with its Russian, Polish and Lithuanian Jews living much the way they had in the small Ashkenazi communities of Europe, only now suffering from the shortages, climate and lack of work. There the Steinbergs encountered for the first time an old-established and serene oriental Jewish community mostly from Morocco or Tunis, and as organically linked to the place as were the Yemenites. There were sometimes sharp confrontations, each group antagonistic to the other, and there were hardly any marriages between the poor Ashkenazi newcomers and the older, more integrated Sephardi families. The clash between western and oriental customs created intransigence on both sides. The two worlds, though both Jewish, were yet so sealed off from each other as to require separate synagogues and separate chief rabbis. Each recited the same prayers and spoke the same Hebrew, yet with intonation and chanting so different that they negated any sense of common identity.

In general, life in Neveh Zedek subsisted on the local commerce. Arab vendors sold coal manufactured from pieces of tree trunks buried in the ground in special pits. Local women crouched on low stools and cooked over primitive, high-powered bronze primus stoves filled with purple vaporized oil, or over closed, slow-burning kerosene stoves. Food was later transferred to heavy copper vessels from Damascus, lined with a white alloy that made preservation possible over a few days. Water was always boiled, meat was rare and stringy, and poultry was obtainable but had to be cleaned by hand, the feathers removed and the bird then singed at home by the women.

From time to time, Arab vendors would bring butter to one's door, but it contained so much grit and dirt that it had to be melted and strained before it could be used. The basis of meals was always the same: tomatoes, olives, onions and bread spread with sesame oil and topped with a generous pinch of salt. The only exception was the Sabbath meal – instead of coarse bread, there was soft white challah and the rich *cholent*, a stew of meat, beans and potatoes cooked overnight on a very low flame and a savoury feast in comparison to the weekday fare. Each housewife kneaded the dough for her own bread twice a week, and took it to the baker, who supervised the communal oven. There was also a common well where the neighbourhood women would collect water for their daily use.

At Purim, the Jewish festival in early spring, the shoemaker came to the house to take orders for everyone in the family, promising delivery in time for Passover which would arrive between thirty and forty days later – a moveable feast. In those days there were no measurements for feet. Instead, the shoemaker would trace the contour of his customer's foot on a piece of paper, and make the shoes to fit the picture! As for new clothes, one family photo shows Gittel's six small children, three boys and three girls, all neatly dressed from the same fabric.

Only now as I look back, does it occur to me how remarkably biblical their existence in Palestine was. Beyond living the simple life of settlers, their daily tasks and even the rhythms of their society were ordered according to the Hebrew calendar and on the basis of religious precepts. As the years passed, they began to establish their own ways of doing things, but those first years were of authentic, Jewish, communal living.

On visits to Neveh Zedek from Ismailia, I found myself fascinated by the different world of Sephardi customs. I loved the exotic, white almond drink, pink jam made from rose petals, jam from unripe dates studded with cloves and sugary pistachio pastries. In an innocent shift of loyalty, I found these delicacies so much more attractive than my grandmother's *cholent*, which we grandchildren disliked but which the grown-ups relished in equal measure, afterwards invariably falling into a Sabbath afternoon torpor.

I was impressed by the Sephardi custom of kissing both hands in deference or gratitude, by the women's ululations at weddings and by the little girls aged five or six, wearing tiny gold earrings in their pierced lobes. I could sense Grandmother Steinberg's strong disapproval whenever I described these sensualities.

In the 1970s I went again to Neveh Zedek, this time on a pilgrimage of exploration, and was touched by its intimacy and smallness. I was met by a little, bent, old woman who remembered me from my childhood visits to my father's parents. The shoddiness of the place by then was terrible to witness, but what remained was a sense of pride in its history. I was shown the school where my father had won praise for his top marks in arithmetic (though not for his daring accomplishment of glueing the rabbi's beard to the desk when the venerable man fell asleep). I saw the grand staircase in the home of the Chelouche family, who had brought commerce and employment to the area, and the barrack-like British Consulate, a leftover from Turkish times when to be a consul was the height of diplomatic status in Palestine. Back then, every consulate was like an autonomous principality with its own postal services and the legal jurisdiction over its subjects. Every consul was preceded by a forerunner, a *Kawass* in his gold-braided uniform, knocking his silver topped mace on the ground. On another corner my guide showed me the humble home of Shai Agnon, Israel's literature Nobel laureate. He had lived there on his second return to the Land in 1920 and had written some of his more famous stories in that very house.

Next I found my paternal grandfather Zalman Ambache's home on Dr Stein Street, named after one of my great-uncles, Dr Menachem Stein. Zalman was eight when his mother died. His father, Nachman, soon re-married, but as his step-mother refused to allow Zalman into the new family unit, he ended up being passed around by his mother's sisters, each in turn housing and raising him throughout the remainder of his childhood. One aunt was married to a Russian-Jewish colonel who lived in Nicolaev and had property there. Another was married to an Austrian army doctor in Vienna. But Charlotte, who married Dr Menachem Stein and lived in Palestine, was the one he felt closest to.

Dr Stein had originally studied engineering in Moscow. When his connection with a secret revolutionary group was discovered and he was down for deportation to Siberia, he escaped to Dorpet and switched to medicine. After graduating he fled Russia for Palestine, becoming the first Jewish doctor of the very first Jewish hospital, Shaarei Hesed, in Jaffa. Renowned as the saviour of Neveh Zedek during Jaffa's cholera epidemic of 1902 and for his kindness to the poor, he became active in community work and was one of the first members of the Jaffa branch of Hovevei Zion.* He also played a similar role in the Vaad Halashon committee that worked actively and inventively on the revival of Hebrew as a modern language.

Dr Stein's brother, Leon, was sent to Bialystok to study mechanics. Zalman was sent along with him since his father then

---

* Literally Lovers of Zion – a charity founded in the 1800s with the aim of encouraging agricultural settlement in the Land of Israel. Some groups were also active in philanthropic work.

lived and had business interests there. Charlotte Stein hoped that the father, and more crucially the step-mother, would now accept responsibility for Zalman but nothing budged my great-grandfather Nachman. He was content within his orbit of comfortable living, was a friend of the governor of the province, not exactly a state common for Jews then, and he remained utterly oblivious to the existence of his only son, Zalman.

Great-grandfather Nachman's new wife had borne him three daughters and ensured that they would be marriageable by insisting her husband provide each of them with a dowry of 3,000 rubles, equivalent in those days to three rivières of diamonds, and completely cut out my grandfather. Blatant discrimination between children and step-children was quite common in those days when women often died in childbirth.

Both Dr Stein and Leon advised my grandfather to come to Palestine, which was only then beginning to greet the technical revolution. The Steins described a land burgeoning with new possibilities: Baron Edmond de Rothschild was building the first vineyards of Rishon le Zion and Zichron Ya'akov, the colony in the north; orange groves were beginning to develop and Jews were starting to work the land; the first deep wells were being dug and vertical pumps imported from France, an advancement that would consequently do away with using animals to turn the wheels of water wells.

At the time there was only one steel factory in Jaffa, the German-owned Wagner Brothers. There were excellent prospects for establishing a useful steel enterprise and my grandfather, succumbing to the memory of their youthful years together, accepted Leon's invitation to settle in Neveh Zedek and work with him in establishing the first Jewish foundry and training a generation of steel workers. The obsession to become a *worker*, and to be useful to the development of Jewish life in Palestine, seemed as extremely relevant then as it would be with every later generation of immigrants.

In 1898, the Steinberg family left Neveh Zedek and moved to Hadera, which had been founded in 1890 in the northern Sharon valley. Mikhel and Gittel had joined an organized group that bought land to establish a settlement in Hadera in hopes of extending the zone of Jewish settlement in Palestine. They packed their children and all their belongings into a diligence one winter day and set out on the road heading north: "I can still feel," my grandmother told me, "how it shook our limbs and insides to travel on the rugged road of those years. The wooden wheels soon stuck in the mud. We slept in the wagon and had to wait until morning for help. It was only the next day that we reached our destination, lucky to have survived the night. And there we discovered marshes, the great annihilators of early settlement."

Hadera, some fifty miles north of Jaffa and slightly inland, is close to nearby Caesarea with its old Roman ruins (and now Israel's only championship golf course). I myself remember the turgid, greenish phosphorescence of similar places along the coast in early, undeveloped Palestine; the stunted flora, the dusty grey banks of cactus that clung to arid clumps of soil and the sickening sulphuric smell of it all. Upon their arrival, Mikhel and Gittel pitched tents on bare ground and when summer came, months later, the parched earth brought forth lizards, scorpions and little snakes writhing in the sand, not to mention mosquitoes. There were 225 original settlers in Hadera in 1898, and only half survived malaria even though the men began each day by planting eucalyptus trees meant to drain the swamps and act as a deterrent to the anopheles mosquito.

Mikhel was the settlers' housing contractor, appointed to build huts that would replace the tents the settlers were all living in. Hadera soon became known as the toughest and nastiest spot in Palestine. "I used to examine the beds every night for scorpions," Gittel recalled, very proud of this initiative. The topics of daily conversation among the settlers were grim: the quinine that everyone took, the "chill-stricken" families, how high was so-and-so's temperature and when was the legendary doctor Hillel Jaffe, who made his rounds on horseback, next expected to visit the sick in this distant, desperate wilderness.

When Gittel's fifth child, my aunt Rachel, was due, there was no midwife in Hadera, so my grandmother had to be taken back to the "great" city of Neveh Zedek where there was a qualified midwife whom everyone called *Bubbé* (Grandma). But because Gittel was from malaria-ridden Hadera, she was not permitted to rent a room for her delivery. When they heard this, some of the local people recalled Gittel's early days in Neveh Zedek and how she had unfailingly sent a basket of food or alms to the homes of needy families every Sabbath eve. Such generosity could not go unrepaid and she was offered lodgings until the birth.

After Rachel was born Gittel returned to Hadera and placed her baby in a trough supported by two wooden poles dug firmly into the sand. Aunt Rachel, who would later become Lady Lauterpacht, the wife of Sir Hersch, the illustrious international lawyer who was also a British judge at the International Court at The Hague, adored telling the story of her exotic babyhood, proudly upstaging the generation of younger women in the family, including myself, who had been born at home.

Very soon, Mikhel himself developed chronic malaria and his condition deteriorated. No matter how much quinine the doctor prescribed, he remained unable to walk, dragging himself around on crutches and looking as if he might be coming down with the dreaded yellow fever. One day, Gittel took him to the German doctor of great repute in the German Colony of Sarona, near Jaffa. German Templars had settled there shortly before the First World War. In a solemn tone that mimicked his voice (she was very amused to have been formally addressed as "Madame"), she recalled his words for me: "Madame Steinberg, if you don't send your husband to another climate immediately, he will die."

And so it was that Mikhel who had returned from South Africa a few years earlier, was compelled to leave for that country once again. His connections were already strong after his previous stay there and he recovered and did well, remaining in Johannesburg for several years. In letter after letter, he begged Gittel to join him, even returning to Palestine in hopes of fetching her and the children. But nothing could make her budge. She had come to the Land of Israel and nothing would ever take her away. She said that if they were once to uproot themselves, they would never come back. "Why had they come here in the first place? What was it all about if they were going to leave? What had they suffered for?" Time after time she refused, and while Mikhel went sadly back to South Africa to continue to supplement the family's earnings, she returned to Neveh Zedek and to her role as strict ruler of her brood, which by then included her sixth and last child, Moshe, born in 1900, just before Mikhel's departure. For a total of seven years, Gittel remained alone in Old Palestine with her children, unwavering in her constancy of spirit. Eventually, she won. Her Mikhel came back to her – and back to the Land.

3

Motza

My mother's family began their involvement with Motza in 1901 when her father bought fifty-six *dunams* of land and his two brothers, Yerachmiel and Shlomo, together bought a similar plot with a mind to settle there. Turkish laws on Jewish settlement were very strict at the time, and as they were permitted only to build stables and cultivate vineyards, so they started a vineyard and kept a stable in Colonia, with two horses, two cows and some sheep. My great-aunt Sheine, married to Yerachmiel, lived in Colonia alongside the Arab peasants, while Gittel preferred to stay on in Neveh Zedek. Shlomo died in a fire in the vineyard when a candle dropped in a barrel of schnapps.

On his return from South Africa, with his new earnings Mikhel built a fortress-like stone structure of a home in Motza. The highest point in the region was (and still is) the Castel from where, on a clear day, the coastal plain can be seen. In the region's history, whoever held the Castel ruled over the plain or controlled access eastwards to Jerusalem. A few kilometres westwards from Motza lay the old Arab village of Abu Ghosh, named after the fearsome Turkish robber who demanded that travellers pay him for the right of passage to Jerusalem, killing those parties who dared to question his self-appointed authority. A generation later, my great-uncle Yerachmiel, as Motza's *Mukhtar*, paid a protection fee to the descendants of Abu Ghosh in order to keep Motza immune from robberies.

While others dreamed of settling the land, Mikhel had another ambition – industry. A site in the Motza area called the *djvir* supplied clay, and Mikhel started to experiment with it. Before long, he decided to establish a real factory in the Judean hills for creation of the bricks and tiles needed to develop Palestine. His own home already built, Mikhel selected two hills among his fifty-six *dunams* on which to construct the factory and sought investors. One hill was earmarked for the factory itself and the other was for the vineyard. In the wide *wadi* under the vineyard, he built a reservoir to collect the rain water which would keep the clay wet. No sooner was the eight-metre-deep reservoir full, than an Arab villager, who in the arid Judean hills had never seen water deeper than the shallow outlets of the local springs, went into the pool thinking he would swim, but promptly drowned instead. There was no point in posting a warning which most fellahin could not read.

It was clear from the start that no one in Motza knew the first thing about building a brick factory. There had been an earlier attempt, but at the hour of the much-anticipated demonstration, every brick had cracked, so Mikhel brought in an expert from Egypt and sent the clay abroad for testing. Under the Turks, no machinery or tools had ever been imported; parts that needed repair, as well as heavier items, such as kerosene engines or the big boilers of steam engines, were put on a rickety boat that plied the coast between Palestine and Egypt, and sent to Alexandria. Mikhel, however, had all the necessary machinery imported into the hills and his brick and tile factory was soon a broad and impressive presence in the barren hills. The main building and its tall, tapered, cement chimney dominated the rural landscape and its bright, coral expanse was known the country over as a landmark on the way to or from Jerusalem.

The large iron factory gate, which was never shut, opened on to a broad, stony, driveway lined with olive trees that led to the back of the property. Midway down this driveway was a slanting, uneven, rough-hewn courtyard that separated my grandfather's stone house, bordered by pink geraniums, from Yerachmiel's, which stood at a lower level and had a huge bread oven occupying an entire wall, not to mention a private synagogue, a stable and the vineyard.

Yerachmiel had set aside for the Messiah the first barrel of wine he produced, and there it stood as a symbol of the family's faith in a better world to come. Bread was baked on Mondays and Fridays, the oven's steel door bolted with an iron bar, and Sheine, my good-humoured, rosy-cheeked great-aunt, milked the cows daily. Once she insisted that I try the milk straight from the cow's udder. From a distance, with a sure hand and amused agility, she directed the udder towards my mouth. The warm taste and strange texture made me grimace in such a way that the story became a family favourite passed down from one generation to the next until even today, her great-grandchildren won't let me forget it!

During the day, the central courtyard resembled a busy village square with trucks, donkeys, mules, workers, family and black-clad, fur-hatted Hasidim who came to collect charity before every Jewish holiday. My grandfather's original dream was of an all-Jewish workforce and at first, there being but a few families in Motza itself, other Jewish workers had been brought in from Jerusalem. Before long however, the daily journey proved too cumbersome for most employees, and they had to be replaced by Arab workers from nearby Colonia as my grandfather set aside his dream to prove instead that Jews and Arabs could work and live side by side in harmony.

Before long the factory was bustling as conveyor belts carrying wobbly bricks in a soft yellow state, rolled up and down the four storeys of the factory with their glass paned windows. Six hundred tons of bricks flowed in pairs on little wooden trays to be stacked later on scaffoldings in dark drying rooms that seemed impregnated with the dank, static smell of wet clay. Every tile had been stamped "Steinberg-Motza" and was ready to be shipped countrywide.

Entering the drying rooms of the factory, you immediately looked for any small penumbral light that could help to trace your steps out of the dark labyrinth. And as you emerged into the blinding sunshine, facing mounds of steel and the debris of factory life, you passed from the "industrial" world held together more by will than by skill, into a pastoral one, as you would suddenly be greeted by the mooing of a cow and the cackling of hens.

It was in the "village square" between the two houses that the bricks, after they had dried for weeks and become firm, would be thrown by hand in pairs from Jewish to Arab workers, from the drying rooms to the trucks that would take them up on the hill, just below the old Roman road. There, like a high, infra-red, open inferno, was the kiln. At night, the Lux magnesium lights gave off a strong, stark light that pierced the thin cotton curtains of my bedroom, restoring to objects something of their daylight familiarity and giving a strange sense of security to this awesomely lonely place. In the whiteness of that obscurity, I would lie between the stiffly starched sheets in my hard, steel bed and go to sleep, lulled by the monotonous chant of Zbeh, the Arab watchman, who, squatting near the far end of the furnace, played on his reed flute through the night to keep himself awake. He played well beyond those hours when the groaning and chugging of the Egged buses as they traversed the seven steep, perilous bends of the old Jerusalem-Tel Aviv road known the country over as the Seven Sisters were no longer heard.

From time to time my family would be invited to an Arab wedding in Colonia, the invitation consisting of two live chickens tied together by the feet and sent to the house a week before the event. One of these invitations coincided with our visit, and I was able to witness the festivities first-hand. Tsilla and I were dressed in our identical, white, Bethlehem-cotton dresses embroidered in a dark red cross-stitch by the Arab women in the village, and we went up the hill for the *fantasia* or celebration. Some time earlier, the bride had her henna ceremony, in which the women's palms were daubed with red dye from the shrub's leaves. The bride's face was decorated with torn bits of coloured foil, and trained mares with their heads covered in white tulle, flowers and more foil, reared up to dance on their hind legs in time to the music. The men had danced the *debka* for seven nights by the time we arrived from Motza, singing the bridegroom's praises and stating that a pretty bride was worth ten camels.

The Makleff family, who lived in Motza's valley, was particularly involved with their Arab neighbours. Chaya Makleff, the mother, worked as a nurse in a Jerusalem hospital and often treated Arab women from the village, and the family hired local Arab workers to tend their sheep on the Sabbath. During the week, nine-year-old Mordechai grazed the flock with his dog Titus, whose ears had been clipped to make him more aggressive. School – a large Byzantine ruin converted to a classroom, where each bench comprised a different grade – did not consume much of any child's time in those days, and so Mordechai was also able to work from time to time as a water carrier for an Arab farmer in Colonia. In the summers he would often be sent down the ten-metre-deep well in the family's property to haul up buckets of water for the chickens and cows, and when he wasn't working, he would help the Arab workers make soil suitable for their vine-growing by removing stones and rocks from the ground.

I remember that old Palestine world vividly, in particular from my years as a student, when I came visiting from Egypt. I sometimes waited at the last terminal on Jaffa Street, at the western edge of Jerusalem, where there was a small shop in which my grandfather bought provisions and picked up his mail. I would then take the grey and battered Jewish bus or the No 25 Arab bus that was far worse, to the gates of the Steinberg property. To signal left or right in the Jerusalem traffic, the driver pushed an inner lever causing a grey wooden arm a yard long, to suddenly pop out sideways at the front of the bus and shoo away pedestrians.

The men sat on the bus in their long *ghallabiyehs* covered by western suit jackets, holding pita bread wrapped in their plaid handkerchiefs. Fellahin women came aboard in a great commotion with baskets of vegetables, and live chickens in crates that were made of dried palm stems and had to be stacked at the back. They dipped into the folds of their wide cloth belts for change, cackling and shouting raucously as they made their way on to the bus. Their clothes had the acrid smell of rancid fat, and before long the odours of perspiration, onions and poultry feathers permeated the bus. Some women sat nestling eggs above their belts, covering them carefully with their long pendulous breasts for safekeeping. Among passengers there were sometimes a few religious Jews in their long black coats, usually headed for Motza, and the occasional kibbutznik, unmistakably identifiable in his khaki shorts and side-buttoning *rubashka* shirt, obviously headed for Arza, the next hill after Motza. The social juxtaposition of it all was bewildering: the extremely religious and the rebelliously secular, primitivism and socialism, Europe and the East, Muslim and Jewish, literate and illiterate, hygiene and filth.

And then came the nightmare.

My grandmother tended to avoid the subject, but every so often she would mention the horrors of the first attack on Motza in 1929, and each time it came up in conversation, I was horrified anew at the terror of that day. On Friday evening, 24 August 1929, all work at the factory had stopped and Mikhel had just returned from Yerachmiel's private synagogue next door for dinner as usual. Suddenly, Maazuza, who lived in Colonia, appeared in the house. Gittel was astonished, because the Arab women never left the village at night, and so she called out, "Who's there?" even though she could clearly see her through the arched opening leading to the kitchen.

Maazuza stood there in the oversized men's shoes that had

helped her come down the stony paths from Colonia. Everything in the house had been set out in advance of the Sabbath. The big *jara* of water was full, the oil lamp above it was already lit, and the circular blue flames of the kerosene stove were burning low behind toy-like mica doors with minuscule coiled steel handles, ready to keep the food hot throughout the Sabbath day. Maazuza entered this serene atmosphere gingerly, stood there in the light of the bulbous silver candlesticks and with a quivering voice, begged my grandparents to leave the place right away. She promised to take the cow to her house early in the morning and look after it for the day, but begged them to leave immediately, for she felt that something was going to happen. My utterly startled grandparents asked, "How can we?" The Sabbath had already begun and as Maazuza knew full well, they were forbidden to travel or light a fire. And in any case, how could they forsake their own home? Maazuza stepped out of the house, weeping, leaving behind her an unmistakably ominous feeling.

That night, my grandparents closed all their steel shutters, something they never did in the refreshing late summer evenings. The next morning, Gittel invited the Makleffs to stay since there was so much restlessness in the country of late, and their house was in the vulnerable valley while hers was up on the hill. The Makleffs had just been discussing the carnage in Hebron earlier that week when sixty-seven Jews had been murdered, and sixty wounded. Mrs Makleff replied, "Here in Motza, where Jews and Arabs work together, the situation is different." They refused to come: father, mother, three out of five brothers, three sisters and two summer boarders they had taken in for a little extra income. Before long, they noticed that the small flock of sheep had not been taken out, which meant that no Arabs had come to work that day, although Friday, not Saturday, was the Arab day of rest.

Around noon, Arabs suddenly arrived by the busload at Colonia. Within minutes, their silhouettes covered the hillcrests. They rushed down the hillsides, some with sticks, others with blunt tools and long knives, to the Broza house, to the Makleff house, coming upon them from all sides like an advancing tide, shouting and screaming, "Kill! Kill!" Among them were Arabs who had worked for the Makleffs. The mother and one of the sisters called out to Tsalah, an Arab they knew, "What do you want of us?" Moshe, one of the sons, went down into the garden, and was hit by a bullet. Chaim, who had been standing nearby, ran into the house to look for their old Turkish gun, came back, shot into the crowd in self-defence and killed an Arab. The gun stopped working, so he jumped on his horse and galloped to Arza on the next hill, to telephone for help from that settlement's new convalescent home.

The Arabs stopped for a while, and then with renewed yells and exhortations, they burst into the Makleff house. Others set the hay in the cowshed on fire. They killed Avraham and raped and killed his two sisters, Rivka and Minna, on the terrace, raped the mother, cut out her eye, hacked her breast off, slashed her face and body, and stabbed her with a dagger. The father's head was crushed so traumatically that his brain literally fell out of a wide hole in his skull. The screams of savagery on that Shabbat were so loud that my horrified grandparents heard them from their hill. By now, the Makleff house was burning.

Mordechai and his younger sister Chana ran to another balcony at the back of the house. They swung themselves along the poles supporting the balcony and dropped down on to the ground. Small and unobtrusive children, they managed to creep along the stone wall of the Brozas' adjoining farm but the Brozas had hermetically sealed the house, and the two small Makleff children, seeing no one, ran instead up to Mikhel's property, where members of the Haganah, the self-defence organization of the Jewish community during the British Mandate, had already arrived. The Haganah had been warned that morning of a threat to the whole area and had sent a few volunteers, but they were too late: they arrived in the middle of the carnage.

Mordechai and the venerable village chief, Yerachmiel, teamed up with two of the young Haganah members, with the aim of rescuing the wounded but before they reached the house they were shot at from the village, and were forced back to my grandparents'. During the exchange of fire, an undercover Haganah armoured vehicle manned by volunteer "troops" arrived from the direction of Tel Aviv, staffed by a young man dressed as a doctor and two young women dressed as nurses. Their report, given after the riots, read in part: "We entered the Steinberg factory and found the local people gathered in the courtyard and heard about the killings in the Makleff homestead. There was no sign of panic, but a strange apathy had seized the people, as if they were waiting their turn to be slaughtered."

In the afternoon, when British soldiers and police arrived at Motza, they piled the eleven dead bodies into a Red Cross British Army bus. Whoever was still alive in the valley was put into an armoured car and led by three soldiers with machine guns to Jerusalem. The Arabs continued to shoot at them, and the British shot into the air all the way to Jerusalem. Yerachmiel was badly wounded while shielding my four-year-old cousin, Ella Japhet, from the crossfire, and was taken to Bikur Cholim hospital where he stayed for three months. After the rescue and evacuation, my grandparents' house was completely ransacked.

My parents never brought up the 1929 riots voluntarily, nor did my grandparents. It was only in the 1970s, spurred by my own insatiable curiosity, that I searched the newspapers from those days, hoping to fill in the missing information for myself. Curiously, the newspapers from 25 August, the day after the massacre, were missing from every archive I managed to find. Finally, I landed on an editorial from *Davar*, the leading Labour Party paper, of 1 September. The same issue contained a shattering list of the nearly one hundred people who had died in various clashes that week in Palestine, sixty-seven in Hebron in addition to the eleven in

Motza. Later I was to learn that the British had closed down the Hebrew papers just after the horrific events, and even the *Davar* articles had been subject to censorship. The *Palestine Bulletin,* the only British daily at the time, printed the news on no less impressive a place than its back page.

An investigation followed and the British police were able to prove that the murderers had retreated to Colonia, from whence they had started. On the other side of the valley, across the convulsed landscape leading to the village, the police had found empty jewel boxes that had once contained the touching mementos Mikhel had brought or sent to Gittel during his South African days.

In November 1929, three months after the riots, the first session of the trial was held. Twenty-two-year-old Chaim Makleff testified, reliving the haunting images of his dead parents, siblings and guests. On 8 January 1930, another trial session was held, in which the child Mordechai was the chief witness. According to the reports in *Davar*, Mordechai was terrified of entering the courtroom and sobbed disconsolately until Judge MacDonald took the boy on his knee and enjoined him to tell nothing but the truth. "The child smiles," reported the paper, "and says, 'I know,' and then tells the full story." The defence lawyer for the Arabs tried to find contradictions in his testimony, but Mordechai did not give him an opportunity to confuse him, insisting on his version until the judge and the counsel themselves burst out laughing at his earnestness. He was even able to identify one of his family's former Arab workers and others from Colonia, as having been part of the mob.

And yet, to our great astonishment and despite the heartfelt testimony of the bereft Mordechai, all of the accused were acquitted. Perhaps, had the trial taken place under the Turks, the people of Motza would have been less shocked. But that a British court should fail them so utterly sent everyone into a sort of despair. I believe this shock to be partly responsible for my family's avoidance of the subject for so many years.

The defendants claimed that they had been in villages outside Colonia on the fatal day, and denied that there had been any unrest in Colonia prior to the massacre. They testified that they had not known about the events in Jerusalem when the Grand Mufti, during Friday prayers, had incited Arabs to riot throughout the land. They even denied seeing the houses burning in Motza, or knowing anything about it before Sunday. Of course such ignorance, given the facts, was impossible: the Grand Mufti, also known as Haj Amin el Husseini, had a summer house in the valley beyond the Makleff house, just below Colonia. He was a violent leader, and used his power as spokesman to incite rioting against the British.

Abandoned for weeks, Motza was now a crushed, phantom settlement, but soon the Jewish authorities under the British Mandate undertook efforts to increase the population there. The Haganah organized a civil guard of *gaffirs*, young men who came after a day's work in Jerusalem to guard Motza at night, and then went back to Jerusalem in the morning. The inhabitants of the valley returned, as did my own traumatized grandparents. Yerachmiel was still convalescing in hospital, where he shared a room with an escapee from the Hebron massacre who did not survive his wounds. Before he died, the man told Yerachmiel about a Torah scroll he had saved from the Hebron riots and Yerachmiel solemnly promised to return it to Hebron at the earliest opportunity. His grandson, Rabbi Ba-Gad, a member of an extremist religious party in the Knesset (the Israeli Parliament) for a number of years, was to fulfil that promise.

The Histadrut (Trades Union Federation) had often criticized my grandfather for employing Arab workers instead of adhering to the principle of Jewish labour. After the events of 1929, however, Mikhel readily adopted the principle without question, keeping only the few Arabs who had been with him from his earliest days.

But even this policy would prove to be mistaken, as he discovered when the Jew he and Yerachmiel had hired to replace the vineyard's Arab watchman was discovered dead one morning, his throat cut "like a cow" as was described by the Arab who came to announce it, gesturing with an index finger across his neck. The Arabs had killed him, claiming that he had taken work away from them. This pattern in labour relations would repeat itself again and again and continues to do so well into our own times, as sometimes Jews and Arabs will work together, and at other times political circumstances will pit them one against the other, in violence and passion.

As horrifying as the year 1929 was for my family, it was the story of 1936 that I remember most vividly. Mikhel and Gittel were visiting us in Egypt that winter, as they often did during the rainy season when the clay could not dry and the factory had to be closed. As in 1929, it was a Sabbath. My parents were informed of riots by a phone call from Palestine early in the day, but they waited until the Sabbath ended before breaking the news to my grandparents. I remember the expression that came over Mikhel's face as if he were standing before me now: crestfallen, mask-like and silent amid the din of grave whispers and pained faces. This time his factory had been burned down.

My mother begged Mikhel to stay in Cairo where we were then living and spend the rest of his years with us. He was already seventy-two but would have none of my parents' suggestion and added, passionately, what became a family classic: "I will give them neither the pleasure nor the satisfaction of a victory." It was now he, Mikhel, who was raising the Motza banner and refusing to leave, just as Gittel had done years before.

And so Mikhel returned to Motza on the midnight train from Egypt to rebuild his fortress of a home into the bare, childless, piano-less house that was the only version I ever knew. He also rebuilt his beloved factory, even climbing the steel ladder on the side of the chimney himself to ensure that the tall cement rings had been reconstructed properly. He managed the factory in full production until he was eighty-four. In 1949, just before he died, he saw the State of Israel proclaimed and, a proud young bride, I remember going to the hospital to tell him that my husband had been appointed the first Ambassador to the United Nations of the *State* of Israel.

"*Die Medine,*" he said quietly. "The State." Those were the last words to pass between us, and I was much overcome. He was very weak, and somehow I knew that this was our parting. I wanted to tell him that although we expressed our Jewish values differently, they were essentially the same. In his last hour, Mikhel called for his brother and great friend, Yerachmiel. They prayed together, and then Mikhel's head gently rolled back and he died. Gittel died three years later.

The three surviving Makleff children, Mordechai, Chaim and Chana, did not return to Motza for almost thirty years. Chana, who had jumped from the balcony with Mordechai, remained an invalid all her life. I visited Mordechai in 1975, some time after he had completed his service as the third Chief of Staff of the Israel Defence Forces. He was then director of the Dead Sea Potash Enterprises, located in an unassuming shack of the *Kirya*, the government complex in Tel Aviv. I was worried that I might tread on his sorrow as we talked, and approached the subject of the 1929 riots cautiously.

After the War of Independence, Mordechai told me he met his Jordanian counterpart during the 1949 Armistice negotiations. He said of that meeting: "He, too, was a man from the Judean Hills. We had walked along the same lanes, we had breathed the same air and we knew the same olive trees and caves. But there was now a gulf between us. Each of us had closed in on his position. He was more, I would say, Islamic. I was also different from then on." I asked him what it had been like to return to the valley of his childhood after all the events that had passed. He smiled. "The big fig tree looked so small," he said.

Today the Makleff house is a ruin. Our family property, which used to look down on the narrow Jerusalem–Tel Aviv road, is still called "The Red House", and is blocked from immediate view by a new multi-lane highway. It is no longer ours, nor is the vineyard on the adjoining hill. The stone watchtower at its centre has crumbled; the fig trees are merely emblematic. Every day, hundreds of cars pass Motza on their way up and down the Jerusalem–Tel Aviv Highway, and when I make this trip, I cannot help but remember our four o'clock walks to the vineyard, my grandfather using his cane to lift the vines that hung too low or to push aside a stone in his path.

I picture my aunt Rivka on these walks, never venturing out without her parasol, and our young cousins who had been rescued from Europe before the Holocaust, through fictitious marriages. They are all balancing their steps on the rocky paths of my mind. We spread a thick old blanket on the ground and are surrounded by vines and bunches upon bunches of grapes. My grandmother Gittel always stays at home, venturing out to her terrace only on Saturday evening for her sunset prayer. Her secret luxury is the row of potted pink and red geraniums around the terrace that runs the width of the property like some imaginary stage. As a little girl, I always wanted her to step off the porch and sing the Hebrew songs my parents had made sure we learned in Ismailia, but she would always recite her prayers instead, or stare at the great natural spaces, awaiting the sight of the first three stars in the firmament to signal that the Sabbath had ended.

On 26 October 1988, nearly one hundred descendants came to Motza to celebrate the one hundred years plus our family had spent in Israel. The local council dedicated a plaque for the front of Yerachmiel's house that commemorated him and Mikhel. The bright Israeli flag, with its vibrant blue star, was startling against the drabness and sadness of the place, as were the bright clothes of the small boys and the flouncy dresses of the little girls, the great-grandchildren who were climbing up and down the external stone steps of the property. Chaim Herzog, the President of Israel, and my sister Aura, his wife, arrived at the ceremony in time to name the original main road in the valley "Rehov Mikhel Steinberg". Although my mother did not live to see her father so honoured, she would certainly have sided with her sisters, my aunts, who gasped in pain when they realized that Gittel was not mentioned on the stone plaque, as if she had never existed.

Grandfather's oil portrait by Pinhas Litvinovsky, the "official" portrait artist of Israel's early generation, is in Cambridge today with my aunt Rachel's youngest son, Sir Eli Lauterpacht. A photograph of Grandfather that once hung in his office, is now on my wall. Aside from the plaque on Yerachmiel's house, there lies in the valley's local synagogue – once a Byzantine ruin, turned school, turned workers' quarters, turned synagogue – the only physical remnant of my family: the Torah scroll my grandparents gave to the village on their sixtieth wedding anniversary, an event I proudly attended with my husband.

I sometimes go back to Arza, high above our Motza, to be alone with my memories and to watch the sunset as its glow, the colour of my grandmother's geraniums, illuminates the place with a pervasive haze. The pink slabs of the stone paths seem to jump out at me, such is the density of the colour there. It is the hour of the last breezes and the last nodding of trees, the only sound a dog's distant bark and the persistent twitter of a few birds. I behave as if I am waiting for the same colours I once saw there, for a special quality of light, for the grunts and echoes of the slow-climbing cars on the mountain road or for that absurdly enlarged yellow moon hanging low and heavy above the undulating lines of the landscape like a naive painting. I come back to the hills my grandparents settled in to recall the rich scent of warm pine and honeysuckle and rosemary, or the scenic arrangement of the red tiled houses and the orchards. Again and again I return, trying to decipher the stern beauty and the changes in the landscape hour by hour, hill by hill, and to observe the last rhythms of that countryside as it closes in for the night. I stand there, drunk with the soft, clean mountain air and find myself transcending the dimensions of our small heroic estate, with its achievements and vicissitudes, into a saga that is my own. These hills are filled with the unbearable sense of time elapsed, a patchwork of many stories, some still untold; dear ones gone, houses decaying, trees dusty and unpruned, and the once narrow and uncharted paths.

My eyes slowly travel down the majestic slope of the opposite hill, its dark silhouette filling my entire field of vision, dark ropes of light appearing on its surface, indicating the mountain roads and homes that I remember from my many visits. Looking towards Jerusalem, the valley of Ein Kerem sits with its old convents and churches, and above it looms Haddassah's modern hospital. To the west lies Mevasseret Zion, a burgeoning suburb.

It would have given the pioneer in Mikhel such joy to see the landscape today, full and busy everywhere, with rows of white houses stacked all the way from our valley to the crest of the hill and the place quickened to life by third and fourth generations. Mevasseret's population has become so dense that its skyline, visible from the highway, includes the distinct yellow arches of a McDonald's perched precariously on the rugged hilltop. It is now more than one would have wished for. The new era is inexorably encroaching.

4

Cairo

When pictures of Egypt are shown on Israeli TV during news broadcasts, I still find myself straining for a glimpse of the places I once knew.

I spent my adolescence in Cairo, my family having moved there in 1936 from Ismailia. My father wanted to broaden his horizons in Egyptian business and industrial enterprises. He would still maintain his connection to the Suez Canal Company for many years to come, but he and my mother had decided that it would be best for my sisters and me to be in Cairo at the beginning of the school year in October. A friend offered us his *dahabeah* (Nile houseboat) to stay in until we could find a villa. We fell in love with its toy-like comforts and with the simple pleasure of sitting out on deck, listening to the sound of wavelets and watching feluccas glide by. We were docked at Giza, on the great plain where all verdure stopped and the pyramids, stark and wonderful, stood like giant stone tents at the gateway of the desert. Magnificent sycamore trees lined the banks of the Nile, while across the water on the island of Gezira, lush tropical gardens, villas, a sports club and a racecourse created an atmosphere of permanent holiday.

On our first morning aboard our new floating home, my father tried to dress, only to discover that the buttons of his trousers had disappeared – eaten by a rat, apparently. These were the days before the advent of plastic, when buttons were made of starch, evidently appetizing to rodents. When the rat performed the same trick the following night my mother was spurred into making up her mind about a house and within a week we left the boat, saving what remained of my father's wardrobe, not to mention his dignity.

My mother had selected a large, imposing house in the residential district of Zamalek on Gezira. It stood opposite the famous Anglo-Egyptian Union, at the corner of a main avenue, Fuad-el-Awal, and a quiet residential street, Kamel Muhammad. The house was enclosed by high iron railings on which grew honeysuckle and jasmine that made the summer night air intoxicating. Descending a few steps, one passed from the entrance room through an oak door and into a library panelled from floor to ceiling in light oak, with a prominent bronze chandelier where smoke from my father's cigars would linger. A stairway led up to a gallery lined with open shelves below which books were kept behind glass doors whose wooden frames were carved with strips of little lozenges. These bookcases held volumes on a variety of subjects: books that related to my father's engineering; sets in beige leather of works on Egyptology and Islam; red-covered collections of such authors as Stendhal, Flaubert and Proust; and dark, stark, faceless Hebrew books.

A vast central hall ran the length of the house and at the front were two great doors of black ironwork and glass, through which, in spring and summer, splashes of vivid greens and the red of flame trees could be seen from our broad stone terrace. During hamsins, the hot winds that blew off the Sahara, this view would be transformed, like the change of a stage set, into a yellow haze with a mysterious luminosity. A film of dust covered the parquet floors and the tabletops, and one dared not touch a curtain for fear of sending more dust spiralling through the air. Some years after we occupied the house, the Saudi Arabian Ambassador and his family took up residence there for a couple of years and I was told that the big decorative glass doors were replaced by opaque ones to prevent the embassy women from being seen from the garden.

Although the house was set back from the main avenue, the

voices of Arab vendors as they cried out, "*La Bourse Egyptienne*", the name of the French morning paper, could be heard against the background rattle of the tramcars that had started at the Pyramids, far away. After crossing the Zamalek Bridge on to our island, a tramcar would give a weighty clang and continue towards the city over the Bulak Bridge – a bridge always associated in my mind with the routine of getting milk for the family.

Buffalo milk, commonly used by Cairenes, was rich and heavy, and we disliked it. At my mother's request, our servant Amir found an Arab willing to bring a live cow to our house each day to be milked on the premises. The cow had to be brought at dawn, before traffic started on the Bulak Bridge; only an hour later she would not have been allowed to cross. Some time between five and six, the sound of slow, dragging, animal steps could be heard. Then there was always a delay before Muhammad, the second servant, came out of his basement abode. The heavy steel gate would be lazily opened, and sleepy sentences exchanged while milk spurted into a bucket. When all was over the Arab and his cow departed, the gate was locked again, and silence fell once more.

My youngest sister Aura took a year off, and instead of advancing to the next class at L'Ecole Morin, she went instead to the English School of Heliopolis at the other end of Cairo. She and her friends would be picked up by the Heliopolis school bus, which would take them across to the other side of the city. The population of Cairo was only three million then, as opposed to more than eighteen million today, and I don't ever remember the kind of huge traffic jams I saw when I returned in 1974.

Tsilla and I had been placed in a nearby girls' school and would travel there each morning on our bicycles. Formally known as L'Ecole de Zamalek, the school was run by a French couple named Morin, and was thus often called simply, L'Ecole Morin. Monsieur Morin, a bourgeois personage out of Mauriac, with a bushy moustache and pince-nez attached to a black cord, was our headmaster. He crowned his solemnity with an incongruous straw boater, encircled by a lush maroon-and-navy striped ribbon, and he got around Zamalek on a bicycle.

The school premises consisted of an old villa on the Nile, and the view of the water and its traffic were destined to divert our attention from the teacher. There were five in my class and I imagine a similar number in my sister's. We wore no uniform and there were no collective activities; we simply spent all our time that first year in one smallish classroom or another, preparing for our first baccalaureate. A year later, in conformity with the secondary education in France at the time, we prepared for the next, the *Philosophie*, comprised of psychology, logic, metaphysics and ethics. Final examinations were sent each June from Paris to all French schools, ours included.

One January evening, the Morins took Tsilla and me to the travelling Comédie Française. As French people, they must have derived great pride from the thought that Cairo depended on Racine and Molière for the hightlight of its winter season. There was the usual flurry about dresses, and ankle-length socks were exchanged for our first pairs of long stockings and medium heels, which the occasion demanded. Seeing our headmaster cast in a different role and doing things for us – closing the car door and rushing to get us programmes made us uneasy: all this Gallic gallantry seemed strange, since we knew we would have to go back to the humble status of being his pupils the next day. The opera house, built by Khedive Ismail for the opening of the Suez Canal in November 1869, had ornate gilt stuccoes, red velvet tiers and crystal chandeliers – an architecture and style of decoration totally unrelated to the surrounding human landscape.

During the interval, we heard a patter of comments about the actors who had performed these French classics on which the majority of the audience had been nurtured. The conversation, intense and high-pitched, cascaded swiftly and was interspersed with "*Ya, mon cher*" and "*Yaani*" (Arabic for "I mean to say") –

figures of speech that, in a breath, transposed the scene from France back to the Middle East. Egyptian society was divided into two categories, with millions of feudally repressed people on the one side, and Europeans and wealthy Egyptians on the other. For the latter group, some European language, generally French, was bound to be the mother tongue. Native English speakers were in the minority – a phenomenon consistent with the fact that the French disseminated their culture together with their political presence, something the British disdained to do. While these two European empires played out their rivalry, the Muslim world appeared to serve merely as a vast, static background against which the various Mediterranean ethnic groups – Armenians, Circassians, Copts, Greeks, Jews, Lebanese, Syrians, Turks – seemed like busy ants running to and fro, carrying morsels of great or ancient civilizations. Though all these people spoke French, through the diversity of characteristics in their pronunciation, expressions, gestures, and laughter came a flavour – an ebullient lack of self-consciousness and a colourful vigour, flashy and at times grotesque – which was to be found nowhere else and which was uniquely the Levant.

On the day after our theatre outing, my sister and I were in class by eight o'clock as usual, having ridden there on our bicycles. On the way, we passed villas with big French shutters, wrought-iron gates and balconies, and apartment buildings, perhaps four storeys high. The latter were neatly bordered with jacaranda trees and guarded at their entrances by dark Sudanese *bawwabs*, recognizable by the deep cuts in their faces, put there as proof of virility. They wore white caftans in summer and black in the winter, edged at the neck and on the cuffs with yellow embroidery. Their feet were covered with red pointed slippers which when they were off duty they would kick off under their benches as they sat in the shade, fingering amber beads and drinking dark, syrupy tea.

Across the avenue from our house, spreading the full length of a block, was the garden of the Anglo-Egyptian Union, shared by the Egyptian Officers' Club. The Union, which had high political and social prestige, nourished the dream of colonial rapprochement – an ambivalent dream, for presumably this fraternization was meant principally to ensure a smooth domination. There were, sometimes, hesitant movements in another direction, such as the Anglo-Egyptian Treaty of 1936, which promised Egypt more independence. But during the Second World War, the British rescinded some of these promises in order to keep a firm grip on the Middle East against German encroachment.

I remember standing on the balcony of my room gazing across at the pageantry of the stag party for the Crown Prince of Persia, Muhammad Reza Shah Pahlavi, on his engagement to King Farouk's sister, Fawzia. Her name, like all the royal names, began with "F", for luck. His other sisters were Fayza, Faika and Fatheya. (It was later said that names beginning with "N" were bad luck for the King: there was Naguib, who would depose him; Narriman, who would divorce him; and, of course, Nasser. But at the time the monarchy seemed secure and high festivity pervaded every royal occasion.) Ropes of lights shimmered around the club, and there were lavish illuminations of buildings and arches throughout the city. Cairo had been, after all, among the first cities in the world to use electricity, as a direct result of the founder of modern Egypt Sultan Muhammad Ali's, ambition to copy the best and latest of Europe.

The future Shah, then a young man of nineteen dressed in a field-marshal's uniform, was received in one of the magnificent quilted tents lined with vivid geometrical designs that are deployed for ceremonies in the East. Every bit of lawn was covered with oriental rugs. For the royal guests there were huge gilt armchairs, gross and ornate in their carvings, and probably weighing a ton, and for the ordinary guests there were cane chairs. After the fanfare and the anthems, the Muslim dignitaries filed by: white-turbaned *ulemas*, followed by *pashas*, *beys* and *effendis*, indistinguishable in their red tarbooshes which they kept on indoors as well. There were people who wore sunglasses even at night to hide the trachoma-damaged eyes so common in the Middle East. I saw a few puckish Turkish moustaches, and men sitting in typical oriental posture, with their legs apart and their hands folded over the tops of the pommelled canes in front of them.

For years, I heard the national anthem, which was based on a melody from Verdi's *Aida*, after every ceremony at the Club. When my future husband came out to Cairo during the Second World War and began to court me, he would sometimes pass by our house later than I was permitted to see him, and would whistle the Egyptian anthem, knowing that those few bars of Verdi, which would be sure to attract my attention, would escape anyone else's notice.

Many Allied troops were sent to Cairo in the early 1940s – British, Free French, Australians, South Africans, Free Greeks, Free Poles and later, Americans. There was death and tragedy in Europe, but here seemingly all was affluence and sparkle. I remember hearing about the father-in-law of a family friend who had played in a poker game with King Farouk in which £45,000 (at the time the Egyptian pound and the pound sterling were more or less the same value) was lost (I can't remember by whom) without anybody batting an eye. At any given party, there might easily be three kings in attendance, for besides Farouk there were the two refugee monarchs of Greece and Yugoslavia who had taken up residence in Egypt.

The wives of Egyptian officers never appeared at the Club, in fact they were non-existent on the official scene. The Queen, the Queen Mother, the princesses and the ladies-in-waiting always wore their white silk-muslin yashmaks in public, although they often covered only the neck and chin, as if offering a token gesture to what tradition expected of them. They used to step out of bright-red palace cars – red was reserved for the royal family –

looking like delicate figurines emerging at a clock's chime to re-enact some exotic episode of the East, perhaps from Pierre Loti's *Disenchanted*. Ordinary women and fellahin wore long black dresses that fell straight to the floor, leaving only eyes and henna-dyed hands showing. The black veil was supported by a bulky golden spool that came down from the forehead to the nose, an encumbrance they bore with servile docility. Despite all this concealment, however, there was a surprising absence of prudery about sex among Orientals. They treated it much more candidly than did Europeans at the time, displaying both a matter-of-factness about the most intimate details, and a great sense of humour. Harem life must have undone privacy and discretion long before.

Segregation of the sexes, however, was strict, not only among Muslims but also within the other communities, whether Christian or Jewish. I do not remember ever going out alone with a young man during my secondary-school years. It would have meant inexorably that we were engaged. Young people used to call each other "Monsieur" and "Mademoiselle", and it was common back then to be engaged at sixteen or seventeen and married at eighteen. In fact, when I was seventeen, a man came to my father's office as an intermediary for a proposing family but my father turned him away, saying that I must make my own choice. The man left in a huff, declaring, "You will regret it when you know who it is," and my father never even told me about the "missed opportunity" until many years later, after I was married. Neither of us ever discovered the identity of my would-be suitor.

A school friend of one of my sisters, the daughter of the Prime Minister of Egypt at that time, married a young man chosen for her by her parents. I remember how progressive she thought her parents were when they allowed her to see him and talk to him (two distinct levels of permissiveness) before the marriage, and even to go to the cinema one evening with him, accompanied by her English governess.

French was the only language spoken at home by members of Egypt's ruling class, just as it had once been among the Russian aristocracy. The girl's husband, a very nationalistic young man who was years later to be a cabinet minister under Nasser, on discovering that she could speak only French, sent her back to her parents to learn Arabic. Imagine the daughter of a Prime Minister of Egypt who was ignorant of her own language, history and literature, yet proficient in the French classics and at ease with French grammar and history, and who even had an English governess so as to be proficient in yet another language that was still not Arabic. Some years later, the girl called to tell my sister that she could not see her anymore, because she would no longer converse in a foreign language, and added pointedly that it would be best for our family to leave Egypt.

My granddaughter Yael possesses my old charm bracelet, which has on it a small twenty-piastre gold coin from a few handfuls that King Farouk threw like rice or confetti during the wedding ceremony of the Prime Minister's daughter. Evening dress and all, I scrambled for one of them, and as I picked myself up, there stood Mme Cattaoui, the Queen's lady-in-waiting, and the wife of Joseph Aslan Cattaoui, a prominent Egyptian-Jewish community leader. Taut and immobile she murmured, for the benefit of her daughter's ears, "Don't you dare move," while the King inspected the female attendance. Many of the women of the court and of the oriental bourgeoisie were very beautiful, their white skin suggesting northern descent, perhaps Circassian or Lebanese. They took immense care of themselves, watching assiduously over their whiteness, never going into the sun or taking part in any sport lest they get sunburned. To be fair-skinned and to be very young were great assets, not to mention having a well-proportioned figure (one sneered in horror at the word "thin", and the man in the street frankly liked a *semina*, or well-rounded female). When these young girls were married, they settled into a world where they seemed to be owned for the specific purpose of mirroring the material wealth that had been, and continued to be, invested in them. At eighteen or nineteen, they were exquisitely set apart to await their special destiny. The primary obligation was beauty, the second money. Education came last.

As my school years neared their end, I became newly conscious of the world around me. Was I expected to share in it, to surmount it, or to simply pass it by? The voluptuous East lay within reach…but what could it offer a young girl? An early marriage, a life of leisure and acquisitions, bridge parties, fittings at the dressmaker and the *lingère* (for even lingerie was custom made then), tea at Groppi's, the Sporting Club and the usual summer months in Europe, where people went for the cool climate. One would exist at the very centre of a pleasurable life, and yet be cut off from any other sort of experience. I knew I could never pass a whole life like that. My parents, by instilling Zionism in their daughters, together with a feminist sense of equality and an interest in higher education, had made it impossible for my sisters and me to live in this customary way. And yet, in spite of their concern for social progress, there had been no thought of equipping any of us to enter a profession.

The war prevented me from studying abroad, as would otherwise have been the natural order of things, so instead I attended lectures for a year at the Fuad-el-Awal University of Cairo where the many student demonstrations gave voice to Egypt's underlying desire for independence from the British. Knowing little Arabic I could not be a regular student and therefore stuck to courses taught in French. The following year, wishing to study social science and literature, I went to the American University, where all my courses were taught in English and I could graduate with a degree. At the same time and at my father's insistence, my sisters and I started learning Arabic privately. Twice a week, the library door would open and in would walk our teacher, Mr Alama, a plump Coptic gentleman, immaculately dressed in a dark suit, smelling strongly of cologne, and twirling a small branch of jasmine, which he left on the table during the lesson.

Arabic aroused no spring of motivation in our lives at the time. Arab life and Arab culture were so far removed from the daily intercourse of foreigners living in Egypt that by silent consensus the effort to learn the language was judged useful only as a scholarly endeavour. To make the task more enjoyable, our mischievous minds made up games in which Mr Alama became an unknowing victim. One was based around his red tarboosh, which he kept on throughout classes, pushing it now towards his forehead and now to the back of his head, leaving his pomaded hair unruffled. We agreed among us never to answer any questions before the tarboosh had been moved – much to the consternation of our unfortunate tutor but to our own constant amusement.

My brother Nachman also attended these private classes for two years. Having achieved a double first in natural sciences at Cambridge, he began to do both research in physiology and a period of clinical work at Kasr-el-Aini Hospital. He sometimes brought home echoes of the people's lives, such as the story of one health inspector who had gone to a village to check on the medical situation there. After calling in all the peasants, the inspector was approached very timidly by a boy who said that he must be ill. After the boy had described his symptoms, it turned out that he was the only person in the village who did *not* have bilharzia.

On Tuesday afternoons, Tsilla and I joined the sightseeing tours of an old Englishwoman named Mrs Devonshire who was a great Arabophile and well known across the Baedeker world. She used to wait for her group on the terrace of the Continental-Savoy Hotel, recognizable by her Edwardian air that came complete with hat with dotted veil, jabot and gloves. We used to set out at 2 p.m. in *gharries*, a number of which always stood in front of the hotel. There would be anywhere between two and six carriages, and the police always helped us through the bedlam of cars and trams as we swung round the Place de l'Opéra, the sides of its buildings dominated for months by luscious posters of entertainers such as Um Kalthum, the great national singer, or Mme Badia, the renowned entertainer.

With one crack of the *kurbash*, the horses would race into the Arab heart of Cairo, full of magnificent Islamic architecture and picturesque streets. Once we had left behind the red-carpeted steps of the Continental's art nouveau terrace, with its straw furniture and potted palms and its red-sashed *soufragis* who could be summoned with a clap of the hands for the usual "whisky soda", we entered another world. Here vendors sold brightly-coloured drinks of tamarind and karkade (hibiscus) to the sound of brass saucers which they clacked like cymbals. There were stalls selling big jars of seeds and nuts, and trays filled with desiccated carobs and bright orange lentils. There were artisan shops of all sorts and hovels for scribes and moneylenders. Cars would rush through the narrow streets honking, for nothing but speed and noise assured any progress. If a car stopped in a side street, Arab lads sometimes slapped its bumper, as if it were the rump of an animal.

A whole wave of humanity flowed aimlessly through the alleyways of bazaars. Amid the smell of musty wood, spices and urine, a man would be selling garlands of jasmine. Standing on the steps of a mosque, one would be pestered by swarms of child beggars crying, "*Baksheesh*" for alms, and old, toothless beggars, eyes streaming with pus and faces covered with flies, moaning, "*Maskeen*" (poor man). In self-protection, one said, "*Imshee*" (go away), nevertheless feeling cruel or guilty, or at the very least, uncomfortable. Mrs Devonshire, tall and stately, carried a parasol as an intimation of protection, but neither this accessory nor the fly-swatter that looked like a small white horsetail, were of much help.

Through these excursions with her, I felt I was able to get some sense of the city's inner life. I could at least get near its colours, its smells and its disorder. We would return at sunset from visiting some of Cairo's most ancient and spectacular sights, and, because of the height of the *gharries*, feel raised to some level halfway between the streets and the minarets. The dark silhouettes of buildings were delineated against a flamboyant sky, and at that hour hundreds of twittering white birds settled down on the trees along the Nile, suddenly transforming the greenery, as if by magic, with a semblance of white flowers. It was the best hour, and in summertime it was the signal for people to go out on to their balconies, settle down in their gardens, or bring chairs out on to pavements and into alleyways, so that the evening breeze could give them respite from the harshness of the day.

There was a lot of activity at our house in those years. My mother had attached herself to various causes, such as the orphanage of the Jewish community, for which elegant ladies often gathered in our big hall to sew baby clothes. With the advent of war, she joined the Soldiers' Welfare Club. Thousands of Palestinian-Jewish soldiers had signed up for the British Army (since at that time Palestine was still under British mandate) in order to fight against Hitler, and these soldiers would come to Cairo on leave from their units. Having been born in Palestine, both my mother and father felt a special solidarity with them and so every Saturday night we held an open house. Our home was very popular because we spoke Hebrew and celebrated the Jewish holidays. In addition, with family roots in Palestine and my grandparents living in Motza at the time, we often had friends or relatives from Palestine staying with us. The train leaving Jerusalem or Lod arrived in Cairo some seven hours later. It was as simple as that.

My sisters and I each practised the piano every day for an hour or two. With only two pianos for three girls, there were always arguments. One day, my father bought a third piano, the second grand. We put it in our playroom upstairs, next to the ping-pong table, which we used as a collective desk surface so as not to have to do our homework in our own room. Mademoiselle Flore, our *femme de chambre*, often sat with us in a corner of the playroom, busily initialling linen, putting in hems or waiting to comb our hair after we finished playing. In Egypt in those days, having three pianos did not seem eccentric. Every afternoon, our house sounded like a music conservatory. Had we lived elsewhere, perhaps we would not all three have played the same instrument, but the piano was the customary choice in Cairo, apart from the violin, which was my brother's domain.

My siblings and I were joined on our many outings and adventures by friends, among them George and Lydia Mizrahi, the children of Emanuel Mizrahi Pasha, the King's lawyer. A small group of us spent a holiday camping for three days near Baltim on the Mediterranean coast. We rode there along the deserted shore, enjoying a commanding view of land and sea from our camels' backs. The Mizrahis' chauffeur had been sent down with us to act as a liaison with the nearby village where, in the name of Bint el Basha (the Pasha's daughter – the letter P is non-existent in Arabic), all our wishes were immediately fulfilled, including camels brought outside our tents and a felucca sent to the nearby shore for sailing. We girls, who were wearing trousers borrowed from our brothers, were delighted when the chauffeur came to tell us that in the village we were thought to be actresses, due to our unlady-like attire.

Lydia's father, as a lawyer, and my father, as a consultant engineer for the Suez Canal Company, had many business dealings together, yet attuned as they were in their thinking on various professional matters, Father and Mizrahi Pasha still disagreed on certain political issues. Mizrahi always poked fun at my father's Zionist beliefs. "We Jews are protected by the King," he would say. Nobody at that time thought to wonder who would protect the King.

Later, when my parents moved from Egypt to Palestine, they heard that Mizrahi had experienced a nightmare of difficulties. Serag el Din, the Wafd* Minister of the Interior, declared that all

---

* The Wafd Party dominated Egyptian politics from 1919 until the Officers' Coup of 1952. The Wafd was banned the following year.

Egyptian subjects other than Muslims and Copts, had to submit a *shehada genseyya*, or certificate of nationality, proving that their families had been resident in Egypt in 1848. The trouble was that in 1848 there had been no registry of births in Egypt. The property of people who did not have foreign passports and were actually Egyptian nationals, but neither Muslim nor Christian, was confiscated. It was clear which minority the law was aimed at. The Mizrahi home was sequestrated and later rented by the Egyptian authorities to the Mexican Embassy. The Pasha took refuge in France, where he later died. Since he was a Grand Officier de la Légion d'Honneur, he was accorded a French state funeral, though there was no one but Lydia and a few others to follow the hearse. Lydia's husband suffered worse than the loss of property. His family owned land in the village of Chibina-el-Anotter and because a son of the *omdeh*, or village headman, had been killed in Sinai in the 1948 War of Independence between Egypt and Israel, the *omdeh's* family hired a man for twenty dollars to kill the brother of Lydia's husband.

Today, there are many Jewish refugees from that period in Egypt; they can be found in Paris, Rome, Geneva, London and New York. Some of them can't bear to talk about what happened to the Jews of Egypt. Others, of a different frame of mind, nostalgically remember the luxury and pleasure of life there. I have heard people recall the feeling of bright promise back in 1936, when young Prince Farouk was summoned home from the Royal Military Academy at Woolwich upon his father's death. He was a mere youngster then, and so handsome! For the coronation party at Abdin palace, he appeared, fair-skinned and gentle looking, in a shiny chalk-white suit and a red cape, ready to receive the diplomats and the aristocracy of the land. The long table glittered with vermeil, and the flowers came from the palace hothouses. Behind the table, in a perfect line, stood the darkest of Berber lackeys dressed in red pantaloons and gold-braided boleros. The festivities were spectacular and seemed to augur a happy reign.

5

Another view

Some time in 1941, in the middle of my university studies, a young officer in the British Royal Air Force contacted my family. John Kendrew had known Nachman both at Clifton College in Bristol and later at Trinity College, Cambridge where he too achieved a double first. A thoughtful, intelligent, hard-working and thorough man, he had participated in the initial steps of the navy's radar project as a junior scientist officer and was now stationed in Egypt.

He joined our family circle with ease, and we were pleased to have the opportunity to reciprocate for the summer long ago when his father had invited Nachman to stay with him and John for a holiday on the Devonshire coast. For his part, coming from a broken home, John had never been so close to family life before so this was a brand new experience for him. I was twenty years old, and in the rare moments my student's schedule would permit, John and I would set out in the early afternoon on sightseeing expeditions. He took many photographs, entering the time, date, lighting, exposure and distance in his little diary – a very methodical young man.

Our driver was marvellously adept at conveying us through the maze of Cairo's narrow crowded streets, many of which John might well never have experienced, nor I have dared to brave alone. John was hardly equipped to face the mentality and habits of the locals living in the poor, dirty quarters where so many of Cairo's Islamic sights are located and where shopkeepers and especially children pestered anyone in a uniform. We saw the architecturally compact and austere Ibn Tulun with its outer spiral ribbon-like staircase, which, dating from 879 CE was popularly known as the oldest Islamic mosque, although everyone knew the Ummayad Mosque in Damascus was older. And no sight had as dramatic a history as the Citadel, a military garrison since 1176 that had an extraordinary view of the city and a gruesome past. Inside these walls, Turkish Pashas had run for their lives, jumping to their deaths over the ramparts one fateful evening when a magnificent banquet in their honour was followed by an order for their massacre: the order was given by none other than their host and ruler, Sultan Muhammad Ali.

Following an afternoon of sightseeing, we invariably ended up back at my house for drinks and dinner, listening to the BBC or playing classical records. Intellectual and emotional attachments were forming between us, and after the family dinner we would sometimes walk along the nearby western bank of the Nile, a walk we specially liked on luminous summer moonlit nights. The cooling temperature and the jasmine and honeysuckle fragrance emanating from gardens after a hot day, left a pleasurable mark on those oriental nights. Only the blue elongated lines of searchlights, cutting like scissors through the skies, and the electric street lanterns painted blue for blackout purposes, acted as a reminder of the war. Egypt was so totally out of the orbit of those suffering.

But there was another view of that same Middle-Eastern world, as seen through the eyes of our new friend. In 1942, after more than a year in Cairo, John was staying in the apartment he shared with two other Air Force officers and recovering from a serious episode of food poisoning. He wrote to me:

> I walked through town and all I could see was the filth and disease. Every face almost a revolting travesty of everything that is human: avaricious, cunning, greedy. Even the Europeans are corrupted by it too. I saw it all as a sort of

foetid manure-heap, crawling with vermin: the sun pouring down and making that vermin fester and multiply – and just as you can only grow marrow on a dung heap – marrow with its glaring yellow flowers and its bloated over-developed fruits – so the only culture that can come out of this town is represented by the corruption and the wealth which flashes past in its large motor-cars – all the materialism which you know so well and which even I have caught glimpses of.

This life did seem a horror. I wanted you out of it, clearly away. I think more strongly than ever before. When I compare it with a civilized country like England, the contrast was amazing. Just look at the book I gave you – *On Foot* – and you will see hundreds of examples of what I mean. The miracle of it is that you – you have kept your purity, your virgin freshness, your quality of spring – in spite of all. It is a miracle. It is.

I would give anything to show you now, just one glimpse of a Scottish moor under the summer sun, springtime by the Thames with the long lush grass and the flowers – sunset from the cliffs of Devon – a dripping, foggy, November day when every object more than 10 metres away is a veiled mystery!

I was attracted to this "otherness" in him – his scientific outlook, and his English characteristic of being calm and tactful, disciplined and proper. He was a gentle young man who loved classical music and literature, one day bringing me a neat little book with his favourite poem, *The Shropshire Lad* by A.E. Housman. It was illustrative of the values he admired, with its utter Englishness, its purity and its deep love of the countryside. I was somewhat taken aback by the choice, as I was more responsive to Baudelaire's sensual poems, and wondered if such a difference in our taste reflected deeper, more insurmountable differences in our characters. Indeed, it was the "otherness" in him that one day would make us part. The only child of an academic couple, John's father was a noted professor at Oxford and his mother, an art historian. When John was only four years old, his mother had left England to start a new life in Florence. She was bitter about England and even more so about academic life, a bitterness that was reflected in her response to John's letter breaking the news of our romance. In an unexpected show of support, she wrote to him that she was very pleased that he had found his potential mate outside England. She felt that neither she nor her son would ever find completion in England, and with a turn of phrase as surprising as it was original, said that with me he would "dip into another layer of emotion".

She saw "the hesitation in giving one's children Jewish blood and Jewish disabilities", but added, "yet what a fine heritage they have too." It did not surprise her that my background was very important to me. "Backgrounds are," she added. "But to those who have none and want one – an adopted background can also be important." She felt that a mixed marriage was one of the most enlightening, widening processes that existed, and that once a person becomes a part of two worlds, he can never again be the denizen of only one. For her part, she would be glad if he was to definitively cut loose from "English middle-class street-ism and from a donnish exclusiveness."

In August 1942, with the Germans coming close to Alexandria after the British set-back at Tobruk, my father decided to send my mother, my sisters and I to South Africa, along with many British families who were being evacuated. I parted from John as an emotionally committed friend, in no hurry to progress our relationship. John, on the other hand, was very set on getting married as soon as possible. Looking back, I think he was driven partly by the unnatural circumstance of war approaching our lives and the fear and uncertainty that were dominant in our minds. Our families on both sides begged for time. We parted from my father at Suez in August 1942, not knowing when or where we would meet again. Escorted by two destroyers, our convoy zigzagged its way through the Indian Ocean to Durban, throwing depth charges throughout the journey.

I was in Johannesburg for the next six months, until the situation in the Middle East following the battle of Tobruk was reversed, when the advance of the Germans towards Alexandria was halted by the British at the battle of El Alamein in November 1942. John and I corresponded over this time, holding on to each other in the terrible circumstances of war, yet I remained free and undecided. On my return, our amorous friendship continued, but we gradually slid into conflict, first over each other's autonomy and eventually over the question of our respective religions.

Mine was an unreservedly Zionist family with the ardent vision of a Jewish renaissance in the form of a Jewish State in Palestine. Personally, I simply could not see myself departing from this belief and could not visualize being taken away from these very profound aspirations that the Jews had carried from generation to generation. Our people had lasted into the twentieth century and we had a presence.

John soon expressed a wish to convert to my faith in an attempt to please me and allay my concerns about my Jewish continuity. At this point, John's mother, who had written almost in a Matthew Arnold vein about the Hebrew civilization (and much about herself), and had been a very liberal and encouraging mother, decided that John had to be rescued from losing his soul and should not be sidetracked from his future career by rushing to marry and taking on the problem of a new religion. She insisted, and my parents also held the same point of view, that we wait until we knew each other better.

Religions were still very segregated in those days. While socially there were very good inter-faith relations in Egypt, such a step as having a priest and a rabbi officiating together at a wedding, as is often the case today in the USA, had never been taken. Nobody had even heard of such a thing then, either in Cairo or Palestine. The norm was either a civil marriage or a full religious ceremony.

As the gulf seemed so wide, we searched for some uncontroversial unity between us. There we were, two young people going against the stream of inter-racial relationships trying almost alone an impossible act. His mother's attitude was that I, as the woman, must follow the man. I knew in my heart that I could not cope with it. Months passed and we lost the happy spontaneity of our relationship.

John continued to fight his intrusive mother by not giving me up; I believe that his eagerness to have a wife and children sent him racing for this fulfilment. Although in my faith the children of a Jewish mother are automatically considered Jewish, I knew that in the pull of the highly developed civilization in which we would live, probably Cambridge, my identity and authenticity would be completely overwhelmed by the power of the surrounding world. I continued to find it impossible to see myself ever abandoning an identity that had survived for centuries, even though I identified more with the nationalist aspect of being Jewish than with its orthodox practices and customs. My personal view of God was metaphysical. For me worship was a communal remembrance and a sharing in the morality, poetry and the ancient messages of my people.

My parents left me total liberty of choice, which was a very wise thing to do, as I eventually did find my way – not by myself, but by the power of another love in my life, more real and more proud. In retrospect, I am more amazed at the time and openness given to me by my startled parents, than by the offensive letters of John's mother. The great dignity exhibited by my parents moves me even today as I read old copies of letters in their handwriting – especially as I know where their sentiments lay.

Although there are many successful mixed marriages, I have often thought that there is always one who is bound to lose some authenticity. We, with youthful intensity, each well anchored in our backgrounds, had taken on huge ethical and social issues, trying to bring these down to our individual scale. Together we probed with such earnestness and joint solidarity, the philosophical, cultural and social issues that concerned us in our two worlds. It is interesting that my parents thought I should study literature at Cambridge and John thought I should study moral sciences!

The truth was that John and I were each too steeped in our own realities and traditions to change for the other, and though we thought the answers would ultimately unite us, they never did. There was now an inevitable growing awareness of our unbridgeable ambition, though we hid the questioning of our deepest inner souls from each other. I think the uncertainties of the times had carried us away into some dream world of our making, but the truth was that while our attachment was true, we would not be able to sustain it and still be completely true to the spiritual essence of our beings and our societies.

If I had been concerned about my identity all this time, John was preoccupied about his future in science. I knew he was very career motivated and that would probably be the final determining factor on his part. Once, having gone to England for consultations and military leave, he tried putting his thoughts down on paper and mailing them to me, and to be the recipient of such ponderings felt quite precious. He was anxious to discuss his future with his family, and to survey his prospects in scientific research. Following the war, he would begin to encounter others who had also philosophically wondered about the future trends of research, but for now he shared his new view of science with me, as it had developed through the special research projects he had undertaken for the air force and navy in the Middle East.

I feel the birth-pangs of a period of intellectual development in myself (a natural consequence of the spiritual development you initiated.)

And in a later letter:

> I will begin to tell you of the new "scientific school" I mentioned the other day. In the past twenty years, there has been a gradual invasion by the scientists of other fields – philosophy, religion, ethics, art and politics. An invasion which has been resented not only by the non-scientists, but by some scientists too. The philosopher, for example, says: what does this scientist know about philosophy, that he should dare to write books about it? And some scientists say: the place of the scientist, like that of the monk, is in exclusion from the outer world: the watertight compartment of the laboratory. Research should be an end in itself, without thought or desire for results of practical, worldly value. But in spite of such criticisms there have been some encroachments, some of them ill-advised. But not all – my own feeling is that the time is nearly ripe for a great new human step forward in human thought. A grand synthesis between the "compartments" I mentioned – philosophy, science, religion, ethics, art, politics etc... a synthesis which will benefit all of them.
>
> And where do I come in you will say? I am not sure that I will ever "come in" at all in the sense of contributing to this step forward (I thought even if I am not a contributor, I hope to be an appreciator). But you will see that the step can be made only by those who are wide in these sympathies and in their culture.
>
> The pure scientist, narrow in his outlook, is no good (and in that class are just 99% of all scientists)...

I personally thought this last remark was a bit snobbish and even going too far.

...and so for the "pure" philosopher, artist, etc., etc., it is breadth that is needed. That is what I must work for. And you come into it too. It is one of the reasons I want you for my life-long partner. For you have things I have not got: you are a complement to me. Together we can do much. That is why we have so much work ahead for us to do together. I must teach you about scientific thought. You must give me insight, into your spiritual world. It is not just a vague programme, this.

Something very definite which will take us hours of hard work. It is sometimes with books, sometimes in the countryside, sometimes in art galleries, sometimes in concerts. It is something so marvellous, so good – doesn't the thought of it make you leap with joy?

As time went on it was clear that John's desire to marry could only run into incredible difficulties and when he was due to leave for South-East Asia I asked that we each go our own way. My change of heart had come slowly and I needed my time. Parting was very painful and I knew that it wasn't I as an individual that was the issue, but that the gap between our backgrounds was overpowering. Nevertheless, we had both retained valuable moments as a result of our relationship, as he once wrote in a note many years later.

John Kendrew, in an indirect way, played a major role in the forming of my identity by accidentally illuminating the path of my aspirations. Some time after I returned from my six-month absence in South Africa, still committed to our friendship and to issues unresolved, a fabulously brilliant Aubrey came into my life, unaware of this picture.

Meeting Aubrey at this time of turmoil helped me see that my life could go in another direction, and clarified for me what it was that I truly wanted. It made it possible for me to make the final break with John, and to open myself to a new life together with

Aubrey. For a long time I did not tell Aubrey what was bothering me, until he pressed me. I received several letters from him "advising me", in particular pointing out the vast differences in John's and my background, including one where he stated: "*it is not easy but you have a fairly clear course to take*".

I continued to follow John's career, and was pleased to see that he did extremely well in his work. Back in Cambridge with an independent scholarship he had received before the Second World War, he joined the Cavendish team that worked on RNA and DNA. He researched and solved the making of the complex structure of myoglobin. In 1962 he shared the Nobel Prize in Chemistry with Professor Max Perutz, who discovered the shape and composition of haemoglobin. Some years later John was knighted for his achievements in the world of Molecular Biology and for the further thrust he gave that subject besides his own discovery. He founded the *Journal of Molecular Biology*, initiated a dictionary on the subject and established the European Molecular Biology Laboratory at the prestigious Max Planck Institute in Heidelberg, Germany. And one day, much to my surprise, I was told that he was on our Rehovot Campus as a member of the Board of Governors of the Weizmann Institute, where he would remain until the end of his life.

Looking back, it is extraordinary to realize that both of the young men who were so dominant in my feelings and development, each had such consciousness about his own capacity to contribute to society's progress and to humanity's achievements in totally different fields and ways. Exceptional people like this carry within them a clear picture of their purpose – the chartered course of their missions as they set out into their adult lives full of uncertainties but on the high tide of their beliefs.

6

Captain Eban

My father had met Aubrey after we left for Johannesburg. He found our usually busy Cairo house lonely and unbearably still, and so he went to Jerusalem for a week. While there, he dined at the home of our very old friend, Dr Julius Kleeberg, who had once saved my mother from some tropical sickness and had remained my parents' friend over the many years since. Dr Kleeberg had also invited the stepson of a radiologist friend from London's Harley Street. The young man was a British captain by the name of Aubrey S. Eban, or Abba as he would come to be known in Israel.

Aubrey was interested in talking to Dr Kleeberg's dinner guest from Egypt and they soon discovered common acquaintances, such as Moshe Shertok (later Hebraized to Sharett), the head of the Political Department of the Jewish Agency, who invariably called upon Aubrey's family whenever in London for political missions or talks at the Colonial Office. This sort of closeness meant a great deal in times of war, when people were away from their home for a long period, as Aubrey would be for almost five years. Sharett had long been a friend of my parents and visited them each time he came to Egypt. However, Aubrey's family and my own knew nothing of each other's existence, although during his years at Queens' College, Cambridge, lecturing on Arabic literature, Aubrey had known of my brother, who was at Trinity.

Initially stationed in Cairo, on his arrival from England at the end of 1941, Aubrey had been sent to Palestine two months later, assigned by British Headquarters to be Liaison Officer of a co-operative war effort between the British Forces and the Jewish Agency, the latter being the representative political body of the Jewish population in Palestine.

Aubrey was no stranger to Palestine. As a young Cambridge don, aged twenty-four when war broke out, he had already been called, at Dr Weizmann's request of his college Master, Sir Montagu Butler, first in 1937 and again in 1938, to replace temporarily the head of the Jewish Agency's Political Department in London. He knew the political background of Palestine and so when both the British and the Jewish Agency wondered who could be appointed Liaison Officer of their new joint war effort, it was quickly agreed to call on Aubrey, whom both sides felt they could trust.

The project entailed the creation of a special training unit in Palestine and the Special Operations Executive, or SOE as it was known, soon had its training camps full of Haganah and Palmach volunteers. Since 1941 Palmach had been the mobile strike force of the already established defence (underground) group Haganah. In the face of their enemy, the two groups put aside any rivalries. By contrast, rivalry between Palmach and Haganah on one side and the right-wing Irgun (Etzel) and Lehi, perhaps better known as the Stern Gang, on the other was sometimes violent. Palmach and Haganah pooled their young forces and encampments together under one commander at Mishmar Ha'Emek in the country's north. It was a large-scale training programme and through these operations Aubrey found himself working closely with some of the top Jewish leaders: the Technion's Professor Yohanan Ratner, Yitzhak Sadeh, Moshe Sharett, Yigal Allon and Berl Katznelson, the deeply-respected Labour leader who, on a visit to Cambridge, had once asked to meet that already much "talked-about" young Zionist, Aubrey Eban.

Palestine's Jewish participation in the war would entail a Jewish volunteer force to be known as the Jewish Brigade which would serve the Allies but remain autonomous; a military legal institution under its own flag. The British Mandatory Authority had long opposed this momentous step, but with the Germans' eastward march along the North African coast becoming increasingly more threatening, they changed their policy and decided urgently to prepare for a possible German invasion of both Egypt *and* Palestine.

As the British began to enlist volunteers, they hoped to see a 50/50 ratio of Jews and Arabs, but the number of Jewish enlistees soon far outnumbered their Arab counterparts. It was understandable. The motivations on either side were so different: the Grand Mufti of Jerusalem had turned to Germany for help and had been received by the Führer himself. But for the Jews, the story was far different. Hitler's advancing troops would spell annihilation. Thousands enlisted. Hundreds of volunteers trained for sabotage operations under the leadership of Yitzhak Sadeh, the visionary commander of Palmach. Chaim Weizmann, the dominant Zionist figure in the world at that time and President of the World Zionist Federation, had negotiated over a long and frustrating period with British cabinet members and other important policy makers in London for the empowerment of the Jewish Brigade and was finally able to see the fruits of his labours.

Following his liaison duties in Palestine, the British Minister of State in Egypt, Lord Casey, requested Aubrey's return to Headquarters. But once back in Cairo, Aubrey found that he missed his new Palestinian friends and the strong connection he had made to the land and to the cause. In a letter to his family dated 10 April 1943, he wrote from Jerusalem:

> I won't deny that it is a bit depressing leaving here after such a happy and fruitful year, despite all the vicissitudes and "headaches" which made it anything but a restful period. However, the last word is not yet written in my connection with this country. I hope.

Unmistakably British as he was, Palestine had touched the fibre of Aubrey's personality. After living in Jerusalem, his previous world took on entirely new proportions. The intense Hebrew learning of his childhood and his Cambridge University education as an Orientalist had now expanded through direct experience. Looking back, it seems to me as if early life had been a preparation for his destiny – to work for his people. When he asked his friend Moshe Sharett to introduce him to like-minded people in Egypt, Moshe suggested he contact my father, not realizing that they had already met in Jerusalem. Aubrey promptly wrote to him:

Dear Mr. Ambache,

May I have the pleasure of calling upon you? I was a lecturer in Arabic literature at Cambridge. I recall meting you in Palestine at the home of my friend, Dr. Kleeberg. Flying Officer Ellenbogen, who is the fiancé of Eileen Alexander*, is also anxious to make your acquaintance.

Yours sincerely,
Aubrey S. Eban

Aubrey sent this note in the spring of 1943, by which time my mother and I had returned to Cairo after a six-month absence – my sisters had chosen to remain in South Africa to complete their year of study at Witwatersrand University. In response, my father asked me to invite him and his friend to tea. I can still remember the two young officers sitting with us on the white stone terrace that extended the width of the house. Steps led down to the garden with its beds of roses and to the lawn on which we played croquet. The ladies were sipping iced tea; my father and the other men were

---

* Both had been close friends of Aubrey's in Cambridge. Eileen's mother was from the very well-known Mosseri banking family in Cairo, her father a Zionist lawyer from South Africa and a friend of Dr Weizmann.

having their whisky soda. Aubrey sat next to my father and they discussed Egyptian politics in which, Father later said, Aubrey was quite well versed. They seemed to appreciate each other's company. At one point, Aubrey looked at me; he simply looked. I still remember the stare. I knew he had taken special notice of me.

Aubrey and Gershon Ellenbogen lived a few streets away from us, also in residential Zamalek. They shared staff and expenses and were both looked after by the Alexanders' cook and their ancient manservant, Sayid. The cook had her parrot with her at all times, an atrocious adjunct to the household and incompatible with the quiet Aubrey demanded when he worked. To his family's query that summer, he retorted in a letter:

Yes, I am still staying with Gershon, but damn that parrot. To my horror, I learn that they live to a fantastic old age.

Aubrey was collected from his flat every morning for work at British Headquarters, as part of the Major-General's staff. His chief was a Bible-loving Brigadier whose expertise was the political Arab world. The office was run by Marjorie Guirgis (always addressed as "Mrs"), an English lady married to a Copt whom nobody had ever seen. She was in great awe of the Brigadier whom she referred to simply as "Him". I once asked Aubrey what he actually did in that office. His only reply was a facetious letter:

Well, first of all, I drink tea out of little pots with broken spouts and OHMS inscribed on their posteriors. Then, I have three files in front of me, marked IN, PENDING, and OUT. Every day, I move the IN papers into the PENDING file and the PENDING papers into the OUT file. My staff sergeant then takes them into the IN tray of the Colonel. The process is then repeated. This is known as efficient staff-work and it is the method whereby wars are won and empires are built.

In reality, his task was the censorship of the Arabic press and Arabic letters, and it was a job he found boring and demeaning.

The next time Aubrey came to our house, he came alone. There were other guests, as there often were during the war years when we extended hospitality to men in the services, but I recall him in particular. I had to leave before the end of the tea party and at dinner that evening, Mother told me that Captain Eban had waited longer than the others, as if for my return, though he hadn't actually said anything to that effect. As for me, I was busy trying to finish the second semester of my junior year at the American University in Cairo. Having done my primary and secondary schooling in French, I was now forced to speak, read and write only in English. One of my professors had a strong American southern drawl, which was an oddity in British-occupied Cairo, where one was more likely to hear English spoken with a clip.

I was looking forward to the summer holidays, when my parents and I would spend August in Jerusalem, taking a break from Cairo's infernal summer heat (air-conditioning was unknown then). We were to stay at the King David Hotel, a Swiss enterprise in those times, partly owned by shareholders from Egypt. The style was art nouveau and has remained so but socially it had a very distinct colonial atmosphere. The servants wore white *ghallabiyehs* with red cummerbunds and red tarbooshes, as in Egypt, and circulated through the halls with little blackboards and a bell to call a guest to the telephone, a charming custom which remains the hotel's system to this day. The hotel was frequented by members of the Allied Forces and by visitors from the surrounding Arab countries. These visitors often came to Palestine for medical consultations, since the war made it impossible for anyone to travel to Europe except on military or political business.

That summer, Aubrey happened to be in Jerusalem again, this time to create the Middle East Centre for Arab Studies for British officers who would serve in the Middle East after the war in a political or business capacity. We met by chance one very windy day. I took out my mirror to tidy my hair and before I had time to put it back in my bag – there was Aubrey coming towards me. The British Chief-Secretary, who was second in rank after the High Commissioner in Palestine, was using a section of the King David Hotel for government offices so it seemed natural for Aubrey to be around. Although my Cairo background, with its social obsessions and restrictions about courtship, made little allowance for frequent visibility together – such a thing was acceptable for a young couple only when officially engaged – I felt much freer in Jerusalem and alleviated of such restrictions. We spent much time with each other, and travelled on a moonlit night to swim in the Dead Sea. Aubrey had begun to send my life into a whirlwind.

I noticed that people everywhere admired him. Yet despite his wide range of scholarship and political experience, Aubrey was curious about my family's history, its early life in Turkish Palestine, as well as my European schooling and Middle Eastern experience. He also seemed to like the fact that I knew Hebrew. He began to share feelings and books and thoughts with me, and frequently left little notes at the hotel desk for me. I began to see him as a special friend. I loved his richness of character, his vast erudition and humour, and his passion for public service.

For two years Aubrey travelled between Palestine and Egypt courting me in total single-mindedness. I did not want to be rushed, although I understood very well that he was in love, and I was beginning to be so myself and ever more dependent on him. However, I still had a year to go before receiving my American University degree. During the second semester after my return from South Africa, I had taken the courses available in French literature at Cairo University, but I knew I could never get a degree there since I did not know Arabic well enough (hence the American University where I could aim for a BA): I felt I was not ready for marriage and needed my own time.

Aubrey, on the contrary, had decided fairly quickly, and his letters during that period of our courtship were like storms. Descriptive and definitive, he was like a blinding light.

> If you feel a "young girl" in my presence, I assure you that I feel like a schoolboy in yours – wondering if I have done anything wrong and if I am behaving well enough to be asked again! Nothing except physical frankness, as you beautifully called it, breaks down that sort of mutual defensiveness – it is not deep or important. What I mean in a practical sense when I speak of my ability to make you happy is that all my interests, pursuits, associations, ambitions (for I don't deny these for a moment), ideals, acquaintances, family – all fall into a framework which would absorb you unquestioningly and lovingly and naturally, and that all I do is comprehensible to you.

> Damn your light burning there so pathetically, and so alone [simply my late-night studies]. It is all wrong. We ought to be together, talking light triviality in some pleasant spot – not alone as you are, as I am, so comprehensively utterly alone.

There were many letters due to so many separations while he was working in Jerusalem and I was in Cairo. They were often amusing and always penetrating – about people, authors, books, and about our relationship. When he came to Cairo, I would lead him to my favourite spot of escape; a walk along the Nile at dusk, an hour I have always liked for reflections at the day's conclusion. We spoke of everything as we pleased and always with an intensity of spirit. But for me, emotionally, the following letter made my heart and soul go out to him. It may be long to quote but I choose to leave it almost in its entirety for its nobility and frankness.

It is headed "The Office" and re-reading it after so many years I smile to myself. Is it from Cairo? Or is it from Jerusalem? Well, it is just Aubrey! But at least there is a date: April 1944.

Sweet darling,

...If I have felt for weeks that you were necessary for my completeness, I knew it only then and know it now for evermore. Oh Suzy, there are terrible solitudes in the capacities of our hearts and there has often been one in mine whenever I felt you distant or beyond access or in the grip of some experience from which I was excluded.

You know me well by now, Suzy dear one; so it is necessary to say again how ardently I seek your happiness and satisfaction and I'm not going to be a hypocrite about it – in seeking your happiness and satisfaction I find my own. It is a selfish unselfishness. For my heart and interests are indivisible and if you divide them I tell you simply and honestly that my heart must break.

...I have reached a point in my life where I can see no horizon ahead of me in which I can be happy alone without love, by which I mean your love, dear Sue – things are too big for me now, I can't achieve them without happiness and support. It is when a man is engaged in things which make a call on all his resources of mind and character that his harmony and completeness are necessary. You are in fact necessary to me in what I do. Is that not good, Sue? So when I feel the need of your support in many, in all things, I don't get irritated by a sense of pride, I feel that I need your wholeness. Think of that Sue, when you are worried about what you call my intensity about you. It means that I need you which is different from "needing a woman".

Well, you asked for it. Sue these are only some reactions. If you come to me we will ascend the heights together. I mean the heights of happiness...

You know at any rate what I offer you. Through no virtue of mine, I have been enabled to keep a mind moving amidst deep and careful issues and a sense of human interest and human welfare and human warmth as the guiding spirit. So we shan't be cold together and shan't be empty, and there is nothing in or out of us to encourage discord.

On Sunday I was left with a sense of balance, reciprocity, a quiet mixture of strength and tenderness.

Why not, Suzy, sweet gentle lady – for Heaven's sake, why not? Say it to yourself with a vision of our common future before your eyes – is it a bad vision, Suzy – and ask yourself, "Why not?" I tell you with the painful ecstatic certainty of my love that there is no answer.

Aubrey's letters, though sometimes flippant, also echoed his deep seriousness. We spoke of the present and of the quite unknown future; though never of the past or of our respective childhoods, as one doesn't when young and so preoccupied with the self. The past became interesting only when we were in the last stage of our life! We spoke of the world of then, he with a sureness about "us" that conquered me. He gave me a sense that we were meant to march forward together, would it be into politics? Would it be academia? I did not yet know for sure. Whatever the direction in which his life would take us, the concern and loyalty to our people would matter – that much was clear.

Aubrey had choices, but Zionism seemed his most prevalent preoccupation. He wanted to see Jewish aspirations *represented with modern diplomatic attributes* and, in fact, had already structured this in his mind. He was dedicated to Zionism, but refused to settle for sectarianism, and seemed well able to offer it his western approach. As our relationship deepened, I came to realize that Aubrey did not simply want to sympathize with Zionism. He wanted to live it.

Of all the letters Aubrey wrote to me throughout our life together, two have always had a special place in my heart. One is about his early choice of Zionism when he was still an officer serving in the British Army during the Second World War. It is dated 22 December 1943 and concerns the necessity of an independent State for the Jewish people.

> I am uplifted by the majesty of an historical performance in every arena of mental and spiritual conflict – and the performers worked sometimes in suspicion and maintained their pride; and the life of any serious society would be imperfect if you took their contribution away. That is what I mean by the call of the Jewish loyalty. That and another thing, for I saw seven hundred children last year who had horror graven in their hearts because we have not been clever or strong – <u>politically</u> – and I am damned if there will be another generation of homeless children if I can make anything of our lives.

> And I will... It is an irresistible pulse, Suzy, it is disinterested too, for there is nothing to be got from it of external satisfaction! And it need involve no narrowness either or any limitation of humanism.

I knew there would be a philosophical and literary dimension to our lives in addition to the primary Zionist vocation, but I never foresaw the full sweep of things to come. How could one guess how all those rich humanistic elements would come together in one lifetime? What I did know, however, was that there was "something different" in this man, in his mind and even more so in his sensibilities. And I wondered if I was capable of meeting the demands of a life with him.

At first I had hesitated about a career dedicated only to Jewish political life. Even Aubrey's own contemporaries were puzzled. Some found his choice among all the opportunities for which he was equally well equipped, to be a reckless mistake. "Too quixotic!" they said. "Squandering a great talent on a parochial scene." Why the Jewish Agency? What was the Jewish Agency going to lead to? They felt that with his triple First from Cambridge (a rarity even in that seat of excellence) in Classics (Latin and Greek) and Oriental Languages, with his successes and the scintillating humour he showed in debate during his two-year term as President of the Cambridge Union, he should have gone into British politics. This was suggested to him by Harold Laski, Chairman of the British Labour Party at the time Labour won a landslide victory in 1945.

Here in the Middle East Aubrey seemed firmly planted in various streams of action – British, Arab and Jewish – comfortably straddling both the political and cultural worlds of East and West. He was my intellectual superior. It was a tremendous awakening to be exposed to such a mind and to his wisdom. I had never trod the political territory, let alone stood within it as a participant. But Aubrey wanted to belong to the new personification of the world of his ideals and into which he had been thrust through the war. He seemed to want to test himself against its issues. It was overwhelming for me later to realize just how much passion would go into his connection with the world of our people.

He puzzled me, this scholarly man, who only once wrote to me about the possibility of returning to Cambridge and yes, seemed totally engrossed in politics! I couldn't envision what his lot in life would be. He was learned, informed and quick – almost impatient. He was also terribly absent-minded, and objects such as pipes and books proved both a pleasure and an encumbrance. He invariably forgot some belonging or other at our house – a tobacco pouch, a newspaper clipping, a book – forcing him constantly to retrace his steps (willingly!) in an effort to recover the lost article. On another level, however, he always seemed to know his direction and purpose in life. For him, the consequence of attributes was action, and he was not immobilized by his intellect. He demonstrated the craft of disciplined thinking right before your eyes, and illustrations or criticism were brought forth from a vast reservoir of knowledge and an amazing memory.

And then, of course, there was his wit, his love of *esprit;* his mimicry. He brought a sense of amusement about life and people and we delighted in fun. He was just as witty as the press would later show him to be, coming out with the most unexpected sallies that would catch us all unawares. I remember how at one of his early appearances in America as guest of honour at some fund-raising dinner, he looked out, poker-faced, at his black-tie audience and said, "I was told that I would speak to an 'Upper Crust' audience. I got out my Webster's dictionary to check the definition of 'Upper Crust' and the following description was given: 'It is composed of a bunch of crumbs held together by dough!'" (American slang for money) The Upper Crust simply loved it!

But just as often Aubrey would be silent, as if his mind had receded into some world of thought which was his alone. He would follow a discussion or glib chatter, and at the same time exercise his mind in some sphere far removed from the surrounding guests, seeming uninterested, disappearing into his private mental universe. He appeared to be totally oblivious to the conversations surrounding him when he was deeply ensconced in these silent dialogues. But if a word or a detail that had been referred to in the earlier conversation came up later, he would invariably return to the scene and conjure up another word or detail relating to it, to everybody's amazement. The family still laughs today, remembering how when my mother asked Father what he thought of the young man courting their daughter, he answered: "I have no opinion. The man can't talk!"

Before Aubrey became "Abba" Eban, I knew we were to share our lives together. We came from quite different cultural backgrounds – I was from the Middle East, with a strict French education. My home had always offered upper-class bourgeois comfort, with servants and a Palestinian emphasis. My parents had taught us to be committed to life's highest aspirations, especially intellectual ones. Aubrey came from the West. He was a handsome British officer from a traumatized home that had left him with an inner reserve. I assume he was also attracted to my Zionist roots and to my very stable home. In turn I was very attracted to this brilliant, kind and lovable person. I wanted to love him and share my days with him.

Aubrey came to Cairo on leave from Jerusalem in late December 1944. A group of young people gathered at our house and we went to the Auberge des Pyramides, a favourite night haunt of Cairenes both young and old where my sisters and I had several times seen King Farouk ogling the women on the dance floor. Aubrey had suggested that we go there to celebrate Aura's birthday on 25 December, each of us with their favourite partner. We all went there again on New Year's Eve, and Aubrey and I danced tenderly with each other.

On 3 January he and I spent the evening together as he was due to leave for Jerusalem the next day. I had missed him deeply every time he left and I could no longer picture my life without him. I also felt cut off from the indelible inspiration of *my* Palestine. He now had fascinating political stories from *his* Palestine. We had already constructed *our world* and had become close, in a more mature way on my part and a calmer way on his, and I told him I was ready to think of marriage. We committed ourselves to each other, to his immediate future and of course to whatever life had in store for us in the distant future, which I sensed in some intuitive but undefined way. I had a feeling that we would be marching forwards not only reactively but because I believed he would be determining situations. He had views and beliefs, a restlessness about him, a conceptual force – and ambition. At that time I was not aware of his oratorical skills. I only knew him as a brilliant and versatile lecturer in politics, the Middle East and Islamic culture. But in Egypt there was no platform for his Zionism! On the other hand, in Palestine the Jewish leaders considered him a British officer with a definite Zionist presence. There seemed to be a kind of hope about him. Perhaps, perhaps he would, yes, take a full step and join the Zionist struggle.

Later on, in our mutual home, I would often feel challenged by the demands of our coming from two different cultures and I assume that Aubrey must have felt something similar, despite his total commitment to Israel and the fact that he chose it and was not driven into it by circumstances. Separately we had each experienced the Middle East from a cosmopolitan reality and now we shared it together. Our separate orientations were sometimes conflicting. Each element would pull us back to our own familiar grounds. However, there was no need to give up anything and we did not, but a magic act was demanded to keep it all together without a sense of renunciation or deprivation. Simply by our love and caring for each other and with our youthful dynamism "we did it".

7

Cape Town

Aubrey was born in Cape Town on 2 February 1915, two years after his sister Ruth and was taken to London when a mere few months old. The next time he saw his birthplace was in 1941 when he spent a few days there during the Second World War. In December of that year, by then an officer in the British army, Aubrey had set out from Liverpool on the troopship *Orestes* which sailed around the Cape. He had a clear idea that his destination would be the Middle East, although one could not be certain in wartime, but he never envisioned that he would get there by the longest possible route. After three weeks at sea they disembarked in Cape Town. The ship was sunk on its return journey to London.

In South Africa, Aubrey had family from his biological father's side. Meyer Solomon was a businessman of Lithuanian origin. Few of these relatives had laid eyes on Aubrey since he was a baby and the prospect of meeting them in that distant place was an exhilarating moment, a stroke of luck, and it whetted his curiosity. After all, this place had deeply affected his personal history.

His father's family had been so welcoming and kind to Aubrey's mother, Alida, when she arrived as a young bride from England; they were charmed by her and she made friends for life. To Aubrey's amazement, that December, he discovered that they had kept a bottle of champagne from the celebration of his birth.

The family took him to the Zionist Office, Dorshei Zion (Seekers of Zion), a branch of Hovevei Zion, which his father had co-founded in 1899. On the wall facing him was a sepia-coloured picture in a heavy wooden frame of a young couple: his father and mother, Alida looking touchingly young and vulnerable, with a gardenia corsage on her shoulder. She had interrupted her studies and married at the age of twenty-one because her father, Elie Sacks, "Papa", the Victorian autocrat who liked Meyer Solomon, had decided on the match.

When we went on a semi-official visit to South Africa in 1982, the community offered us this picture which is now in Aubrey's study in Herzlia. One day, before we had hung it on the wall, I saw Aubrey alone in his room, the picture flat on his desk where he was sitting. He was looking intently at the portrait of the father he never knew. I believe he must have been searching for a resemblance or the link of some common feature between him and the man he was staring at.

From that visit, we also came back with the only photos of the Hofmeyer Street house in which he was born. By then there were tall buildings all along the street, except for that one remaining small house with its two flat panels of wrought iron at the front. It seemed an extraordinary coincidence, almost as if the house had been waiting all these years, holding out for his visit.

When Meyer Solomon became seriously ill a few months after his son's birth, since it was wartime, Alida received special permission to travel with her husband and two small children on a troopship back to London in hope of finding a cure for her husband. Mostly confined to her cabin, the sea journey with noisy soldiers on board, a very sick husband in bed, a baby boy and a small girl of two and a half to take care of on her own, was pretty dreadful. Two months after their arrival in London, in January 1916, Meyer Solomon died of pancreatic cancer.

And now in 1941, here was Aubrey in Cape Town – again on a troopship – and again there was a world war after an interval of twenty-seven years. He said to me once that it had been strangely personal and yet impersonal to find oneself in one's birthplace never seen or known before, and yet a place that had left such a strong imprint on his life.

A few months after we were married, we talked about his childhood. When Aubrey said, "I was brought up like an orphan," I was shocked. From the security of my own childhood I was wrong to dismiss this feeling simply because his mother had remarried a few years after her loss. I protested, "You can't say that, you had your mother." I have always regretted that sentence. He had, in fact, been sent away from home several times, starting at the age of three and a half to attend a boarding school in Herne Bay on the east coast of England. A Dr Hochsbaum whom Aubrey did not remember despite his wonderful memory, ran the school.

When we were with Ruth one day, Aubrey said, "Nobody ever came who was called Daddy," and she added, "And nobody ever told us anything that was going on. In 1917 there were air raids over London, and we were sent away with Alida's mother, Grandmamma Sacks, to Belfast with no explanation as to who or where." They came back either in December 1918 or January 1919. Grandpapa Elie Sacks started teaching Aubrey, who was not yet four years old, the Hebrew alphabet. As Ruth was disruptive and a nuisance they sent her back to Belfast to their relatives, the Eliott family. Gittel Eliott had two grown-up boys who went into medicine and no daughter so she loved having Ruth. After the school holidays Aubrey was sent back to Herne Bay and Ruth was returned from Belfast and sent to Brunswick College for Ladies in Hove. "If only we had been kept together! There was total fragmentation in our life," she said.

"You were always in somebody else's room," exclaimed Aubrey. All this was stated in a succinct but devastatingly personal way. Aubrey and I had not approached the story of his childhood that closely: he had never gone into his emotionally deprived childhood. Before our modern education theories, the British used repeat "children should be seen and not heard", but in this family they were hardly even seen.

In the summer of his eightieth year, Aubrey, Ruth and I sat together in London and, prodded by me, they reminisced about their childhood. It was all new to me to discover in them this depth of inner feelings about their family life and Ruth's presence had occasioned this. She said, "We never lacked food but we were emotionally starved."

Alida went back to South Africa, probably in 1919, to wind up her home, since she had left many practical matters unattended. Before she left, and after a school holiday, she took Aubrey, who was four by then, back to the boarding school in Kent, and once more left him in the care of Dr Hochsbaum. Kissing her child goodbye, she said she would come back soon. When she did so – a year later – her first sight of Aubrey was of him sitting on the radiator in his room, other children sitting cross-legged at his feet, and he was reading them a story. He looked up at her and quietly remarked, "Your hair is different."

Now Alida had to find a job. Her parents lived with her brother, Dr Sam Sacks, and he invited her to live with them as well, and offered her a job taking care of his patients' waiting room and dispensary. (In those days, patients would get their medicines right there at the doctor's surgery.) She also found a Dr Isaac Eban installed in her brother's home at 13 New Road, in the East End of London. He was Sam's assistant and assistants then lived with the doctor.

In South Africa Alida had studied languages and knew both French and Russian from her childhood in Lithuania which were to prove extremely useful. In the evenings she also worked at the Zionist Office and one afternoon an emergency call came for her to go immediately to the Zionist Federation Office at 175 Piccadilly and translate the Balfour Declaration into French and Russian, a request which made her very proud. Aubrey always said that the excitement engendered entered the family and his consciousness very early. He heard so much as a child about the active struggle for statehood, which was then a new political theme, and the promise of 1917, a victory so full of hope for our people, and the name of Weizmann glorified in millions of Jewish homes.

After dispensing at Sam's practice, Alida expressed a desire to study medicine but she was soon dissuaded: Grandpapa saw that Dr Eban was charmed by her and after the young man asked to marry Alida, he simply told her, "We won't study medicine, my child, we will marry medicine!" And so it was. Alida and Isaac were married in June 1921. As a medical student, Isaac, who had graduated with the Eliott boys in Belfast, had been very sweet to Ruth, giving her coins and sweets. After the marriage, Ruth commented, "I can't call him Daddy. He is my friend and I knew him before Mummy."

There had been many previous suitors but one man she was in love with would not marry her because she had two children. Some fifty years later, when Aubrey was Foreign Minister and we were in London on an official visit, that particular suitor called Alida and asked: "That famous man Eban, is he Eban's son?" "No," she said, "but he could have been yours." Isaac Eban loved children and was happy to inherit two of them: he would give them "their" home and his name. But the condition of the marriage was that he would also have two children of his own.

Sam bought a practice for Isaac and set up the new family in a house on Kennington Park Road in south-east London. The house had to be decorated so Aubrey was once more left at Herne Bay and Ruth, who was brought back from Belfast, was returned to the "School for Ladies". When the house was ready, Isaac Eban and Alida went together to fetch Aubrey and Ruth from their respective boarding schools, and for the first time they lived as an established family. Isaac Eban's two children with Alida, Carmel and Raphe (Rafael, later also a doctor) would follow.

A doctor's life, never easy, was even harder then. After a day in the surgery they were expected to get up at night whatever the weather and visit sick patients in their homes; sometimes Aubrey said, "these old London brown brick 'frowzy homes'".

Aubrey was never effusive with "Daddy", forming a more distant relationship than Ruth who, despite her earlier protestation, had quickly learnt to call Dr Eban "Daddy" and would always very sweetly address him that way. In family conversations Aubrey talked about him as Daddy, but would rarely call out for him. I think the relationship was also partly due to the English habit of more daily separations between parents and children. "Daddy" was wonderful at coaching the children in mathematics and algebra since he had taught mathematics at a Glasgow school.

Isaac Eban loved his classical music after dinner, and he had a great collection of long-playing records. He was pedantically orderly and had an extraordinary memory. By the time he was watching carefully over the young family's mathematics, he was already a general doctor, later specializing in radiology. When I first knew them, Dr Eban was a well-established radiologist in Harley Street. He still read and studied Hebrew well into his eighties for the pleasure of the mental exercise.

To Aubrey school was everything. He simply loved St Olave's which he attended from the age of six. It was rather exciting to hear him describe the school's atmosphere and standards. Every single teacher was an Oxbridge graduate (they even wore academic gowns over their suits in class). They all had done Latin which was then an essential part of English public school education. As well as academic subjects there was a great variety of sports and, as a grown up, Aubrey would still talk with deep admiration about the headmaster, Mr Abel, as a great educator.

Subjects which Mr Abel taught were all the more stimulating as Aubrey measured up extremely well. School brought elevation and was also a compensation for his personal life, although only in his eighties did Aubrey say that he did not like his home. When I asked why, he simply said: "It was not the kind of home I fancied."

When he was not at St Olave's, Aubrey spent weekends with Grandpapa Sacks, continuing to receive Hebrew lessons. This absence from home added to the somewhat reserved connection between stepfather and son. Whatever personal matters Aubrey had to talk about, he did so with Alida, or in any case, with Alida first. Aubrey continued to absorb the Hebrew language during his childhood, and its literature in his adolescence. As a young boy he had no free weekends and knew nothing of play. Ruth would go out to play with their two cousins, Howard and Neville Halper, and they would watch Aubrey through the glass panes of the door, sitting alone in a room with his grandpapa, whose sole ambition was to cram more and more knowledge into his grandson: Hebrew verbs, tenses, punctuation, the Bible and, later, modern writings. Grandpapa literally scooped Aubrey out of a normal childhood, determined to set him apart. Within a few years, he knew most of the Bible, first in Hebrew from Grandpapa and then in English from St Olave's, and of course Latin. Nobody knew what Grandpapa had in mind for Aubrey and when he died Aubrey, aged fourteen, was left feeling free for the first time after eleven years of private tuition. I am almost sure that with British reticence, nobody in his family ever discussed with Aubrey how he felt. Neither did I.

His mother always loved evenings with friends at home where political discussions were the theme and from the early days of my own marriage I remember how *The New Statesman* was read weekly and analyzed thoroughly: they all had Labour sympathies.

I loved Aubrey's joy in his books, his pride in his library. He so enjoyed the smell of new books and to be the first to leaf through them. We always travelled across continents with the inevitable two cartons of books – his and hers. They added a special dimension to our interests which of course did not coincide. His preferences were technical: in his own domains of policy, strategy, historical biographies, and first and foremost diplomacy per se. Mine were art history, literary essays and biographies of special women. We, especially he, would feel as if on a desert island without books. He was not interested in owning objects, art or antiquities, unlike me, but he took pleasure from them. He loved gadgets and very early on acquired a TV set, a computer and an electronic calendar. His musical tastes ranged from classical music to songs by Naomi Shemer, a gifted Israeli composer and lyric writer, and the Yemenite singer Shoshani Damari who was renowned for her authentic oriental pronunciation. He was very pleased that both our children went in for musical careers – as it was *their* choice: Eli, after ten years with the Israel Philharmonic, is a performer and professor of clarinet at Indiana University and also with the Indianapolis Orchestra. Gila is a classical guitar builder, a rare profession for women.

Deep in Aubrey's heart there was always a sense of incompleteness about his family life, a silent curiosity. Pictures of his biological father Meyer Solomon, or of his mother's first marriage were never shown by her, just as she never said a word to Ruth and Aubrey when there was a baby on the way and kept them away from home at that time. Ruth, one day in July 1922, was summoned by her headmistress, and wondering what terrible thing she had done, was informed that she now had a baby sister and was shown the announcement in *The Times*.

When discussing her mother, Ruth always maintained that Alida was not particularly interested in her children and that it was Dr Eban who took them to the park, to the Serpentine in Hyde Park, or to the circus. There always remained around her the aura of the woman "too young to be a widow", of the mother left traumatized at the age of twenty-three, with not enough material resources for bringing up a family on her own and the humiliation of returning with two small children to the family fold after everything had looked so promising in South Africa.

The attachment to her brother Sam and his family always remained strong. He had branched off into his own full life. Elsie Landau, his wife, was an unusual person: she had trained as an obstetrician in Paris because in England no woman was accepted for the study of surgery. Their three sons became doctors and one of them is the renowned neurologist and writer Oliver Sacks. Ruth married a doctor, Robin Lynn, who provided the family with much amusement as they affectionately mimicked his strong Scottish accent. The family's sense of humour and literary creativity was noted not only in Aubrey but also in Ruth's son Jonathan Lynn, the co-author of the extremely popular British TV series *Yes, Minister* and *Yes, Prime Minister* to which Aubrey was able to contribute two or three bon mots. Sam's granddaughter, Caroline, a strikingly beautiful young lady, who became Viscountess Bearstead, is also a doctor. She goes once a week to the surgery in the district where Sam attended daily to so many. Sam was loved for bringing into his patients' homes his joviality and cheerfulness and a great fund of Jewish anecdotes. Aubrey once said that no matter what international fame he had, for some people in London he would always remain the nephew of the beloved Dr Sam Sacks.

One day, when our relationship was close enough for Alida to be able to talk about the sad past, she and I sat alone on the embassy lawn during her visit to us in Washington, and it seemed as if in spite of the long time which had elapsed, the scars had never healed for her and probably never for Aubrey, who I think buried the tragic event in their lives under layers of academic successes and achievements.

I always felt that even as a fully mature man Aubrey was still trying to prove himself again and again to his mother, and as he accomplished much in his far-away world he liked to share only the best and most successful news with her. It was a continuation of the fears of childhood that there was a mother who would never come back. They had the same quick impatient mind but she had more agility and spontaneity. He loved in her an equal distribution of wisdom and insouciance, her sense of fun, and her quick repartee.

Although we did not discuss Aubrey's childhood in any depth until we had children and grandchildren of our own, it was this Aubrey, the sensitive and deep-feeling man who emerged from a sad childhood of self-defined orphanhood, with whom I fell in love. It became apparent to me in very little time that the independence with which he was forced to grow up, and the rigorous standards of education to which he was expected to rise, combined with his outwardly calm disposition and his deep inner restlessness, had helped to shape him into the passionate and sincere leader he became.

8

Entering the political struggle

Luckily, Aubrey came to Cairo mid-way between what was to be our last separation before our marriage; we became officially engaged and set our wedding date for 18 March 1945. Since he was leaving very early the next morning on the long desert journey back to Jerusalem, we became involved in a torrent of plans and suddenly realized how many practical details were facing us in our decision to marry. So much would have to be worked out in the following months by letter and cable – then the most practical method of communication. Telephone calls for civilians between Palestine and Egypt were not permitted to exceed three minutes.

Aubrey wrote to me every day. I was now beginning to understand that marriage to him would involve exposure to the public; in my heart I resented this involvement in my personal life. But when the wedding preparations began to unroll, it actually pleased me and I was proud of my partner now being acknowledged publicly as mine, and I as his.

British Army regulations entailed an obligatory interview with the prospective bride before granting an officer permission to marry a foreigner. Therefore, because of my Egyptian nationality I had to undergo this "ordeal". The assignment of the military matrimonial inspector was probably to prove that our engagement was nothing more than an officer's war adventure. He must have come away with no such information and on departing he said only that the tea was very good!

Our wedding was due to take place at my parents' home in Zamalek. Amir, our head servant, knocked on my door very early in the morning, before I had even woken up, to say that there was something from the *ostaz* (the Arabic word for scholar, Amir's appellation for Aubrey). He brought in a charming basket filled with sweet-peas of all colours. The accompanying note said: "Good morning darling!" A shiver of delight ran through me. It was an auspicious way to begin the first day of our life together.

Some of our guests had arrived seemingly out of the blue, including Aubrey's best man. A day before the wedding, when I was busy with my own preparations, Aubrey was out looking for books. While in the bookshop, he was utterly surprised to discover there his London cousin, Dr Neville Halper, a medical officer on leave from Iraq. Neither of them knew where the other was during the war and, on seeing Aubrey, Neville exclaimed: "What are you doing here?" Aubrey replied, "I am getting married tomorrow – come and be my best man."

I wore a long, dropped-waist *peau d'ange* white dress, covered with the sheerest of sheer lace moulded over it from the neck to the hips. A tulle veil flowed from the back of my floral head-dress to the ground. Aubrey wore his Staffordshire regiment dress uniform with a thick brown leather belt across his chest and smartly shined brass buttons. The crown on his epaulettes indicated that he was now a major.

Our spacious central hall accommodated the 120 guests and the two big wrought-iron doors at the end of the room provided a wonderfully decorative background, forming a veritable picture frame for the lush green foliage outside. My father stood at the bottom of our wide oak staircase, and as the tune of "Here comes the bride" filled the hall, I came down those same heavy stairs that, in my girlhood, invariably creaked when I surreptitiously climbed back to my room later than my parents liked me to.

Aubrey was waiting for me under the chuppah, the traditional white silk canopy, which had been erected on the elevated parquet platform at the end of that central hall and served as a sort of stage where I stood with my bridal party, surrounded by a mass of white flowers. The Chief Rabbi of Egypt, Nahum Effendi, nearly blind behind his dark glasses, officiated on my behalf while the Jewish army chaplain, Rabbi Fabricant, officiated for Aubrey.

After the service and the guests' congratulations we approached our three-tier wedding cake from Groppi's, and our British and Palestinian military friends raised the roof with a resounding "Hip, Hip Hurrah!" and toasted us, the newly weds.

David Ben-Gurion and his wife Paula, as well as Teddy Kollek, the future Mayor of Jerusalem, also happened to be in Cairo at the time of our wedding. Ben-Gurion (or B.G.), the then Chairman of the Jewish Agency, had come to Cairo for political talks at the British Middle East Headquarters and Aubrey invited him to the ceremony, where he stood next to General Iltwyd Clayton, Head of British Intelligence in the Middle East, and Aubrey's chief. Clayton accompanied by Marjorie Guirgis, came resplendent in his dress uniform with medals and red bands on his cap, and the decorations on his lapels indicated a top commander. Surprisingly he held his own Catholic prayer book during our Jewish service! Even on his wedding day Aubrey did not miss creating the opportunity for a political discussion after the ceremony. Paula Ben-Gurion, coming down the receiving line in the drawing room after the service, congratulated me in English and I, wanting to show off my knowledge of the language, thanked her in Hebrew. A minute later she rushed back and asked me, somewhat puzzled, "Where did you learn it?" and I answered, "Here in Egypt and in Jerusalem."

For our honeymoon we left for Luxor and Aswan in Upper Egypt. In the mornings we would set out with a guide to look at the Pharaonic antiquities, which Aubrey had never managed to see before, and in the afternoons we sailed in a felucca on the Nile. We were so carefree now that we were on our own, and intimate in a picturesque and fascinating world. We lived in a closed box of time, untouched as yet by the realities, dilemmas and personal as well as national struggles that would later invade our life.

The second part of our honeymoon was a little catastrophic to say the least! We had returned to Cairo to be with my family for the Passover Seder. It was strange to be in my childhood home as a married woman, but after two days I felt strongly connected to the routines of the house, although in many senses apart from them. Aubrey and I proceeded to Palestine with the intention of ending our honeymoon on the Sea of Galilee (Lake Kinneret). But, on the stopover in Jerusalem, I suddenly felt as if I was getting an enormous boil on my cheek; when I went to see the doctor he declared that I had mumps! I was taken to Hadassah hospital where I was ordered to remain for a week.

What a terrible anticlimax that was but it was crucial that Aubrey not catch mumps from me. After the silk and tulle of the wedding and the specially nice honeymoon, the hospital nurse immediately tied a much less beautiful cloth around my face, and I sat in bed swollen-cheeked, looking like a bunny rabbit and feeling very miserable about what I was doing to Aubrey. All our plans went awry, especially as Jerusalem society was expecting to meet the "imported" bride. My cousin Ella (we always remained close) immediately came to see me in hospital, since we had made plans to meet that day. Unknowingly, she rushed to kiss me, and she too came down with mumps two weeks later, the exact period of incubation.

During the war years it was very hard to find accommodation in Jerusalem but somehow, even before my recovery, Aubrey had managed to procure a suite for us at the American School of Oriental Research in the eastern part of Jerusalem. A year before we married, he had been appointed chief instructor at the Middle East Centre for Arab Studies. The Centre had been established in the Austrian Hospice in the Old City of Jerusalem that the British sequestrated during the war. Affiliated with the British Foreign

Office, its mission was to prepare the Middle East for even greater control by the Empire after the Second World War. Aubrey had prepared a curriculum for the teaching of Arabic by Arab instructors to some twenty carefully-selected officers, while he familiarized them with Middle Eastern politics, history and culture. They would later be assured of political or business posts in the Arab world. It was obvious what the thinking was: the British Empire would rule the deserts forever and for this reason Aubrey had been kept in the army for more than a year after the war in Europe had ended in June 1945.

Aubrey's immediate boss was now Colonel Bertram Thomas who had been Finance Minister and Wazir, or Prime Minister, to the Sultan of Muscat and Oman from 1925-32. Thomas once proudly displayed for us his impressive collection of magnificent Arab robes which he wore as Prime Minister.

British control of these Gulf countries seemed to be taken for granted then – Bertram Thomas as British Prime Minister in Arab Oman – how odd it sounds today. Thomas was the first westerner to cross the Rub' Al Khali (Empty Quarter) from west to east by camel, in a totally different direction from T.E. Lawrence's initial exploration of that vast desert, and had received many honours for this spectacular achievement. Although no real Arabist, from 1942-3 Thomas served in the army again, this time as public relations officer in Bahrain. From there he was summoned to Cairo, with the rank of lieutenant colonel, to open the new Centre and it was then that Aubrey met him for the first time – from that point on B.T., as we and Aubrey's officers called him, shuttled between the Egyptian capital and Jerusalem.

A few months after our wedding, B.T. asked to come and visit us at our new home. We had moved to the Jewish district of Jerusalem called North Talpiot, off the Bethlehem Road behind St Claire, a Catholic nuns' convent, which partly illustrates how mixed the populations were and still are. It was an isolated place with no more than seven or eight houses, fantastic fresh air and a stunning view of Jerusalem. On the hill facing North Talpiot was an Arab village whose inhabitants robbed every house in our neighbourhood one night. By a stroke of luck, Aubrey had left some small change on the window sill and woke up at about 2 a.m. when he heard it tinkling. All our neighbours came out into the square in their nightclothes. There were guards in the area, *gafirs* (the Jewish volunteer force of the time), who were supposed to be protecting Jewish houses, but they managed to sleep through the entire incident, only rising two hours later!

When separating our two blankets one morning, I found a scorpion snuggling between them at the level where my toes would have been. Our house was obviously cheaply built, but we had taken it because it had a piano. To my horror, one evening as B.T. sat comfortably in his armchair with his inevitable whisky, two field mice scampered across the living room in procession – luckily *behind* the Colonel's armchair. They daintily perambulated further, saving us embarrassment and these socially correct mice put me in a hilarious mood after he left.

B.T. had come to plead with me for Aubrey to stay an extra year at the Centre beyond the year already added on to his military service. On a business trip to London, he had even visited Aubrey's parents in Harrow, and as a result he was now describing to me how, after living in Palestine, we would not be able to cope with the harsh conditions of housing in the vastly bombed out London, the deficient heating, the hardships of food shortages and – the atrocious cost of whisky! All true, but it left us unfazed as, with young confidence, our considerations were already different. We were pondering other issues.

Yet by early 1946, Aubrey had still not decided which of the various career options he would choose after his demobilization the following September. I was wondering what he would do with that academic record in Classics. And what about those oriental languages? We had never discussed the possibility of going back to Cambridge in the way we had other matters.

Aubrey and I travelled to Cairo for a weekend with my parents to deliberate the situation in Palestine. He also wanted to discuss with them what he would do after his demobilization, but he was worried about me, about what might happen to his young bride if the situation deteriorated even further. My parents, sensing his wish to enter the political struggle of the Palestine conflict, encouraged him to abide by his intention of joining the Agency and assured him that if he ran into unpredictable difficulties in his efforts, they would take total care of me!

Britain was in a state of moral contradiction. Perceived as an exemplary liberal country, it was behaving in an unbelievably cruel manner on the issue of concentration camp refugees yearning to reach Palestine. What was it now? Oil? Appeasing the Arabs? Power per se? Inveterate Foreign Office Arabism?

There was deep bitterness, profound resentment and despair in Palestine over the British policy of limiting immigration. The Jews of Palestine wanted to take in the sad, starved, ghost-like, battered and displaced survivors of the concentration camps. There were endless curfews. The Jewish population was tense as the British relentlessly chased illegal immigrant ships on the Mediterranean and off the coast of Palestine. We were devastated when they returned a boat of camp inmates to its port of origin in Hamburg. Barely sea-worthy vessels were hounded and sunk, refugees drowned. The British Government's White Paper quota of 75,000 immigrants over five years was tragic, intolerable and inhuman. This infamous Paper was issued on 17 May 1939 in the name of the British Colonial Secretary, Malcolm MacDonald. In defiance of the White Paper there were many secret operations on the Kfar Vitkin, Tel Aviv and Haifa coasts, where illegal immigrants were bravely brought into the country, often by beaching the vessels, and immediately dispersed to kibbutzim and other Jewish settlements.

In one of the most violent protests by any underground movement, on 22 July 1946 the Irgun blew up the wing of the

King David Hotel in Jerusalem where some British Mandate offices were housed: British officials, Arabs and Jews were killed. In all ninety-people died in that blast. An extremist movement, the Irgun considered the representative political body of the Jewish population (the Jewish Agency) and its defence arms, the Haganah and the Palmach, too ineffective.

Aubrey and I were due to meet at the King David that afternoon, as we so often did to make a telephone call to my family in Egypt, since we did not have a phone in our rented house. Thankfully, I was delayed on the day of the attack because of some absurd reason that nonetheless turned out to be life-saving. I had decided to buy pastries since I was in town as Talpiot had no food shop, and Aubrey was late because . . . he was late! We walked all the long way back to Talpiot under a smoky sky and only because of Aubrey's British officer's uniform could we get through. A curfew had already been imposed. Frightened citizens were running in all directions to get home.

That same year some of the executives of the Jewish Agency were jailed, including our friend Moshe Sharett, and Moshe Dayan, who was not a part of the Jewish Agency but a member of the Palmach, as well as a few other "suspects". Menachem Begin, who would become a Prime Minister of Israel many years later, had gone underground as had Yitzhak Shamir, another future Prime Minister, because they were very much on the "wanted" list. Begin headed Irgun and Shamir was the head of the Stern Gang. Relations with the British administration were embittered with their stance of inhuman repression, their cage-like policy of frequent curfews imposed throughout the country. Despite the fact that different political groups within our population violently disagreed on how to cope with the situation, they were nonetheless united in deep pain and anger.

Aubrey, in spite of all this, and more certainly because of the waves of violence and antagonism between the Jewish population and the British rulers, initiated a luncheon with Moshe Sharret to discuss his invitation to Aubrey to join the Jewish Agency in London after being demobilized: Moshe was head of the Political Department. We waited, and waited, assuming that Sharret was delayed by urgent political matters as would be quite plausible in the circumstances, until we heard on the radio that he was in the Latrun jail! On receiving his one-word message, "*Nu?*" smuggled out in a tiny note (originally Yiddish, *nu* has become part of Hebrew slang and means "So?"), Aubrey sent his own one word response: "Yes." He would join the Jewish Agency.

I completely went along with his decision and my parents continued to respect his aspirations and choice. There was a certain logic in the fact that we, much closer to Palestine and its tough political issues, identified more with the poignant immediacy of the problems than Aubrey's family and certainly his friends in distant England. But even though surprised, they never interfered with this decision.

I have often thought about the first letter I wrote to Aubrey's mother – I preferred to express myself in French at the time. In case she doubted it, I assured her that I intended to be a full partner in Aubrey's ideological decision to advance the cause of our people. Even then, in a general kind of way, I sensed the future, but I was not so prophetic as to foresee that we would have a sovereign state within four years of our marriage.

I did understand that we would be striving for an enlarged Jewish autonomy within the British political system. There already existed a Jewish infrastructure within the British Mandate and this ambition would need new and incisive defenders. Aubrey thought much further ahead, like his mentor Chaim Weizmann and his friend Moshe Sharett, the two top titleless diplomats of the Jewish people at the time.

Even in his Cambridge days, Aubrey had been known and described as having adopted Zionism when other students were involved with Spain and Communist Russia. From his work with Dr Weizmann before the war and his own understanding of the

Balfour Declaration's skilfully crafted dual meaning, he and that generation of early diplomatic founders never wavered from their interpretation that the promise of "A Jewish Homeland" meant nothing less than a state.

9

London 1946–7

In the summer of 1946, we were still in Jerusalem and totally steeped in the tensions between the British government and the Jewish community of Palestine, with political conditions deteriorating at an accelerated rate. By September, following Aubrey's decision to join the Jewish Agency, Moshe Sharett wanted him urgently in London to head the Agency's Information and Middle East Departments. The Information Department was actually called the Propaganda Division, a word with such strong fascist connotations that Aubrey remarked angrily that the name was totally unacceptable to him, and insisted the Division be renamed the Information Department. He also felt that the British specialists the Middle East had not been appraised fully as to the real complexities of the region after the horrific events in Europe.

Before we left Palestine for London, Dr Weizmann asked Aubrey if he was coming to work for him, and on hearing "yes", replied that he was very happy. Aubrey had already made himself quite a reputation amongst British officials, not to mention Palestinians, Jews and Arabs alike.

The new assignment was due to start in September, after Aubrey's demobilization. After much paperwork to secure a passage and move our belongings, we left Jerusalem. I knew I would soon have to face all the concerns of daily life on my own in a very battered, very deprived England. I had not been to London since my childhood. During those visits we would stay with my mother's sister Rachel and her husband Professor Hersch Lauterpacht.

Earlier that year I had sent some of my lingerie (part of my trousseau) home to Cairo to be shortened because the hand stitches had to be small and because only a real lingerie-maker could be trusted to do this nicely! I am rather ashamed to acknowledge this now, but it was part of the incredibly feminine mentality we women had in the absurdly luxurious life we led in Egypt. This was of course in sharp contrast to the way of life that was about to follow.

We had heard about the austerity England still faced after the Second World War, but to live it was a different story. We stayed at first for three months with Aubrey's parents in their house in Harrow until our belongings arrived. Alida enjoyed gardening and grew her 100 beautiful roses with utter love. She and Dr Eban continued to listen to music every evening after dinner. I was rather self-conscious about playing the piano there although I had some serious pieces in my repertoire. I was sure they assumed that if Aubrey had fallen in love with me, I must be at least as good as Myra Hess.

Eventually Sigmund Gestetner – whose father had invented the duplicating machine that still bears his name and who was a close friend of Dr Weizmann – found an apartment for us in Highpoint, a property he owned in Highgate, north London. The living room had huge glass panes from where my winter view for months would be only snow and more snow.

Statistically, that winter of 1946-7 was the harshest in England for fifty years (or ever, as some thought); grey and bitterly, bitterly cold and damp. One night the fog was so terribly dense as we came out of the theatre that we had to abandon our recently acquired new car, a Standard, in Piccadilly. Many drivers showed some initiative and stepped out of their cars to guide others. There was no traffic noise, only the calls and exclamations of people bumping into each other. Eventually we succeeded in making our way to the nearest underground station and, after climbing a snow-covered Highgate Hill, we reached our comforting but cold apartment at 2 a.m.

My parents left a xenophobic Egypt for Palestine in 1947, and Tsilla joined me in Highgate for a year to prepare for her entrance exams for Oxford or Cambridge. In between studying she was fantastically kind and helpful to me, sharing in all my responsibilities after Aubrey left for the ancient, gloomy Jewish Agency offices now at 77 Great Russell Street, very near the British Museum. Before Tsilla arrived, I had been so totally alone doing endless chores that I was driven to real despair. As I wrote to my parents, "I don't do anything, but just try to exist."

Everything was a struggle that year, not only obtaining food, but keeping warm, or even managing a lukewarm bath. When we went to Oxford one weekend, as no cars had heating in those days, Aubrey made Tsilla and me travel with hot water bottles under our feet. Even at the hotel in Oxford, where we stayed for two fascinating days, I could not achieve more than a ten-inch "slipper bath". We went to a debate on Palestine at the Oxford Union where Aubrey was due to give the Zionist point of view. The next day Tsilla and I looked at colleges and enjoyed Oxford's architectural splendour with David Samuel, the grandson of the first High Commissioner to Palestine, now Lord Samuel (ironically an Israeli member of the House of Lords). Meanwhile Aubrey had a meeting with Isaiah Berlin (then a Fellow of New College), followed by an important talk with Professor Reginald Coupland, as the initial author of the idea to partition Palestine into two independent states, one which he had already presented to the British Mandate's Peel Commission in 1937.

These were times when we were all so close as a family that we never let more than a few days pass without each of us – father, mother, brother, three sisters and respective spouses – keeping in contact with the others by either writing or phoning. My brother Nachman lived with his bride Stella, also a Cambridge student, and a doctor – in a bombed out house in Chislehurst in Kent, for that was all one could get then. We shared details of our daily lives, which were now so difficult and full of uncertainties, especially after my parents went back to Palestine, their country of birth. They later came to London for Tsilla's engagement to Peter Castle whom she met when they were both students in Cambridge, and stayed a month in order to prepare for the wedding. Sadly Aubrey and I could not attend as we had already been called to New York.

During what was our relatively short stay in London, I often marvelled at how disciplined the British were, how resolved to accept the hardships. They spoke in muted tones, were very polite and courteous to one another, and the women did their errands wearing a hat, though I could never work out if it was for warmth or for respectability. I remember, too, standing for long hours in queues for our rations, hearing British housewives' angry grumblings about "our innocent boys" and about these "dreadful Jewish terrorists in Palestine".

The coal crisis was extremely serious. Everyone tried to reduce their usage of heating or lighting in some way, although there was hardly the need – electricity was cut off at specific hours. All the same, at the Highpoint apartment it was not too bad in comparison with other places but there were many times when I had to go up and down six flights of stairs in darkness. It was a struggle to get the laundry dry in front of a little electric stove between the permitted hours of 12 and 2 p.m. I needed a coat round the clock – a strange feeling for a Mediterranean person, and Aubrey's aunt, Lina Harper, promised to get hold of some fur-lined boots for me since my dozen pairs of thin-soled Egyptian shoes were completely useless.

Another challenge was finding some way or other to entertain, and the person who did me a wonderful turn was Aubrey's old friend from Cambridge. Chatty, exotic Eileen Alexander gave me the address of a butcher in Dublin from whom I was able to receive a small, neatly nailed wooden crate with *real* meat kept fresh by the cold weather. This solved my problem of a main course for dinner guests each time, and was more than all three of us could receive on our coupons.

Despite all the hardships, there were also worthwhile occasions, such as my exposure to London's exceptional theatre. We admired Laurence Olivier in two breathtaking performances as Julius Caesar and King Lear, and then again in *Antony and Cleopatra*, this time playing with Dame Edith Evans. This marvellous actress had the clearest enunciation, but could no doubt have better kindled Antony's passion some ten years earlier. We didn't miss seeing *Les Enfants du Paradis* on New Year's Eve. London was in a joyous mood and I was struck by the capacity of the English to let their hair down and behave like very rowdy children. Age seemed to have no bearing on the festivities.

At about this time we also attended a dinner hosted by the Anglo-Egyptian Union under the patronage of the Egyptian Ambassador to London, Hussein Nahat Pasha. I described the ill-fated evening in a letter to my parents (written to them, as always, in French).

> On both sides, English and Egyptian, the speeches were extremely inappropriate, considering they were meant as expressions of friendship! The English were condescending and quite directly staked a claim on Egypt dating back to the Second World War, when the Allied troops at El Alamein victoriously pushed back the Germans before they could reach Alexandria. The Egyptian Ambassador responded with a series of carefully chosen sentences that were a real cold shower! For him the notion of "Anglo-Egyptian" was a social concept and involved only personal relationships.

The newly elected Labour Prime Minister, Clement Atlee, had been due to attend but the coal crisis forced him to be away – or perhaps this was being used as a welcome excuse to avoid the sensitive issue. Notwithstanding the austerity of the times, the women wore long elegant gowns and beautiful furs. I, too, held my own in a turquoise-blue moiré evening gown from Egypt and the long, white-kid gloves which protocol then demanded for official dinners.

Swimming against strong antagonistic currents, it was a busy time for us and Aubrey felt that had we started a year before, the picture might have been different. He analyzed and expressed Zionist views in an equal, intellectual dialogue both with British officials and the press. Nevertheless, even when intellectuals on both sides used similar turns of phrase, the contents and emotions were miles apart. The British Government never budged from its 1939 White Paper policy with its quota of 75,000 immigrants over five years.

Aubrey was developing an impressive chain of contacts at the Colonial Office but he often came back either depressed or angry or both. I wrote home on 4 January 1947.

> Negotiations are in full swing morning to evening with the press pursuing us on the telephone. It is Tsilla and I who are the willing victims since we two are usually in the apartment.

Aubrey reached out to editors in the British press, went to universities and spoke to both Conservative and Labour MPs. A task assigned to him was to write Dr Weizmann's speech for the Basel World Zionist Congress of 9 December 1946. The details and mood of the Congress were fully reported in *The Times* in two long columns the following day and I remember how my young husband rushed out of Highpoint early that morning to check if that prestigious newspaper had adequately covered the speech.

Aubrey remained in London to look after the hour-by-hour situation in the capital, and the day after the Congress opened, he influenced the editor of *The Times,* Dr Rushbrooke Williams, to write an editorial favouring a Jewish State which would strengthen the moderates at Basel. Years later when they came to have tea with us in Jerusalem (when Aubrey was Foreign Minister), and we discussed the Egyptian boycott of the West, Mrs Rushbrooke Williams mentioned that nevertheless Nasser's children were dressed in Marks and Spencer clothes. I asked how she knew and she answered, "because my children wear the same". About Basel, Aubrey wrote in a letter to my parents, "I was officially informed that the Secretary of State was vitally interested in strengthening Dr Weizmann's position." (This, I believe, meant that the USA was in the picture even then, since it had participated in the League of Nations planning of a British Mandate for Palestine after the First World War.)

Sadly this was to be Dr Weizmann's last Zionist Congress. As he criticized the people who sat in comfort in New York and grumbled about the intransigence of the Jews of Palestine, some right-winger from the crowd shouted at him: "Demagogue!" After a moment's astounded silence, Weizmann passionately retorted: "I, a demagogue? I who have borne all the ills and travail of this movement? The person who flung that word in my face ought to know that in every house and stable in Nahalal, in every little workshop in Tel Aviv or Haifa, there is a drop of my blood." There was tempestuous applause; the delegates all rose to their feet (except the Revisionists and Mizrachi), as he continued like a shaming prophet. Then, leaning on his wife Vera's arm, Dr Weizmann walked out, never to return to his position as President of the World Zionist Organisation.

For Aubrey and I, although not present, this was our first view of a personal and explosive drama in political leadership. Aubrey, so involved intellectually and emotionally with the Zionist issues, was shocked and deeply affected by the tragic spectacle of the Congress and wondered whether he could have influenced the outcome had he been by Weizmann's side. I can't help thinking today how television would have made a dramatic difference in the world's cognizance of the conflicts of Zionism – not that it would have helped right there in those incredibly tense moments. When it seemed as if Zionism was turning into a state of acrimonious bickering, Aubrey and I never lost the conviction of our cause and the belief that we must fight on.

After Dr Weizmann's walk-out, Paula Ben-Gurion busied herself and claimed to B.G.'s entourage that the situation must be corrected right there and then. She even thought of procedural corrections but to no avail. Blanche Dugdale, Balfour's niece and biographer, and very close to the Weizmanns, clamoured for an immediate retreat by the opposition at the Congress. But Weizmann had stumbled and when he called for Aubrey on his return to London said to him, "You wrote me such a good speech that they fired me after it!"

In the year and a half that we resided in London, I entertained Aubrey's Cambridge friends. A real quartet they were! Joyce Nathan and Bernard Waley Cohen, who later married and years after became Lord Mayor and Lady Mayoress of London, and Eileen Alexander and her husband Gershon Ellenbogen. There is a different kind of seriousness and humour between ex-college students, and Aubrey's friends were no different.

I became well acquainted and loved to be with Aubrey's family. He found great moral support in our encounters with them, sharing events amidst the difficulties. All of them, even Dr Robin Lynn, Ruth's husband, the one Conservative member of the family, were dedicated Zionists, unquestioning Weizmannites and faithful readers of *The New Statesman*. No less well informed was Aubrey's half brother, Raphe, who fully participated in the discussions about British politics within the family while observing them all with a supercilious smile. They were proud that Aubrey mattered in decision–making circles. Even after a five-year absence serving in the British Army, he already had good communication with his public who would listen carefully to what he had to say. They always knew in their hearts that it would turn out this way, though not what would be the ultimate outcome of his activities.

One day, as Aubrey was working assiduously at keeping his contacts with the Colonial Office and the press, he again received an urgent request from Moshe Sharett, to explore with the prime ministers or foreign ministers of France, Belgium, the Netherlands and Luxembourg whether they would support us in the presentation of our case for the "Partition of Palestine" at the United Nations. Aubrey was most impressed with the charismatic Léon Blum, the French Socialist statesman, and the first Jew to become Prime Minister of France (from 1936-7). Léon Blum was deported to Buchenwald concentration camp in 1943 and subsquently was sent to Dachau from where he was liberated in May 1945. He served again, briefly, as caretaker Prime Minister in 1946. Joseph Luns, the Dutch Foreign Minister, was as immensely tall as Charles de Gaulle and, if one may compare, more sympathetic to our cause. Aubrey also spoke to Paul Ramadier, the French Foreign Minister, and Paul-Henri Spaak of Belgium who was both Prime Minister and Foreign Minister, the latter addressing Aubrey as if he were a public meeting!

10

America

With great foresight, Aubrey decided we would go to the United States together. Within five days we closed our London apartment and on 8 May 1947 we departed for New York. Neither of us had ever set foot on the American continent, and that in itself was exciting and quite special. There were no direct flights between London and America then: planes invariably stopped at Shannon in Ireland before the huge leap across the Atlantic to Gander in Newfoundland and then to La Guardia, at that time both the domestic and international airport in New York.

Believing that we would be away for a maximum of six weeks, those six weeks were to become twelve years – years that would prove to be particularly significant for us as we discovered a completely different scene politically and personally. More importantly, these were critical times, strategically, diplomatically and economically, for the Jewish people. It was almost two years since the end of the Second World War and yet every day there were shocking new revelations about the Holocaust.

We arrived in New York during the day: it was spring and the visibility was extraordinary, giving us the first aerial images of the city that we would see again and again over the years. Aubrey's youngest sister Carmel – whom I had not met before – came to greet us. After she had been demobilized from the WRENS (Women's Royal Naval Service) Carmel took the adventurous step of asking to serve as part of the United Nations staff in New York. Although not a lawyer, she was on the legal side and was part of the British quota for UN secretarial staff. It was all a bit anomalous. Here was Aubrey, after five years in the Middle East, coming to lobby for a Mandate-free Palestine. His sister was working as a British subject, as was Aubrey himself, and I, as his wife, also travelled with a British passport. It is hard to believe that at the time the British allowance for travelling abroad was only £75 per person.

Carmel had left England before Aubrey and I arrived there. She was dynamic, well read, with high literary standards; she was crazy about the theatre and worshipped Shakespeare. She had studied acting at RADA, and English literature at Oxford in the hope of becoming an actress. We were to develop a good and friendly relationship.

There was much to do, see and learn in this extraordinary new country politically and journalistically with its informal, casual speech and behaviour. The city had its own beat and travelling there was like running impatiently through one's music scales on a keyboard. It had a totally un-European character in its population's mixture of races and colours, although I learned quickly that the mixture was of tribal or cultural entities.

The Jewish Agency housed us first in some bombastically titled Empire Hotel on Broadway and every three days we had to move, as at that time after the Second World War no hotel offered a reservation longer than this span of time. Our first encounter with New York City seemed more like reading Damon Runyon, whose stories of Broadway and of the typical American, and especially the New Yorker, had inspired many a Broadway play. It was a world full of colour, zest for life and frenzied activity. Its buildings could not have been more different to the solemn buildings of London, nor could the brisk, tangy vocabulary and the curt answers of the people have been more at odds with the muted intonations of British speech and reserve.

I was fascinated by the functional and much accepted procession of food rushed through the streets in brown paper bags at all hours of the day, as well as a new novelty for us, "drug-stores", which were placed in specially targeted spots where an abundance of humanity dropped daily on to the street from their high-rise offices above. On the sacrosanct Fifth and Madison Avenues, elegant and conservatively dressed women wore hats and gloves. Perched on high heels, they carried stiff, shiny shopping bags, bold evidence that shopping was still part of the American system, an economy so different from British rationing and an emaciated Europe – even after the war. And then there were the white-haired old ladies, brazenly wearing bright red dresses or jackets in the restaurants. At the edge of the pavements, under heavy steel grids, rose the sound of the subway. On Third Avenue, the "subway" traversed the city's sky as if suspended in mid-air. There was something energizing and liberating about the clearly stated size, length and width of New York's avenues so that to get around, it was sufficient to use numbers! Unlike the solemn black taxis of London and the battered versions in Palestine, here the cabs were a cheerful yellow. The speed at which they travelled down those avenues was nerve-racking.

During one of my first cab rides, the driver remarked: "You have a foreign accent, Miss, where are you from?"

"The Middle East," I replied.

"Young lady, you are wrong," he replied. "There is no Middle East, there is only a Midwest," he responded. When I got out of the cab, I wondered what had made me say Middle East instead of Palestine. Probably to avoid a discussion on what we were living through from morning to night – as well as night to morning.

New York brought a great breath of a refreshing reality into our lives. The city had been left physically untouched by the Second World War and we had just come from bombed-out London, yet the unforgettable share in and sacrifices of the United States in that war had taken its soldiers to the continents of Europe and of Asia.

By 1947 Aubrey was known in England but was quite unknown in America. Indeed, he had previously been turned down as a speaker by the Jewish Agency New York Speakers' Bureau.

However, the President of Hadassah* in New York, Rose Halperin, who was also on the Board of the Jewish Agency and therefore more knowledgeable about the active Jewish scene abroad, had heard a lot about him. On our arrival she asked him to attend a meeting in a private home and address Hadassah's board about the situation in Palestine. This was to be his first contact with Jewish leaders in the New York community. Through a detailed analysis of events in Palestine and his first-hand impressions of talks in Whitehall with British government ministers and senior Colonial and Foreign Office officials, Aubrey asked the politically eager ladies seriously to envisage that the British would leave Palestine. The logic was that since the British were going to give up India, they would no longer find it necessary to keep 100,000 British troops in a country with as many problems as Palestine. It had been valuable to them only as part of the route to India, he told them. The ladies were flabbergasted to say the least! I had very inconspicuously seated myself in the back row and I remember reporting to Aubrey later that people in the audience had sneered outright at his prediction. I witnessed that the stately, pince-nezed Etta Rosensohn, long-standing President of the organization and widow of Judge Samuel Rosensohn, was the first to stalk out after Aubrey's presentation, muttering angrily under her breath: "Schoolboy stuff!" as though she had been personally insulted. But on the whole we were received with friendliness and some curiosity and felt welcome in America, where great concern was shown for events in Palestine.

On another occasion, when we first went to San Francisco, then a stronghold of assimilated Judaism, the audience was informed that a lecturer from Palestine was available to give a report on events there. They told us later that they had expected some

---

* The American Women's Zionist Organisation founded in 1912 by Henrietta Szold and others.

impressive presence in a long black coat and hat, and what a shock it had been to see a man in a modern western outfit, who addressed them in impeccable English!

That's how it was at the beginning – that's how we started. People had completely wrong impressions: they didn't know that Palestine had a modern side as well.

That first flight to California gave me a great linear view of the United States, east to west. Aubrey as usual would take a look only every now and then as he was getting through his *New York Times*, *The Times*, *Le Monde*, *New York Post*, and the Hebrew newspapers that Jerusalem provided a few times a week then. I was stunned by the sense of space, the vast unexplored stretches of emptiness that were so naively "reassuring" to me. The real New World was endless. There was so much to discover, to take in and to appreciate, and when one tried to compare it to anywhere else one quickly discovered it was truly incomparable.

I was spellbound by the American art world that was soon to be an added anchor outside my Zionist world and was just starting to break away from conventional views in an inventiveness of its own. It was the beginning of the New York School (of Abstract Expressionism) watched over by its guru, Clement Greenberg, and the new wave of collectors. Later the exposure to extraordinary museums, brilliant art collections of Impressionists and Cubists saved from Europe and contemporary American art in American homes was literally inspiring. I remember my first encounter with a George Segal sculpture proudly shown off as a full-length white plaster figure standing at the last curve of a "found" old-fashioned wooden staircase on a dark parquet floor. Years later we met the sculptor and became life-long friends with him and Helen, his wife. George sculpted a stunning white plaster wall-piece of me and after he moved into dark greys, almost blacks, he donated to the Abba Eban Centre for Israeli Diplomacy (part of the Harry S. Truman Institute for the Advancement of Peace at the Hebrew University of Jerusalem) a dark-grey sculpture of Aubrey seated.

Behind this sculpture is a detailed map of Israel with a striking red line as if an approximate territorial partition had created the State and the approximation of that line gave me a feeling of an undefined conclusion.

Another great surprise came on my first ever visit to the Modern Art Museum, discovering Jackson Pollock and his drip technique, a disarming confrontation with all the premises acquired in old established museums. The galleries provided us with a wealth of special discoveries and proved how art was an essential constituent of New York life. Later, during our diplomatic assignment in the USA, there would be uniquely large and spectacular shows such as the Van Gogh exhibition, or the Cubists, completed by the relevant Hermitage part of its own Cubist collection – the first time it was shown in America.

Although we had come to the US in the service of our cause, it was mostly I who had the incredible satisfaction of being able to make time for getting acquainted with the new creativity and the intellectual search of American artists boldly seceding from the artistic domination of European art and relating to their own light and scale. They used unconventional, daring materials and techniques and were well on the way to expressing themselves with the power of their own civilization and even more so with their individual personality.

Whenever my thoughts turned to our national problems I wondered if I should have had a sense of guilt, but here was such a unique enrichment to my life, a call of celebration. Here was a different kind of viewing of the human mind, new expressions of artists relating to their own world. The New World was beginning to grasp its own realities and debated its need of an expression relevant to itself, sensing where it differed in its way of seeing and projecting its subjective world. It was an education not to be missed and I was so thrilled to be touched by it.

I also knew that in this "short stay", as we first thought, in this new country, I was from now on going to live on two parallel tracks. The art in museums and galleries would display new works for weeks, but UN debates were like a flowing river, never the same from one moment to the next. I decided I would be constant to both: the United Nations in its make-shift first home, the abandoned gyroscope factory at Lake Success, where the Jewish people's lives and future were at stake, and then there was my world of artistic appreciation.

So, when Aubrey went to Lake Success I, too, attended sessions because I was unwilling to forgo the privilege of seeing and hearing first hand the debates in which the future of the Jewish people would be decided. The days had a unique quality, charged with heavy existential responsibilities, and I was conscious that because of Aubrey's role I could witness the actual diplomatic creation of that future. We were actively aiming for a sovereign state – a legal shelter for thousands of homeless survivors of the Holocaust confronted by the games of the Great Powers. Our strategy was still exploratory. Aubrey would be developing much of it, step by urgent step, supported by Moshe Sharett, so as to be in accord with the UN Charter and the nations sympathizing with the humane and diplomatic side of our work, while confronting our virulent Arab enemies. As the representatives and defenders of the Jewish people, our Mission had definite political aims and an obligatory moral reckoning so charged emotionally. It demanded a huge, concerted effort of our new breed of diplomats, press and public relations to reach the inner powers of a world too readily willing to forget the vast human tragedy that was the Holocaust. What nerve-racking hours we passed in that abandoned gyroscope factory! We shared dramas and fears and moments that sixty years later are almost impossible to imagine.

For months the members of the Mission worked together in solidarity with the men working frantically to get the necessary votes for the Partition scheme. We were suddenly operating with urgency on a world scene: besides Europe there was now Africa, Asia and Latin America, whole regions where Zionism had never functioned on the political level before. Latin America became an important bloc. Mostly Catholic, many citizens had been indoctrinated to feel a certain antagonism towards Judaism. It was important to present, in parts of the world that had not suffered directly from the Holocaust, our undertaking for salvaging and sheltering the battered remnants of our people. Primarily this had become a political issue, running alongside a humanitarian track of urgent rescue and rehabilitation, and demanded constant effort to find the channel needed to obtain the necessary vote for partition in each capital. And to think that the United Nations had only fifty-seven members in those early years!

Since, of course, we had no embassies at that time, every day necessitated new efforts in the search for the sources of power in each country. It was like a treasure hunt with immense ramifications for the winning team. Certainly Aubrey's eloquence and articulation of thought was an asset in communicating with nations that had no prior interest in or understanding of the devastating issues of Palestine. We had a most knowledgeable and hard-working Argentinean colleague on our Mission, Dr Moshe Tov. He took over the daily contact with the South American countries and was extremely helpful in the preliminary contacts with countries of almost a whole continent so that Aubrey could fully apply himself to his own daily semantic struggles and dealings with Arab delegates and their sympathisers.

On 15 May, during a special session of the UN, Andrei Gromyko, the Soviet Union representative on the UN Security Council, stunned the delegations, journalists and radio stations of the world by proposing the Jewish State. Aubrey and our delegation were ecstatic about this incredible turn around in the balance of power. The Russians, of course, made their proposal because it suited them at the time: anything to diminish the influence of the British.

Following this event, the UN recommended there be a thorough, balanced study of the situation in Palestine and established a Special Committee on Palestine – UNSCOP. The Arabs decided not to co-operate, although it was to their detriment as well as leaving a real political vacuum in the field. David Horowitz, the economist (later Governor of the Bank of Israel), who always had the facts and figures at his finger-tips, and Aubrey were appointed liaison officers from the Jewish side. The British Government had already announced the termination of its mandate to take place on 15 May 1948.

During the summer of 1947, I accompanied Aubrey on the UNSCOP mission to Palestine. The Chair was Judge Emil Samdström of Sweden and the committee consisted of eleven members: the two South Americans in particular, Guatemala's Professor Fabregat and Uruguay's Gracias Granados, were quite passionate about our plight. The other members were from Australia, Canada, Czechoslovakia, India, Iran, Netherlands, Peru and Yugoslavia. I was struck by the fact that there was not a single woman. Diplomacy was a man's world then.

The idea of the visit was to show this select committee the situation "on the ground" and create a two-state solution in the area: they had to choose between partition and a federal state. Aubrey hit on the idea that the delegates be shown the ship *Exodus* in the Port of Haifa and observe the cage-like conditions of camp survivors – 4,500 refugees crammed on to a small ship. All were cruelly returned by order of the British Foreign Secretary, Ernest Bevin, to Port de Bove near Marseilles. After the passengers refused to disembark, they were forcibly removed at Hamburg, their port of origin.

During a visit to a kibbutz, I was struck by a lack of awareness when one of the members of the committee, trying for impeccable balance, asked, "You have shown us a Jewish kibbutz, will you now show us an Arab one?" After ten days, the UNSCOP members moved to Geneva where, with Aubrey and David, they worked together with the UN Secretariat at the Palais des Nations on the preparation of their report and recommendations for the next UN General Assembly session in mid-September.

I was grateful for those ten days in Palestine as they gave me the opportunity to see my family, my grandparents, and my sister Aura who had married Chaim Vivien Herzog in May 1947. Chaim was the eldest son of Yitzhak Herzog, the Chief Rabbi of Palestine, and before that the Chief Rabbi of Ireland. He was also Aubrey's childhood friend. Back in 1946 and a Lieutenant-Colonel in British Intelligence, Chaim was serving in Germany. One day he had come to tea with us when we were living in Jerusalem's North Talpiot and told us that he was due for a stop-over in Cairo on his return to Germany but knew nobody there. I suggested a visit to my family and when he called on them Aura opened the door to him – it was love at first sight!

We spent a tension-filled summer not knowing the outcome of the UNSCOP recommendation. Would it be a federation or partition and two states? Just before midnight on 31 August 1947, the report's deadline, Aubrey and David Horowitz were waiting outside the committee's room like expectant fathers. Dr Ralph Bunche, an American and assistant to UNSCOP, opened the door wide and announced: "It's a boy!" The committee had opted for partition. (Today such an announcement could not be made – the feminist lobby would have made itself very vocal!) The verdict was a political victory for the point of view of Weizmann, Ben-Gurion, Sharett, Aubrey and their colleagues but was a bitter disappointment to those activists who would not compromise and would only accept – be it on the Arab or the Jewish side – nothing less than the whole of Palestine. Now, in the twenty-first century, when Israel's international status is accepted almost world-wide, it is difficult to impart the stuggle and pitfalls of those times. This status would be established step by step as country by country started recognising the sovereign State of Israel.

On their return to New York, Aubrey and his team next had to lobby many more members to ensure the obligatory two-thirds positive vote of the General Assembly scheduled for 29 November 1947, to ratify the Geneva committee's recommendations. Palestine, after the British relinquished their mandate, would be partitioned into a Jewish state and an Arab state. Strong nerves and all-out efforts of persuasion were demanded to lobby this time for the implementation of the UNSCOP decision and this without the basic facilities of an embassy. Up to the very last minute there was extreme tension in the air. Would all the countries that had promised to vote in favour of partition do so? Some tried to delay the vote for their own political purposes. For example, under the pretence that he could not miss his connection via Europe, the delegate of Thailand, Prince Wan Waithayakon, embarked on the *Queen Mary* twenty-four hours before sailing time to avoid the negative vote he was instructed to cast.

The chief of the three rapporteurs of UNSCOP to the General Assembly was Ambassador Thor Thors, the Icelandic delegate. When Aubrey, early in the morning of the day of the vote, urgently explained to him the importance of his support for the partition (Resolution 181) in his presentation of the Geneva recommendations, Ambassador Thors was literally stunned to discover that his small country, with a population of a mere 150,000, had such a major role to play in this drama. Yes, we could count on his support and he bought with him a significant number of crucial votes.

There were some amusing anecdotes about getting the votes, including one about a delegate who had promised to vote for partition but on the day wasn't there. Moshe Tov happened to go to the men's room and, to his great surprise, he recognized the delegate's two-tone shoes. He got him to come out for the vote.

The hall was tense. Thousands waited outside the building in anxiety and hope. The Jewish world held its breath, and so did its supporters: they counted each and every "yes" or "no". I shall always remember the rhythm and sound of these calls and the pathos of their meaning. There were absentees, there were abstainers, but at the end of the dramatic count we had thirty-three for, thirteen against, with ten abstentions. We had won by the requisite two-thirds majority.

Afterwards Aubrey and I, joining Moshe Sharett, drove back to Manhattan, one hour from Flushing Meadows where the vote had taken place. Emotionally drained and not unaware of the immense task still ahead, we three sat in complete silence. Aubrey was thirty-two and I twenty-five. It was just incredible for me, having lived with every detail and every step taken along the way, that at such a young age Aubrey had had a truly determining role in a unique event for the Jewish people.

I I

From delegate to Ambassador

The Egyptian Secretary-General of the Arab League, Abd al-Rahman Azzam Pasha, and Aubrey had met for tea at London's Savoy Hotel during the summer of 1947 when Palestine was still under British Mandate. Azzam told Aubrey then that the Arabs would not accept partition. They might lose their case, but they would most likely fight us. He was right. Immediately after the vote of 29 November 1947, all hell broke loose and terrible attacks by Arabs against Jews flared up in Palestine. The War of Independence had begun. For us, the human cost, coming on the heels of the Holocaust, was already bringing much sadness and much loss of life.

There were continual dramas of cease-fires achieved and then broken numerous times, but a sense of purpose and deep faith at every stage and in every action, sustained the fighters' sacrifice and hope. It was clear, indeed, that this time a state must emerge after more than 2,000 years of prayers and when that happened the following year, in May 1948, a sense of magic radiated from our Mission building, with its flag at full mast and its sign proudy proclaiming, "The Permanent Delegation of Israel to the United Nations", next to another which read: "Consulate General of the State of Israel". People sometimes stood in front of the building at 66 East 70th Street just to stare at it, trying to take in that these words really meant what they said.

Immediately after the War of Independence started, Aubrey worked furiously behind the scenes at the UN trying to broker a truce. At times there were fears that we were losing the support of the Americans and others. The US State Department, never relenting in its opposition to partition and trying to manipulate the size of the country after the UNSCOP report, came up with the idea of a temporary trusteeship, which would include the Galilee but not the Negev, which was included in the UN partition. It was here that the international status of Jerusalem was included. Dr Weizmann, always kept informed by Moshe Sharett, had caught on to the threat of an international trusteeship over the whole of Palestine – even if defined as "temporary". This was as late as 13 May 1948, less than forty-eight hours before the British were due to leave: the Jewish leadership was very worried. Desperately concerned, Dr Weizmann called Aubrey out of the UN Security Council meeting. But Aubrey was able to reassure him: at a dinner we had attended at the home of Trygvie Lie (the first Secretary-General of the UN, from Norway), Andrei Gromyko, who had, after all, proposed the Jewish State, came towards us, shook Aubrey's hand and said solemnly, "Good! Good! You have killed trusteeship. Congratulations!"

Everything had to be in place for Israel to take over sovereignty of the country, and for the nascent state to be recognized by the international community. What dramatic days and what anxieties and fears! How our fight for freedom riveted millions of radio listeners. The threat of trusteeship for *all* Palestine was still circulating around the UN and in much of the press. To interpose an international trusteeship during what was by then a fully-fledged war and with the clear ambition of a sovereign state, was making the situation perilous for us and would defeat independence. The urgency to run a society with its gates wide open to immigration and give, at last, an autonomous response to our social and religious traditions was immutable. Trusteeship was not acceptable. A passionate race was on in our representation at the UN to defeat it and we were completely single-minded about our one ambition: a sovereign Jewish State.

We debated between ourselves what moves to take and which people to activate next. If only President Truman would meet Dr Weizmann! American Zionist leaders remembered that President Truman had a Jewish friend, Eddie Jacobson, from the time the two of them ran a haberdashery shop together in Kansas City. Jacobson had never ever made any request of Truman as he advanced in the world of politics to become President, just as he had always been a perfect associate in their earlier joint business. At this crucial time for Palestine, the Zionist leaders decided to ask Jacobson to arrange for Dr Weizmann to be received by President Truman. Truman at first opposed the request. He thought the Jewish lobby had been energetic enough. But Jacobson would not give up. He knew no other person in our leadership had had access to the President so, as a last resort he said to Truman, "Andrew Jackson was always your hero, Dr Weizmann is mine. I ask you to please receive him." The President thought for a moment and then said to his old friend, "You bastard – you win!"

So it was that they met at the White House on 18 March 1948. There was a genuine rapport between them, each with his own style. President Truman from then on called Dr Weizmann "the Old Doctor". After this talk, the President heard that the US delegation was still functioning on the basis of the original premise of trusteeship and this angered him. He exclaimed, "The Old Doctor will think I am a plain liar!"and there and then the White House contacted the US Mission's Ambassador, Warren Austin, and ordered that recognition of the independent State of Israel under its Provisional Government should be given by the USA. Warren Austin, startled by this change in policy, called back the White House to make sure it was true. He had been on the point of proposing trusteeship in the name of the US in accordance with State Department policy. What a dramatic political reversal this was as, within seconds, Warren Austin announced that instead of a trusteeship over the whole of Palestine, the USA would support an independent State of Israel as per the UN Partition Resolution. The new instruction reverberated around the world as the policy of the premier world power; journalists scrapped their forecasts while our own Mission savoured the taste of historical justice and "lived" the great political moment.

So did I in my own seat in that awesome Security Council Hall. I had been privy to the preparatory juggling of ideas by members of our UN Mission since Aubrey shared so much with me. And as I recall this extraordinary chain of events, it flashes in my mind as the equivalent of some ancient king or ruler granting a request to his people, certainly in terms of the modern structured diplomacy of our State.

A General Assembly vote was scheduled to take place in May 1948. Aubrey had quickly requested that Moshe Sharett deliver a speech against the trusteeship proposal. As usual, Aubrey set about drafting the speech, working long into the night of 30 April. At that time, we were living in Meyer and Shirley Weisgal's apartment for a few months while they were in Palestine. (Meyer was the Chairman of the Board of the Weizmann Institute.) Early the next morning, the phone rang. It was Moshe Sharett. He said, "I have read the speech. Since you sat up all night writing it, it is only fair that you should deliver it."

It was thunder from the sky. We looked at each other in total surprise. Such a brief conversation for such a momentous occasion! And when we simmered down we still could not believe the gesture. I cannot think today of anyone who, even if he had followed Aubrey's career and attachment to Zionism, would have put such complete trust in a man junior to him in age and rank and given him the world's stage with such certainty and utmost belief in his abilities to conquer this illustrious forum of the Security Council.

Aubrey delivered the speech – "Against Trusteeship and For Partition" – that same day, 1 May. Not only did the content cause an uproar but the eloquent young man was received with great curiosity. Where did his articulate English come from? The expertise? The lucidity? The passion? Endless questions. It seemed a new star was born.

After Aubrey's speech, Moshe Sharett mysteriously disappeared from the Assembly Hall. To our surprise, we learnt a few days later the reason why: he had gone to send a cable to Aubrey's parents in London.

HAPPY BE ABLE CONGRATULATE ON AUBREY'S STRIKING MAIDEN SPEECH IN APPEARING AS OFFICIAL SPOKESMAN JEWISH PEOPLE IN INTERNATIONAL COUNCIL STOP HIS EXTRAORDINARY BRILLIANCE IN THOUGHT AND EXPRESSION POWERFUL COGENCY OF REASONING DIGNITY OF PRESENTATION DID OUTSTANDING CREDIT TO OUR CAUSE AND MADE US ALL IMMEASURABLY PROUD STOP SPEECH MADE PROFOUND IMPRESSION ON ALL STOP FRIEND AND FOE LISTENED WITH RAPT ATTENTION MANY CHARACTERIZING IT AS ONE OF THE HIGHEST WATER MARKS OF ENTIRE SESSION STOP WARMEST REGARDS.

Some time later I went to a UN meeting with our friends, Dewey and Anne Stone. Anne asked me: "Aren't you nervous when Aubrey speaks?" and I replied: "No." But after he finished I apparently gave a sigh of relief, although I knew in my heart that he would succeed. Anne very quizzically commented: "Who says *she* is not nervous!" It is difficult to describe now my feelings about Aubrey's public speaking. He had a tremendous power of concentration while preparing a speech and would obliterate anything that did not concern his task. People were carried away by the form of his presentation; but it was the analysis in preparing the arguments that was so important – they too-often skipped that part. He worked late into the night preparing his drafts; sometimes he would ask my reaction to some sentence or idea. I was then the public. At other times he had to speak virtually off the cuff. I always felt that those who worked with him on whatever national issue respected his distancing from his environment as his pen rushed onwards in that small handwriting, the words at times written in full so that he could keep their cadence mentally in the construction of his sentences. Sometimes the thoughts ran so fast or, more often, the situation was so pressing politically that he would jot down a few headlines and count on his capacity for spontaneous expression. For instance, during the Sinai War of 1956, he had very little time to prepare his speech for the emergency meeting of the Security Council. He went to the Westbury coffee shop, across from our Mission, sat scribbling headings for about twenty minutes, and then made an incredible speech. When he went up to the podium he carried a bunch of papers, as if it were his well-prepared text. Afterwards, one of the team, Esther Herlitz, asked, "It must have taken you hours to prepare. Can we use your material?" Aubrey replied: "No, I just did it very quickly. There's nothing here; I just picked up these papers to give the impression that I had a written speech."

On 1 May 1948, I sat for hours at the General Assembly. The Trusteeship Membership Resolution for the *whole* of Palestine was defeated at the tense deadline of 6 p.m. (midnight Palestine time) and the United States officially recognised the new "Provisional Government of Israel", not yet an official state. Not only the Israel Mission but those who participated or attended had by now become experts in international law. We knew we had been recognized *de facto* but not yet *de jure*! Israel would in fact be the first diplomatic creation of the UN. There followed phenomenally hectic hours as the whole world watched and wondered whether the Jewish state surrounded by so many enemy states would last. Aubrey always said it would be a convergence between his diplomatic tasks at the UN and the triumphant feats of Israel's forces in the field. The two were so closely and inseparably intertwined. We, the Jewish people, knew this was our hour, our one and only chance. It would never be regained and must never be lost.

On the morning of 14 May 1948, before the official deadline for ending the Mandate, the British left Palestine. There was a dramatic picture in the press. The British High Commissioner in his military commander's uniform, standing in the launch that was taking him towards the destroyer waiting at Haifa port, was giving a last salute to Palestine as the Union Jack flapped in the air.

That afternoon, before the Sabbath, a carefully selected group of heads of various political parties gathered in the small Tel Aviv Dizengoff Museum to hear Ben-Gurion make his Declaration of Independence, announcing that the new state would be called Israel.

The next day, not quite sure of his status, Aubrey sent a telegram to Sharett (who had hurried back to Tel Aviv for the Museum vote), asking: "What should I do now?" The answer was he should remain in New York as the new State of Israel's first Head of Mission at the United Nations. We should have thought: "Weren't we in fact the first diplomatic assignment of Israel?" but we were too caught up with the immediacy of events and procedure. I felt Aubrey was almost jumping out of his skin. It was an immense moment in our life! Telegrams and good wishes poured into the consulate; the telephone rang non-stop and the staff had to be increased immediately. It is with great emotion and a deep sense of those historical moments that I remember as I write … and ever will! We hurried to the Waldorf Astoria on Park Avenue to congratulate Dr Weizmann who had just been appointed the first President of the newly born State of Israel.

Sadly, but not to our surprise, within hours the first shots were fired at Israel as Arab armies began to pound, harass and invade the newly born country. Jerusalem came under siege. Without water and food supplies, there was real famine as the city was brutally cut off from the rest of the country. I worried about Aura and my parents on Mount Carmel in Haifa. By chance, Ambassador

Azcarte of Spain, a member of the UN Conciliation Commission during the War of Independence, offered to take a food parcel to my sister. She later told me what a great event the parcel's arrival was, with a wonderful smell of coffee in the house, and how she and Rabbanit (Sara) Herzog distributed some of the contents to friends in Jerusalem, as I had requested.

I realised that our "temporary" stay in New York might stretch out longer than we had expected in light of Aubrey's new position. Although he was the new State's UN chief representative, we were still not official members of that prestigious body – and that was the next diplomatic battle to be waged in New York at the same time as the War of Independence was being waged in Israel. Indeed, on the diplomatic front he and his team were working day and night trying to establish a cease-fire or truce.

Aubrey continued to use the co-operation of the people who had worked with him. Now, as a sovereign state, it meant that its representatives had to take up Israeli citizenship, and this posed a dilemma for our American team. Most decided to retain their American citizenship and slipped into the background. As Aubrey succinctly puts it in *Personal Witness: Israel Through My Eyes*, "We 'backroom boys' were now out front." Until an Israeli passport could be printed (only after our official admission to the UN) I would travel with a *laissez-passer* which seemed to give me a non-identity for a while.

At the same time, things were sometimes very difficult; juggling the responsibilities was a challenge. There was little time for personal life and the endless tasks took their toll. And yet one never dared to complain. In Israel a war was raging and attacks were constant on all fronts. People were dying just for the right to exist in their sovereign state. Our battles were of a different nature and we had to persevere.

A truce was observed from mid-June to mid-July 1948, after which hostilities broke out again. Finally, a more stable truce was negotiated and fighting stopped in December 1948–January 1949, after the conquest of Eilat. The young state had defeated armies from five fighting Arab states, the cost was cruel and hurtful, but the sense of purpose was supreme.

Aubrey was a slave to his deepest ambitions. He so wanted the centuries-long yearning of our people to be channelled after the Second World War into an autonomous modern national system. To many of us at that time, it was nearly impossible to reconcile ourselves to the inexplicable cruelty, perverse hatred and death of those years. Such monstrous acts had left many terribly vulnerable. The horrors could not be explained – neither the purpose nor the means. Aubrey opted for dedicating himself to the cause of Jewish homelessness which was calling out for our next "diplomatic" step.

In order to obtain Israel's admittance to the United Nations as a full and sovereign member, the rounds of negotiations and lobbying started all over again. That summer we took a short "working holiday" in Geneva, where my parents were residing for the summer and where Aubrey had meetings with Chaim Weizmann. One day, just before he departed for lunch with Weizmann, an unbelievable cable arrived from Sharett:

PLEASE DON'T FORGET TO APPLY FOR MEMBERSHIP IN THE UNITED NATIONS.

Aubrey did have a reputation for forgetting scarves, gloves newspapers, books, etc., but to think he would "forget" to apply for Israel's membership to the United Nations! And now the subsequent irony: that same afternoon, a telephone call from our embassy in Paris, where the next UN Assembly was due to take place, startled us: Count Folke Bernadotte*, the UN Mediator, had been assassinated, presumably by one of Israel's extremist military

---

* The Swedish-born, UN-appointed peace mediator who had proposed that the Negev be given to the Arabs. He was succeeded by the brilliant American mediator and former assistant to UNSCOP, Ralph Bunche.

groups. The instruction was that we leave immediately for Paris from where Aubrey was asked to travel to the funeral in Stockholm. I hurriedly pushed all our clothes into suitcases in the most uncaring way to make the night train.

I waited for Aubrey's return in Paris where Sharett, now the Foreign Minister of our provisional government, had gone to prepare for the Assembly. It was a tough moment for Aubrey to represent the country where the assassination had taken place. The civilised Swedes, shocked as they were, managed to rise above making any accusatory expressions towards our official representatives.

Back in New York, the following months saw intense negotiations to gain formal recognition of the Jewish State by the member states of the UN. Finally, following Aubrey's speech on 11 May 1949, Israel was admitted to the United Nations as a member state by a vote of thirty-seven for, twelve against and nine abstentions. Immediately afterwards, people applauded (which is not usually considered acceptable in the Assembly Hall), embraced, laughed and many cried. Outside, thousands waited in the street: the vote had such a deep historical dimension.

I wrote to my mother:

> Our admission to the UN has been a very moving episode. I can tell you Aubrey's speech was a "monument!" Rarely has a speech had such impact. Somebody from the British delegation said: "After this I am ready to recognize Eban but not yet Israel." The Canadian delegate told Aubrey, after the vote for our admission, "You have won by your personal prestige."
>
> The UN Assembly finished its sessions two days ago and we have [already] taken part in international debates other than ours.
>
> The resolution against Franco's Spain was won by two votes, Australia and Israel. The next day there was already

an attack against us in the Spanish press. They did not jump on Australia but on us!

For the Italian colonies, it was strange for us to find ourselves on the day after the most stormy Arab protestations against our admission, united with all the Arab and Asiatic bloc, all of us voting together against British trusteeship for North Africa. So, just for a few days we cast our eyes on horizons further than the Mediterranean and the Jordan River.

Our first major reception, held at the UN, to give expression to the fact that we were now "on the scene", was on the occasion of the first anniversary of Israel's independence – May 1949. Arthur Lurie, who had represented the Jewish Agency in New York and had been appointed Consul-General, also gave a party. We entertained 250 people – mostly heads of Mission, and stood for a total of five hours shaking hands – the Jews were so excited! It is difficult to find the right words – exhilarated, euphoric, stunned, incredulous. I was so proud of our Mission and doubly proud of my husband. He had given his all to the struggle.

A story that I also recall from these early years in New York concerns Eleanor Roosevelt, the widow of the American President, Franklin D. I quote from a letter to my family:

> Sunday, 27 March 1949: Our visit to Hyde Park was of extraordinary interest. We had lunch at the country estate of Mrs Roosevelt. She behaves with a striking informality. There is something pure in her personality. In her own way, with patience and tenacity she tries to improve the human cause. She talked at length about the Negro problem and all the injustices that have gone with it. Franklin D. Jnr., who had invited us, was also there, and another son, Eliott, married to the actress Faye Emerson.

After lunch, Franklin took us around the historic property of Hyde Park – the little house that FDR had ordered to be constructed according to his own plan. The view from the principal room and the terrace is breathtaking. It is there that the famous "Hot-dog garden party" for the King and Queen of England took place. Apparently the Queen, who had never eaten a hot-dog in her life, did not know how to handle one! It was said, she had asked, picking up the hot dog: "From which end does one start?"

Conditions in post-war New York were difficult, and we were constantly moving to and from temporary accommodation. I was pregnant with our first child and our living conditions were still not satisfactory. Finally, the consulate found us a nice two-bedroom penthouse through the Rudin family six weeks before Eli, named after Aubrey's grandfather, was born in the middle of a snowstorm on 17 January 1950.

Immediately after Eli's birth, Aubrey was asked to leave for the UN in Geneva where all the most important discussions about trusteeship, this time for Jerusalem were taking place. Israel again wanted to avoid trusteeship and certainly a vote on it. Most countries never recognized this and have embassies in Tel Aviv instead. Aubrey brought me home from hospital, left a couple of hours later and stayed away for two and a half months. Overseas calls were very scarce for us then and, sadly, he missed the first few months of Eli's development – something we both felt very keenly. But I wrote to him often and described our baby's progress. The solitude after Eli's birth was terrible for me. I was alone for so many days and nights although I received concerned telephone calls from Arthur or Jeanette Lurie and Rachel Tov the wife of Moshe Tov. On Aubrey's return from Geneva our reunion was great and Eli, in the meantime, had made sweet progress.

Eight months later, the Foreign Minister, none other than our friend Moshe Sharett asked Aubrey if he could take on the additional appointment of Israel's Ambassador to Washington, to which we agreed, moving once again. It was at this point that Aubrey's name was hebraized to Abba, as an Israeli ambassador had to have a Hebrew name.

It was quite arduous for me to wind up our stay in New York as a little family of three at 240 Central Park West. Our black maid Bertha was so enamoured of Eli that, although apprehensive about Washington with its even stronger colour segregation than New York, she decided she would come with us. This was to be a great help for me as she was very personable and devoted to us. It seemed that as we prepared for the move, we would have a respite from our nomadic life and at last, at last, we would have a proper base.

אמצא

Above   Construction of tile factory, Motza, 1904.

Below Left   Suzy's parents, Le'a and Simha Ambache, 1932.

Below Right Suzy (right) with her mother, sister Tsilla and brother Nachman, 1923.

Above Left Sailing to Europe, 1932. Suzy, eleven years old (right).

Above Right Suzy and Abba's wedding in Cairo in 1945.

Below With Meyer Weisgal (left) and Secretary of State General Marshall (right), 1950.

Above   A moving visit to an isolated immigrants' camp. An elderly woman offers Suzy a bunch of mint, the only plant growing there.

Below   Arriving at the UN, New York, 1951; (from left) Paula Ben-Gurion, Abba, Suzy and Jeanette Lurie, wife of the Consul General of Israel in New York.

Above   Suzy with Janet (left), the wife of Secretary of State, John Foster Dulles, in Washington DC.

Below   Under Stalin's picture in the Soviet Embassy, Washington DC, 1950s.

Above Suzy and Abba with their children and her parents, Washington DC, 1956.

Below With the Israeli Inbal dance group and Gila at a party given by Suzy, Washington DC, 1958.

Above   At a UN farewell dinner for Suzy and Abba, New York, 1959 with Sir Pearson Dixon, the British Delegate to the UN, and Lady Dixon.

Below   Suzy and Abba with Eleanor Roosevelt and Sir Pearson Dixon at the same dinner.

Above Left   Leaving for Israel with the children in 1959.

Above Right   With David Ben-Gurion at the opening of the Rehovot Conference at the Weizmann Institute, August 1960.

Below   Suzy with (from right) Ben-Gurion, two guests from Africa and Golda Meyer (centre) at the Rehovot Conference.

Above   Suzy with President Ahidjo of the Cameroons at the Rehovot Conference.

Below   Looking at Abba's bust by Robert Berks at the Ebans' home in Rehovot.

Above   On a trip to Greece in 1962 when Abba was Minister of Education.

Below   On tour in Thailand, March 1967.

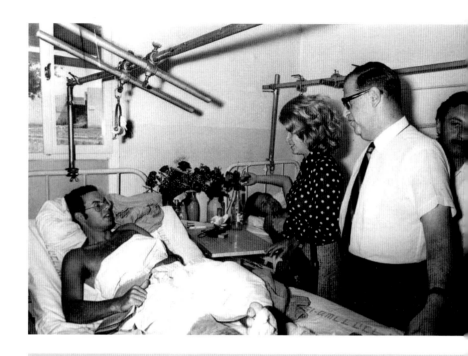

Above   Visiting the wounded at the Hadassah Hospital, Jerusalem, June 1967.

Below   At a dinner Suzy gave for Nancy Kissinger (left) at Mishkenot Sha'ananim, Jerusalem, shortly after Nancy's marriage to Henry Kissinger in 1974.

Above   Suzy with Yigal Yadin.

Below   In conversation with President Anwar Sadat of Egypt, Ismailia, 25 December 1977.

Above   On the same visit; (from left corner) Egyptian Chief of Staff General Gamazzi, Suzy, Vice President Hosni Mubarak (later President), Prime Minister Menachem Begin and President Anwar Sadat.

Below   On a camel at the pyramids on Suzy's second return visit to Egypt, April 1979.

Above   On the banks of the Nile during the same visit.

Below   With Queen Noor of Jordan, Amman, 1995.

Above   With King Hussein of Jordan during the same visit.

Below   Suzy and Abba in May 1989 at a lunch they hosted in New York for Beit Berl,
         Israel's largest academic college.

12

Washington, DC

I flew alone to Washington, DC at 10 p.m. on a September night in 1950, a young and newly appointed ambassadress with an eight-month-old baby in her arms. On arrival we were taken to our new home, which was to be the first residence for the Ambassador of Israel in Washington. A house had been prepared for me to view at 1673 Myrtle Street, N.W., a few weeks earlier, and since I did not express any opposition, our government bought it. It was a very pleasant place with its garden and its panelled sitting room, but in no time it turned out to be too small for Aubrey's new position and hosting members of Congress. Thinking of the hundreds of thousands of immigrants in Israel living in tents and transit camps, I did not have the gall to ask for a bigger residence.

I took on a butler to help with serving at Abba's all-male dinners held to explain Israel. When he decided to display my silver wedding presents I told him that I liked a simpler set-up. He answered: "You cannot do that. The house will look as if it has been burgled!"

We had hardly managed to settle down when Teddy Kollek, minister at the embassy (number two to the Ambassador) called me in great glee: our government had been given a house with four floors as an embassy residence into which we were meant to move. It was a most impractical and unsuitable building, tall and narrow, totally out of accord with what we needed. The interior was neglected, the furniture was flashy, with the colours of furnishings clashing. The sitting room credenza had antique mirror doors on which had been painted huge black roses. Equally bad was the fact that the house consisted of many small rooms, the last thing needed in an official residence when entertaining.

I turned the gift down and expressed my desire to stay right there in the first family-size house we had lived in, but Teddy said I must not refuse since the donor had just agreed to be the first chairman of Israel Bonds in Washington. This was a new venture we had helped to launch in the US only a while before. It was much opposed by the United Jewish Appeal (UJA) leaders, who thought that it would badly hurt their venerable organization, the main fundraising body for Palestine and then Israel created in 1939 on the eve of the Second World War.

They claimed the loyalty of donors would be split but, on the contrary, projected as an investment Israel Bonds raised huge sums for the development of Israel and continue to do so to this day. Aubrey and I did our best, fox-trotting and cha-cha'ing our way through the main cities of the USA with the fund-raising "Ambassador's Ball".

When I saw that Teddy would not budge from his position, I suggested that I would move only if the house we were already occupying was sold and the proceeds used to reconstruct the interior and furnish the new residence in a modern style – in fact to redo the interior of the place entirely. He agreed.

Now I had to formulate my ideas as to how the young State of Israel should present itself. We all opted for a modern style residence and it was Teddy's idea that the furniture should be custom-made in Israel. We knocked down walls, and the old brick house breathed modernity inside. It aroused much curiosity. The outcome was striking and unknown in the conservative diplomatic circles of Washington. When it was completed I invited the press for a viewing. *The New York Times Magazine* gave it notable coverage. The two Washington papers with large circulations had different views on the subject. One printed that, "for a poor country, how did [they] dare spend [so much] money on decorating the house", while the other paper came out with: "How come there are no crystal chandeliers and dark red velvet curtains as would be expected from an ambassadorial residence?" And some of the young Israeli staff complained that I was not running the place like a kibbutz, i.e. eating all our meals together (on benches) because the kibbutz was, after all, the unique pride of Israel. Everybody seemed to have a definite opinion about how I should run the place.

On the first floor Abba's study was spacious, as was our third-floor bedroom. But the dining room, which was so important, even after knocking down partition walls to enlarge it, was suitable only for small groups. Years later, on Israel's tenth anniversary, Abba decided we would give a dinner in honour of Secretary of State John Foster Dulles and Mrs Dulles and so, to accommodate a table of twenty-two, we emptied Abba's study and turned it into a dining room for the occasion. The bookshelves taking up the entire length of the long wall only stressed that the Ambassador was an incorrigible intellectual. No embassies had books in their dining room! The kitchen was on the second floor, but with efficient and caring helpers we managed it all.

An embassy's representation carries great significance and that includes the physical space and its portrayal, and is in direct relationship to the diplomatic obligations of the head of mission. An embassy without a proper official residence might diminish the prestige of a country and most importantly, it hinders the social scope of one's work. Of course, I felt that the diplomatic residence, with its many social events, must primarily act as a stage for political dialogue. The modernity of the new house went some way to compensating for its most impractical structure.

All pictures on the walls were Israeli. When we held a reception in honour of our Minister of Religion at the time, he looked at a very abstract nude by Pinhas Litvinovsky, where the lady was a turquoise blue. I had turned the picture sideways to obliterate the subject. He gazed at it and said to me: "What a lovely landscape of the Sea of Galilee."

Some of my first obligations as a newcomer were the usual half-hour calls on wives of other ambassadors so we would get to know each other, and then the ladies made return calls on me. This made it possible at official functions immediately to be on friendly terms with the people on the scene, and sometimes it was expected that we women introduce the husbands. In Abba's case, since he was already known from his appearances on TV, the recognition was instant.

At a tea party given by Mrs Eisenhower at the White House for ambassadors' wives, the Egyptian Ambassador's wife, Mme Aziza Hussein, recognised me – we had both studied social sciences at the American University in Cairo. However, Israel and Egypt were enemies at the time so Aziza and I did not allow ourselves more than conventional civilities. In the course of the tea, the wife of the Iraqi Ambassador asked her in Arabic who I was, assuming I did not understand. Aziza poked her elbow into the woman's ribs with her elbow and said, "*Escoty!*" "Keep quiet!"

Besides the two jobs of Ambassador and UN representative, there was another essential challenge: to visit Jewish communities throughout the United States and create a vital link between Diaspora Jews and the State of Israel. We gave it all we could – both physically and emotionally – and our efforts were worthwhile, the outcome was both reciprocal and heart-warming.

There were many formal dinners and events in the various cities where the rehearsal for the seating arrangements on the dais would be lengthy and, later, the presentation of the speakers no less lengthy. Sometimes the whole function would stretch out to four or five hours. Abba, frequently the last speaker, once opened his speech with the following remark: "As you see me come up to the podium to speak, you know your ordeal will soon be over."

Finally, the numerous invitations from Jewish organizations to speak about "the situation" in the Land became too much for

Abba; he never wanted to say no and – God forbid – offend any one organization. So he wrote to World Jewish Congress President, Nachum Goldmann, suggesting: "Why don't we collect all the organizations into one and then I'll come and speak to them." This was the beginning of AIPAC* which fostered the principle that all the organisations work together. Abba couldn't help but remark: "AIPAC represents the major Jewish organizations. I'm still waiting to hear of a minor Jewish organization."

In 1952 I lost a baby girl of twenty-six days from what is today known as cot death. Abba was in New York when he received the dreadful summons to return to Washington and left immediately. There had been a terrible snowstorm and he had difficulty getting to the train station, arriving home only after dark. Aura and Chaim, who was military attaché at the embassy at the time, were tremendously supportive, and contacted my parents in Israel to tell them the tragic news. For months afterwards I could not sleep with the door to the corridor leading to our bedroom closed. This was true trauma.

The Washington period of my life placed me squarely in the defined role of a diplomat's wife: creating channels of communication on every level; hosting official functions and serving as part of my country's public relations effort, promoting our crafts, travelling and appearing on my own.

Our daughter, Gila, was born in 1954 and she brought great joy to us both. Together with my own responsibilities which came with the two diplomatic missions Abba headed, the Jewish communities across the US and my new family, I was completely overloaded. The role of the ambassador's wife in Washington was much more demanding than at the UN, not to mention that our house was away from the mainstream of embassies, which made

* Amercan Israel Public Affairs Committee

the mingling a bit more complicated. I became involved in Washington social life, often having to give "greetings" from Israel to women's organizations. I must confess I did not always enjoy those occasions when I had to get dressed up – but it was all part of the job.

For what was required of me I had very little staff: Nanny Gates to help care for the children, a maid, and a French cook. We employed a caterer for the bigger parties and receptions. Abba had a driver, of course, but I drove my own car, which was simply necessary. I am sure I made a few mistakes at the beginning – despite the fact that there was a protocol section at the State Department that gave out strict instructions regarding table planning and invitations. I was told: "Whatever you do, it must be in the papers, or it is as if it didn't happen."

"The wife of" is a full-time job and yet not a defined one. The woman is an adjunct and yet plays a necessary role because, in my case, Abba had such major responsibilities and it was essential that as his wife I embraced the human relationships around his assignments. I was expected and required to open our home as the representation of Israel and this often meant relinquishing our privacy. Our home, the decor, the food, and even the children, small as they were, had public visibility. The assignment was often a disruption for them as they grew up, in terms of language difficulties and strange customs foreign to their own culture. I believe that we, the diplomatic families, never felt as if we were in our own private lives and homes.

I believe, too, that at times, the wives must resent this lack of privacy in the home which exists almost always as an active extension of the office. In addition, despite her essential role behind the scenes, the wife of a public figure can be made to feel diminished – she is part of the same process as her husband, she represents policy too, and yet should never try to proclaim her own ideas publicly, especially if they are a fraction different. Hers is a domestic role, even if she feels she could be an ambassador in her own right, and many became so as the field of diplomacy opened up to them.

The wife is expected to ensure that the home relays pride and precise organization for its multi-functionality. She must take care of her own appearance, be knowledgeable about current political and diplomatic issues and well read on world affairs. Furthermore, she must take care of her family's personal needs as any mother and wife would. The multi-layered responsibilities are often brutally overwhelming and leave few options for personal interests.

There are times when skilful evasion and diplomacy are required in dealing with the press, such as when articles portray clear opposition to one's nation's point of view; when things are skewed to make them sensational and less than truthful; when not all the facts are accurately presented. And then on the social level, strange, almost amusing errors, are printed, such as when I attended a women's club luncheon and was described, after some fumbling, as the wife of the Ambassador of "Saudi-Israel". The Middle East, which was part of the British Empire then, was far from the consciousness of American citizens. On another occasion, the description in the social columns of a cocktail party Abba and I had attended read, "The Ambassador of Iraq and Mrs Eban left the party early."

Despite the small size of the household staff in Washington, there seemed to be many problems which I had to deal with, such as when our black driver had an affair with the French cook, then with another staff member, a Danish girl. One day, along came his wife brandishing a big knife; she seemed more concerned that his liaison was with a white woman than with the fact he was having an affair at all! I did my ambassadorial duty and calmed the situation.

Abba had to find his way around Washington and combine his two jobs, which meant commuting between the capital and New York. His one advantage over other new ambassadors was that he was already very well known: if he was running late in Washington and had to catch a plane to New York, *in extremis*, his secretary would call the airline and say, "The Ambassador is running late for his UN appearance, can you delay the flight by seven or eight minutes?" And they did.

Abba sometimes found himself at odds with the decisions and instructions emanating from Israel. He occasionally had a more complex foresight regarding decisions and actions the Israeli government wanted to take. Diplomacy is a profession, or comes from specific experience, and due to original inexperience, some of the politicians in Israel occasionally took decisions without carefully weighing the ramifications.

A typical example of this was in December 1955 when the Syrians fired on an Israeli fishing boat on the Sea of Galilee. Although no one was hurt and there was very little damage, Ben-Gurion ordered a massive response (some would say disproportionate). The attack on Syrian positions caused the deaths of seventy-three Syrians and six Israelis. This was just at the time when Abba was negotiating the political side of an important military deal with the US and Canada. He was furious and wrote to Ben-Gurion telling him so. Publicly, of course, he had to defend the Israeli government's action. Just to add salt to his wound, he received the following note from Ben-Gurion:

> I myself thought we had made a grave mistake, but when I read your great speech in the Security Council defending my decision, I concluded that we had acted correctly. I have nothing more to add...

We managed, at times, to have a personal and social life. It was easier in New York where we made friends outside our official sphere. We both started to play golf, often getting up at dawn to play or just to walk and be on our own.

On one occasion Arthur and Jeanette Lurie invited us to join them for a weekend in Stanford, Connecticut, as guests of their recently widowed friend, Rebecca Shulman, whose lawyer husband had won the case for Pepsi-Cola against Coca-Cola. Rebecca had accessed the pinnacle of the vastly influential Hadassah Women's Zionist Organization. Her eighteenth-century property was a place to which we would be invited many times for relaxing weekends. In winter, surrounded by a snow-covered landscape, we would sit in front of a huge log fire in the sitting room where we saw our Eli stand up and cross the room by himself for the first time. When we first drove there in the spring, the landscape was abundant with white, flowering dogwood trees on both sides of the highway, simply part of the natural scenery. Water was plentiful, even wasted with insouciance, and the Americans were taking it all for granted.

When President Nasser declared, in July 1956, that the Suez Canal Company had been nationalized, the British immediately announced that the single power control of the canal was unacceptable. In August, John Foster Dulles put forward the Western Plan for an International Board to run the Canal. Because I had grown up in the Canal region I was fascinated by all the debates and what nation or group of nations would exercise authority there but the Americans were extremely upset to have been left out of the "collusion" between France, England and Israel: Abba was immediately criticized for having "gone behind America's back". For a long time there was a strained relationship between the author of the "collusion", Shimon Peres, and the US administration. It was always believed that Shimon Peres had greater affiliations with France than with America which could not emotionally absorb that she had been left out of the game. This was a very difficult time and we were hounded by the press who demanded to know if there was indeed "collusion".

Towards the end of the 1950s we had already started discussing returning to Israel. Had we waited any longer it would have meant another four-year period of ambassadorship. We thought this would be too long, and we particularly wanted the children to live and be educated in Israel. Importantly, Abba knew that David Ben-Gurion expected him to become involved in politics and specifically in the election due to take place in November 1959.

In November 1958, at the annual Weizmann Institute dinner at New York's Waldorf Astoria, the guest of honour was Senator Henry Cabot Lodge of Massachusetts, then head of the American delegation at the United Nations. Abba made an elegantly critical and brilliantly witty speech about Lodge who was no friend of Israel. Meyer Weisgal, Chairman of the executive board of the Institute and for decades Weizmann's confidant and loyal advisor, was elated and ecstatic. In his impetuosity he drew Abba away from the congratulating crowd that had gathered, seized him by the lapels of his dinner jacket and said: "You are a genius, I must talk to you!" He then offered Abba the presidency of the Weizmann Institute. I could see how his mind was galloping away with his idea as he swore us to secrecy, mostly to upstage the governors of the Institute who, after seven years, had still not come up with any candidate.

When I said to Abba that night, "But you are not a scientist," he answered, "This is very much meant as an extension of Weizmann's political side." Shortly after, Abba gave Weisgal his positive answer. To the Weizmann devotees who formed the Board of Governors it was still considered important to buttress the Weizmann legacy. There had been bitter rivalries and animosities between Ben-Gurion and Weizmann, less about political views than about the ultimate power of the Zionist movement. For us, keeping the planned appointment a secret over months was somewhat embarrassing, as our close and dear friend Dewey Stone was the Chairman of the Board of Governors of the Institute.

At the Governors' meeting held in London, Abba was elected President of the Institute – all forty governors, including Mrs Weizmann, stood up to record their unanimous assent. A luncheon was held in our honour on 6 November 1958 at the Weizmann Institute in Rehovot and Meyer formally announced the appointment. We would return to Israel the following year. In his letter to Ben-Gurion of 11 February 1959, Abba resigned as Ambassador to the United States and on the following day, he wrote again, advising the Prime Minister of his forthcoming resignation as Permanent Representative in the UN.

The presidency of the Weizmann Institute was not hugely unusual for that place or for those times. Chaim Weizmann, who had made significant discoveries in organic chemistry as a Russian émigré in England during the First World War, had run his life on two parallel tracks: science and politics. When the Balfour Declaration had lifted him on the crest of a wave to the unchallenged leadership of the Jewish people, he had not abandoned science in spite of constant calls upon his diplomatic skills and contacts. This had resulted in the long sea journeys of those days to America, South Africa, England and Palestine for the Jewish cause. He was acknowledged much more as a political figure; science was an additional and prestigious asset.

The Board of Governors, though proudly identified with the Weizmann Institute, was now suddenly involved with a revitalization of Rehovot's political role in Israeli life: they wanted Abba for their institution. When he expressed his intention to enter the Israeli political arena, they offered a solution – he could do both.

For many, their attachment to Israel transcended their affiliation with its potential for scientific development. The governors wanted to express their full support of Abba and encourage his move from diplomacy into politics. It was therefore understood that he would head the Institute and also enter the domestic political arena of Israel. When the time came, the communiqué issued by the Institute had a clear political connotation. Provided laymen did not interfere in the decisions of their scientific council, the scientists had little to say about the choice at the top. The appointment was thrust upon them as a surprise. The view was that although Abba Eban belonged to the humanities, in the strongly pragmatic and practical world of an Israel that was still creating its basic structures, his range of experience and intellect would add international prestige and contacts to the Institute.

We had a long and comprehensive farewell tour. At every point we had a caring public who had followed Abba's diplomatic skills with appreciation and, I think, admiration. New York and the UN sent us off after a farewell dinner with many superlatives and tributes.

As we felt the first gentle lilt of movement as the ship moved away from its anchorage, Abba sat down and exclaimed: "Thank God!" "Thank God for what?" I asked. "Thank God I didn't make a mistake."

It was then that I fully realized what a terrible strain our years in America had been on him, carrying the single responsibility of all the speeches, negotiations, constant political playing and national representation, despite the great achievements won. In the destiny of the Jewish people he was called "the right man at the right time". This is how I concluded it all in my heart as the *SS US* sailed slowly past the Statue of Liberty and took us into the future.

It was exciting still to be young and to have been thrust so forcefully into the centre of world affairs without the customary process of diplomatic promotions. Would there now be a chance to spread our wings in the Homeland and be given a further chance of service for our people? How far away the full edifice of our national dreams and ambitions still seemed.

13

Return to Rehovot

At 2 a.m. on a warm July night in 1959, Abba and I were driven from Lod Airport to the residential compound of the Weizmann Institute of Science in Rehovot. Eli, nine, and Gila, five, were to follow with Nanny Gates. In the hush of the night there was no sound and the house we stepped into was stark white and marvellously empty. Coming in from the dark, I felt as if I was entering a huge sugar cube – this was our new home. Our luggage was dumped downstairs and we went to bed but it was difficult to sleep in the hot, muggy atmosphere, uncovered, with the windows wide open and the blinds up, in the hope of a breeze. We talked for hours: there was the excitement of a fresh start, a new place, with no personal objects and an unknown future. The feeling of suspension in time and direction was overpowering.

Restlessness and curiosity made me step out on to the large bedroom terrace and into the opaque glow of tropical moonlight. The rhythmic noise of water-sprinklers working in the night to save evaporation could be heard and the black surface spreading under the terrace was a lawn bordered by the silhouette of dark trees. A constant hum originated from a heavy water plant, part of the highly secret nuclear energy research project, and we were to become used to sudden rings day and night which would grip the place as if in a seizure. Twice a week, the blaring music, the amplified calls and energetic foot stomping of the folk-dancers on the roof of the San Martin Faculty Club reverberated loudly in our residential neighborhood – a circle of houses where the heads of scientific departments lived. Otherwise, the place was all serenity and peace.

The morning following our arrival, my first view was of an open cart loaded with tall tin containers of milk parked near the entrance in front of the kitchen path. A frail-looking milkman was coaxing his donkey with a flip of his whip to move on. This would have been an unlikely sound down any "Embassy Row", where the kitchen was always at some invisible end of one's living quarters. I went to get acquainted with the butcher and on the way met the wife of Professor Michael Feldman, an eminent cancer researcher at the Institute. She said to me, "Why do you have to come yourself?" I answered, "Well, what do you do?" "Oh!" she said, "I send my husband!" and she chuckled.

After Chaim Weizmann's death in 1952, Meyer Weisgal had decided there should be a living memorial to him, encompassing the laboratories, houses and institutions. This was to be Yad Weizmann, or the Weizmann Institute. After the traditional thirty days of mourning, bulldozers were sent to slice the land, uproot orange trees, and create a central avenue. Never one to miss out on an emotional moment, with grief still fresh in people's hearts, Meyer felt this would be good timing.

The entrance to the Institute is on the main Rehovot highway which also leads to Beersheba and the Negev. The old white marble façade, with its emphatic bronze lettering "Yad Weizmann", used firmly to separate "town from gown" but later, the emblem of the Weizmann Institute of Science, in Hebrew and English, replaced the original and Yad Weizmann refers to the Weizmann home and archives, managed by a separate board, under the auspices of the Weizmann Institute.

The first administrative director, Dr Ernst Simon, came from the prestigious Kaiser Wilhelm Institute (now the Max Planck Institute). Dr Ernest Bergmann, the thirty-one-year-old scientist to whom the Weizmanns attached themselves very strongly and whom it was assumed would be the first scientific director, was also from Berlin: he was fluent in Hebrew, and he foresaw our future scientific needs, stating early on that Israel should work at desalinating its water and developing atomic energy.

Dr Bergmann's insights had won him the complete trust of the military-scientific establishment of the newly created State, which on the morrow of the Declaration of Independence found itself attacked by all the surrounding Arab countries. The country needed the urgent co-operation of every single scientist available like Bergmann, Aharon Katzir and his brother Ephraim, Israel Dostrovsky and others. The Institute was immediately put on an emergency footing. From those times onwards, autonomous as it was, there would always be a great closeness between the Institute and the government. And years later, in 1952, in an act of recognition, Ernst Bergmann became the founding Chairman of Israel's newly created Atomic Energy Commission.

As Dr Weizmann continued to choose his top scientists, notwithstanding the envy of other academic centres, he carefully selected a very exceptional group that included Professor Isaac Berenblum from Oxford University's cancer research campaign and Professor Joe Gillis who, like Abba, was already affiliated to a Zionist society in Cambridge. During the Second World War, he had been part of a team of brilliant British mathematicians at Bletchley Park who worked on "Enigma", the decrypting of Germany's secret codes. From Princeton came Professor Chaim Pekeris, former head of the scientific team at Columbia's War Research Section, to organize the department of Applied Mathematics with Professor Gillis. It must have been extraordinary for Pekeris to find the awesome Weizmann on his doorstep at Princeton, offering to uproot him and claim him professionally for a much humbler world. Yet Pekeris knew that his spiritual choice would be no less important than his scientific contributions, and so he bypassed research in pure mathematics in favour of prospecting for water and oil in Israel. He was the first to conduct a geophysical survey of the land and to train geophysicists since there were none in the country.

There were others who, for the same ideological reasons, had not recoiled from the decision of going to that small place, Rehovot, beyond the sand dunes of Rishon le Zion, which was as far south as Baron Edmond de Rothschild, the father of Jewish settlement in Palestine, had supported development. The Negev was as distant in their minds as a lunar landscape. Even so, these men had willingly parted from the physical and cultural amenities of the well-established centres they belonged to abroad – the rich museums, the historical sites, splendid surroundings, and higher standards of living – to live and work in Israel.

The town of Rehovot, founded in 1890, is one of the twelve original colonies. The town ran its course at a slow rural pace, but for the menacing highway bisecting it. As you came out of the serene isolation of the Institute, there rushed at you a frenzied traffic of cars, trucks, vans, buses and communal taxis called *sheruts* – and there were no traffic lights. Battered donkey and horse carts of the local agrarian population would weave in a defiant and disorderly manner in and out of the traffic. In Rehovot's streets can still be found steel loops embedded in the edge of pavements to which farmers tied their donkeys or horses as they went about their errands. Shops on either side were so small that, due to lack of space, they would display their shoes and kettles and cuckoo clocks in their single windows. I would buy greeting cards for the New Year or to send abroad for Christmas, each card with its pale, sepia calligraphy and its few dried wildflowers from the Galilee on the inside page: a standard card in those days. Orange growers came to re-supply their hardware at Harlap's store, with its Wild West look, its arrays of tools and its earthy smell. Wives of scientists with their net shopping bags came to Horn's grocery, owned by the German refugee couple who turned grocers, and whom everybody addressed in old European fashion: "Mr and Mrs Horn".

All the dairy prides of the land, pasteurized Tnuva cheeses, and "Kfir", buttermilk sold in one-litre pitch-black glass bottles were on sale. Dry goods were wrapped for you in newspaper. There were always children around who had been sent on bicycles through the inner road to fetch the one forgotten item. There they passed the early orange planters' old houses with their weather-beaten wooden shutters and the patterned lace curtains, or the house of the Israel Prize laureate, Izhar Smilansky, who wrote under the name of S. Yizhar, with its enormous mulberry tree under which a woman helper sat and did the laundry by hand. He was the one humanist luminary of Rehovot: a man with the look of the Romantic poets, erudite, an educator who always had the ear of Israeli youth, a great master of Hebrew prose, and a moral voice. He preached preserving the character of the landscape and reminded the young generation of the purity of motive and the idealism of early pioneering. Perhaps his principles were unheeded then, but they have resurfaced, modernized and are part of that global concern now called environmentalism.

Between 1 and 4 p.m. all the shops closed. Parents and children came home for lunch. Nobody called during the afternoon: from Ben-Gurion down, the country took a siesta. Or almost nobody. Sometimes, there would be a surprising ring at the front door at that time, which I would assume to be an urgent message. But there, standing and smiling, would be a Yemenite woman in her deep-toned native costume and pantaloons, her exotic head-gear edged by rows of clanking silver coins just above her eyebrows. She came from Shaarayim, the Yemenite quarter at the end of Rehovot, and sold handmade straw baskets densely woven in colourful geometrical patterns which I still use. We were once invited to Shaarayim for a Yemenite wedding. The ceremony, with the prayers and chants, had a character quite unlike anything we had ever witnessed before. On this occasion, the bride stood in the family home in a hired white-satin dress, having abandoned the idea of the traditional Yemenite bridal costume, heavily laden with a mass of silver jewellery in typical Yemenite patterns, and the sensuous dance with the large round tray of burning candles balanced on one hand high above shoulder and head at the henna ceremony. The palms of her hands were not to be fully dyed with henna, but only dotted with it. The pressures of modern society would have made her uncomfortable about this custom, and the henna-covered palms would not be practical in any job. For the celebration, the music was provided by a small group of players using silver thimbles over strings (not typically Yemenite), and giving the beat on an empty kerosene can. The men were chewing *Qat*, the herb that is supposed to heighten male virility.

At the other end of Rehovot was the Zarnuga *ma'abara*, the immigrants' transit camp. I wrote to my friend Anne Stone:

> I went to a Chanukah party there. It was exciting to see the development of some of the youth through education and army service. They had a nice programme. We sat out of doors at 4 p.m. in December and I thought of the Institute. It seemed fantastic that such an earlier neglect in general education (though the men did have a religious education) and such intellectual sophistication should exist side by side. Within five minutes of each other are centuries of intellectual development.

In the *ma'abara* I felt a strong sense that the collision of backgrounds was the challenge in creating our new modern nation. There were losses such as the dissolution of the family's closeness, a strong feature in oriental society, and gains, such as acquiring the rhythm and attributes of a modern society. The Hebrew language and concern for the nation would be the great cultural unifiers. Every new wave of immigrants, with its special characteristics, was the subject of jokes by the previous wave. The veteran East Europeans were taken aback by the quick-tempered Moroccans and the Moroccans were utterly puzzled by the precise and meticulous Germans who, in turn, were baffled by the Romanians – who regarded the Anglo-Saxons as incredibly complicated in their understated ways. Later, the immigrants who came off the planes carrying violins and yet more violins, were undoubtedly Russians. The immigrants about whom there seemed to be no criticism were the sweet-natured Yemenites with their authentic oriental pronunciation of Hebrew.

As work developed at the entrance of the Weizmann Institute, the main avenue was bordered with two rows of ficus trees with trunks covered up to the branches in a chalk whitewash to repel insects. This gave the long avenue a stately look as if the trees were costumed to stand on parade. The building erected in the years we were there, is the impressive Dewey and Anne Stone Administrative Building. Dewey – with his portrait by Boris Chaliapin, the son of the Russian opera singer Feodor Chaliapin who painted so many personalities for *Time Magazine* covers – was the founder and first Chairman of the American Committee of the Weizmann Institute. A staunch Democrat, with Weizmann's devotees he followed both President Truman's policy and the steps that led to the recognition of Israel, very closely. The Weizmann supporters had worked extremely hard at counter-balancing Truman's antagonism to Rabbi Abba Hillel Silver, the Republican head of the American Jewish Committee, a great orator, but who had once brought his fist down on Truman's presidential desk about a Zionist issue. Anne and Dewey's arrival in Rehovot was always important to us as we could discuss Israeli politics and problems with them as well as strategies concerning Abba's political position, all of which Abba called a "situation review". They cared deeply about his progression in politics. During our years in the USA, when possible in the summer, we stayed with them for weekends at their East Brewer House on Cape Cod and played golf.

Further along the inner main avenue of the Institute, behind a beautifully kept lawn, stood the Wix Scientific Library with its ultramarine façade breaking the monotony of the invariably off-white buildings and houses. In the early years it housed a museum containing the Weizmann papers – some 20,000 letters – a great many of them of historical importance, and handwritten in Weizmann's habitual green ink: the signature tidy and legible, loop by loop every "m" and every "n". His one hundred patents were kept in box files and his vintage table-microscope behind glass – rather touching when compared with today's several electron microscopes at the Institute that magnify ten million times. There were family memorabilia from his childhood in the Russian village of Motelé (also known as Motol), from his science studies at Fribourg University in Switzerland and early research in Manchester, and a copy of the Balfour Declaration, with an absurd smudge next to Balfour's signature, for millions to see. That single-hall museum was so special and intimate, and so illustrative of the unusual connection between scientific discovery and statesmanship that had existed in one individual and one nation.

In 1998, the contents were moved to a separate archive in the Barbara and Morris Levinson Visitors' Centre which also houses a small theatre showing documentaries about the Institute's history and current scientific research. It is an invaluable addition.

Opposite, the Wix Auditorium remains the cultural centre where members of the Institute listened to concerts, robed ceremonies conferring honorary degrees took place there, and sometimes there would be a more unusual event, such as when the French Nobel Prize-winner Jacques Monod gave a lecture to which "the public is invited". A Yemenite shepherd in his nicest, Sabbath robe attended. He listened to a mass of incomprehensible foreign words, came down the auditorium knocking his shepherd's staff on each step, bowed to the lecturer, crossed the podium behind him and walked out, leaving a stunned lecturer and a silent and mesmerized audience. Sometimes, a Walt Disney film for the children from Rehovot and the surrounding areas would be thrown in, as if a yearly bonus for parenthood. *One Hundred and One Dalmatians* was an exciting event for the region, in the time before television.

The last building along the main avenue, the nuclear physics department, had a free-shaped pond that looked so pristine and important with its tender, beautifully curved weeping willow bending over the water in poetical reflection. It was a favourite spot for the children. They would sit on the cement ledge for a respite from their energetic outdoor games, and chat and confide. Occasionally, a military helicopter (there were never any civilian ones then) would mysteriously land on a bare stretch behind the department, much to the children's delight, but nobody asked questions. Once a year, in preparation for Lag B'Omer – the one joyous day during the devotional fifty-day period known as the Omer, between Passover and the Festival of Weeks (Shavuot) – the children would ambitiously drag tree branches, much bigger than themselves, for bonfires and sit up till dawn roasting their potatoes and marshmallows, singing and joking through the night. Israel is dotted with bonfires during this holiday, giving a friendly glow to the countryside, while recapturing an ancient tradition. Nobody seems to mind the smoke.

By the time we arrived, the grounds of the Institute had become an enchanting sight. Alongside its scientific mission, the Institute had fulfilled the idea of settling on the land with great panache. A low-growing jasmine covered spaces between buildings in a unifying greenness. Hedges were cropped to perfection and borders of timid verbenas added touches of vivid purple and carmine red to the sprawling scenes of verdure. Mauve wisteria and honeysuckle hung languidly from walls and trellises. There were jacaranda trees, Australian brush-trees, and flower beds of luminous red and white polyanthus rosebushes covered long stretches bordering garden paths. There were roses in every garden and an infinite range of snapdragons and sweet peas in spring, and vibrantly colored zinnias in the summer – yellow, orange, red, purple and pink. It was dazzling with a vengeance. I used to see the inseparable trio of professors, Michael Sela (the biologist) of "copaxone"* fame, Michael Feldman (the cancer researcher) and Amos de Shalit (the nuclear physicist), walking together up and down, passionately debating some subject, totally oblivious to the beauty of the surroundings which were cultivated to encourage inspiration in scientific thought.

It seemed impossible not to compare these tremendous bursts of creativity in science and the beautification of the landscape and to marvel at how, while we were so busy fighting for the national cause in the world, the national cause had made enormous strides here at the Institute. What a contrast these two worlds were! Science dealt with the predictable, since scientific results must invariably be proven correct, whilst we in politics would often have to deal with the unpredictable behaviours of men and nations. We had all moved forward together in our concepts and efforts to develop the world of scientific research and defend the diplomacy of Israel while helping to shape its politics. It was exciting to find myself in the midst of both creations.

As time went on, the number of Israelis who concerned themselves with scientific pursuits increased. Those who worked at the Weizmann Institute as well as the Hebrew University and Haifa Technion, became aware that they formed a new, specialized Israeli community. Hundreds of scientific researchers, engineers and technicians involved in the exploration of natural phenomena seemed to give Israeli society a new and unexpected dimension.

Beyond what was a deserted area in 1959, and viewed from a ridge above, is now a solar energy field. The visual impact is tremendous – sixty-four giant mirrors, set in the soil and driven by computers, quietly tick away, and turn like automated sunflowers towards the sun in imperceptible moves at an angle that gives them

---

* Copaxone is a drug for multiple sclerosis sufferers, discovered by Sela.

3,000 times the strength of sunlight. The energy is stored in a huge rectangular tower and eventually it is hoped a chemical heat pipe will carry that clean and economical energy.

At the end of the main avenue the plaza is dominated by a massively symbolic sculpture by Dani Caravan of a fallen, burnt Torah scroll – lest we forget, in this seat of science, the horrendous destructions of bodies and minds in the Holocaust. It is a silent reminder of an immense potential, cruelly lost. Two to three thousand people used to assemble in the plaza on or near 2 November (Weizmann's birthday) to mark Weizmann Day.

In the early days, in addition to the heads of state – the second President, Yitzhak Ben-Zvi and the then President Zalman Shazar – the Israeli cabinet, Ezer Weizman, the nephew, officials and the diplomatic corps, presented themselves faithfully, along with members of the Institute's board of governors, who would come out to Israel at that time for the bi-annual international board meeting. Every President of the State has since continued the tradition and attends what is now a short memorial at Weizmann's grave.

It is a place of great silence. Most times a gentle breeze wafts over the treetops that delineate the far border of the Institute against a vibrantly blue sky. In winter, during the eight years that we lived there, we would end an occasional walk by sitting on the long marble ledge that encloses the plaza. The sun-baked floor radiated delicious warmth. A stone path surrounded by pine trees and bushes leads to a natural elevation of the ground and there, at the end, stand the marble tombs of "The Chief" as Weizmann was called by everyone in his immediate entourage, and "Vera" as only a very few intimate friends of her generation were ever allowed to call her. A short distance above stands the Weizmann House.

At the time we lived in Rehovot, Weizmann's tomb was regularly used as a military rallying point for the Women's Army Corps. I used to be invited to attend the ceremonies by its commander,

Mina Ben-Zvi, who was very friendly. The many platoons of girl soldiers would be brought in army buses to the Institute grounds when they had finished their initial six weeks' training and then, in a very dramatic ceremony, they would be sworn in at night, amidst rows of flickering torches. The martial orders of a sergeant major commanded in a loud, clipped voice, "*Smol/yemin*" (left/right) and the girls' boots echoed on the marble. We mothers would stand watching, knowing that our then small daughters would one day have to carry the same Uzi guns, give the country the same two years, wear the same gross-looking shoes and the same flat folding khaki hat, awkward on any hairstyle, and see them get fat on greasy army food. The girls really hated their very un-feminine accoutrements and called their boots "Golda" shoes, because Golda Meir, old by then and heavy as she was, had to wear orthopaedic shoes.

The obligatory two-year army service was a challenge to the young girls. There was a new pride in reaching out beyond the family framework into national necessities. Young Jewish women were now being cast differently. The majority would not conform any more to the centuries' old image of the "woman of valour", heroic in her complete servitude to her man and her home. There was instead a deep national commitment and the indication of a potential escape from a life of total domesticity. These girl soldiers would increase the labour force of Israel in a significant way.

Mina made me share other special experiences, like the annual march of the girl soldiers from the army barracks of Tsrifim in the coastal plain, to Jerusalem. Her driver would take us to the highest hilltop and we would stand together up in the Judean Hills, way above Ein Kerem, and watch the battalion of girl soldiers come up from the valley in a huge, serpentine formation through the hills. They would be singing and tapping firmly on tambourines to maintain their marching rhythm. The sound echoing in space and the unit's slow, curving progression around the hills gave a singularly biblical character to the scene.

After Mina retired from the service, she went to the Ivory Coast to advise the government of President Felix Houphouet-Boigny on a project for training women for a similar women's corps. It was a time when Africa was very close to and admiring of Israel, and preferred to turn to us rather than to western countries that were too reminiscent of colonial times.

Large functions were sometimes requested of us by the Ministry of Foreign Affairs or by the Institute for their own political reasons. These would be at the San Martin Club House at which Abba and I would be hosts as when King Mahendra and Queen Ratna of Nepal visited. The Queen sat in a magnificent, gold-edged, violet-coloured sari, saying not a single word. The explanation given to me was that the Queen is never allowed to speak when the King is present in the room. For more intimate occasions we used the small dining room of the San Martin where I remember an African chief whose helper came bearing a sack of gold coins as a donation to the Institute in return for its hospitality and advice, and which was heaved on the lunch table before his speech.

The Weizmann Institute was pragmatic about its official guests. In the early years of the State, many famous people felt the need to pay obeisance to Israel for its gallant efforts. They liked it. They liked the fact that it transcended its meagre space, and its lack of natural resources; they admired too that with its lack of established frameworks to fall back on, it was absorbing immigrants from all corners of the world. Nobel Prize-winners came to the Institute such as Professor Christian Anfinsen from the USA, François Jacob from France, Sir Robert Robertson from England, who became a member of the Board of Governors, Ernst Chain, with his "pageboy" hair style and Professor Isidore Rabi of Columbia University, who also went on to the Board and who strongly believed that only a scientist must be the head of a State. It was quite a development from the time of Dr Weizmann's gleaning of a few Jewish scientists from Europe in the 1930s.

Of all official visits, the most highly charged and discussed in every home in the country as well as at the Institute, was that of Konrad Adenauer, the first Chancellor of the Federal Republic of Germany. Historically, it was Ben-Gurion who had dared make the first official move regarding establishing contact with post-war Germany. He met Adenauer at the Waldorf Astoria in 1960. This spectacular and unique encounter of two such charismatic figures, swimming strongly against the stream of their countries' political history, gripped the news media the world over. However painful and politically dangerous this was for Ben-Gurion at the time, and however shocking for Israelis, the two men coalesced in a determination to initiate a dialogue at their level in spite of pained and sincere opponents on the one hand and demagogues on the other.

Adenauer had put the whole weight of his personal prestige, his devout Catholicism and not least, his own experience during the Nazi period (he avoided imprisonment on several occasions but was arrested and briefly incarcerated after the assassination attempt on Hitler), to re-creating contact between "the new" Germany and the Jewish people. You had to have devastating humanitarian credentials to contemplate such a move, and he knew he would have to do it through the State of Israel.

In 1966, aged eighty-eight, and out of office by then, Konrad Adenauer came to the Institute as part of a three-day visit to the country. It was strange to behold this legendary figure with his wise face, and skin that seemed made of crushed parchment, standing there of all places, as true as his photographs. He came with his daughter who was very solicitous of him and, to us, she exemplified a new German generation we would soon have to accept. Neither of them spoke much English and interpreters had to be used. Of course there was no dearth of immigrants who could have an immediacy of communication with them.

Abba was then Foreign Minister and protocol dictated that as the Minister's wife I be seated next to Adenauer, but no one had provided an interpreter. His daughter, having just come to Rehovot from an earlier wreath-laying ceremony at Yad Vashem's National Memorial for the Holocaust in Jerusalem, said to me in her very limited English: "It was a lovely visit."!

Dr Nachum Goldmann, the German-speaking President of the World Jewish Congress at the time, a rather controversial political figure and a man with a strange love-hate relationship to Israel, but close to Dr Weizmann, was now helpful to Meyer Weisgal. Taking advantage of the Adenauer visit, Meyer was attempting to create a scientific bond between the prestigious Max Planck Institute in Heidelberg and the Weizmann.

There had already been contacts between the defence establishments of Israel and West Germany at lower levels but this was the first official contacts with Israeli science. There would later be many significant scientific collaborations as a result of that mutual recognition.

The scientists' homes in Rehovot were the traditional refuge of intellectuals. Bookcases could be seen through the windows and often the ubiquitous picture of Einstein was on the wall, just as in the late 1930s and 1940s Van Gogh reproductions seemed a uniform choice in non-scientific homes in old Palestine. There was little modern Israeli art in those days in homes (I brought in the first abstract painting to the campus) and very few could afford extending their budgets in that direction. As I walked along I would hear children practising *Für Elise*, and thumping bravely at Diabelli and Czerny that bored them to tears.

I enjoyed knowing the wives of the heads of departments because we all lived in the same part of the residential compound that separated us from the laboratories. There was Olga Gillis, wife of the British mathematician, Joseph Gillis who had received his doctorate from Cambridge. Olga had come from South Africa and was a well-known Afrikaans poet, a talent which she could hardly use in Israel, so she became an English teacher. Dafne

Dostrovsky, whose husband, Israel, was head of isotopes, was English and drew and painted in the manner of a well-brought up English lady. She executed an exquisite portrait in crayon of Eli. Rosalind Sheleznyak, whose husband dealt with the disciplines concerning birth control, funded so early by the Rockefeller Foundation, was American. She brought a breath of the avant-garde to our neighbourhood and painted in the abstract manner.

Mathilda Krim, then Danon, who was to become famous for her clarion call for public education and fundraising for AIDS, was the campus showpiece: she has played a central role in alerting the world to the threat of AIDS. Short, blonde and pretty, Mathilda, who spoke both Hebrew and English with an endearing French accent, had arrived in Israel as a Swiss scientist detaching herself from her anti-Semitic background. She joined the ranks of the Irgun after the Second World War and became deeply involved in rescuing survivors of the Holocaust. Her first marriage to an Institute scientist ended in divorce. Arthur Krim, Chairman of United Artists Films, visiting Rehovot, fell in love with her and took her away to the USA.

One evening Mathilda had a party. The first man who asked me to dance turned out to be the owner of an American-style restaurant in Tel Aviv. I knew Mathilda loved to have fun but I was taken aback by the sudden explosion of the sedate, inbred, academic norms of the compound. Years later, after she had departed from the little Rehovot world, that restaurateur, Abie Nathan, one of the first pilots of the Israeli Air Force, turned out to be a great proponent of peace with the Palestinians. He had an offshore radio station on his boat, the *Voice of Peace*, that played music and popular songs interspersed with news. Then he chartered a plane, flew to Tunis to meet Yasser Arafat, our avowed enemy then, and was promptly jailed on his return. Years later, Ezer Weizman did the same thing, but he was only reprimanded; his credentials were more powerful.

Nina Katchalski, wife of the renowned scientist, Professor Ephraim Katchalski/Katzir who was elected the fourth President of Israel many years later (Abba being one of his supporters), was a very sensitive and tormented person, and experienced great tragedy when her daughter, an aspiring actress, died young, poisoned by the fumes of a heater. Nina once said to me how hard it was not to be able to share in her husband's work since he could not possibly discuss with her the daily progression or problems of his biophysics or biochemistry research that was so totally absorbing to him. Wives of other scientists often had the same feelings.

Victor Rothschild (Lord Rothschild) used to come for meetings of his family foundation, Yad Hanadiv, which resulted in many extraordinary benefactions, the most spectacular being the entire funds for the Knesset building willed to the State by his cousin, James de Rothschild. Later, there would be another breathtaking gift to the nation from Victor's son Jacob: the Supreme Court. Jacob, who inherited the title and the role of head of Yad Hanadiv on the death of James's widow, Dorothy de Rothschild, later offered some of the funds for the restoration of the Weizmann House.

Victor, himself a scientist, would also come for the distribution of the Rothschild prizes in Jerusalem and would invariably make a point of visiting Mrs Weizmann. Since the Balfour Declaration was addressed to Walter, the second Baron Rothschild, the family kept a constant relationship with the Weizmann name. Victor was rather touching in his guarded informality and desire to be a part of the scene of the Institute. He would elegantly take out his gold cigarette case, tap his cigarette on it before lighting it and slip the case back into his pocket in an almost dandy-like gesture. He once came to us for lunch in a blazer with oval leather patches on the elbows – the latest men's fashion in sportswear in the 1960s. Reverse snobbery must have given him a great sense of fun and, in democratic Israel, when he departed, he sat next to the driver.

When Abba took over the presidency of the Institute, the place was still viewed with strong ambivalence: it was a source of both pride and some criticism, commonly viewed as a gathering of distant, detached academics. It was a distinctly western kind of place in its interests, values, ambitions, and attitudes. Its scientists seemed different from the rest of the country in their social culture, isolated in their world of neatness and rationality within a country that was still somewhat primitive and provincial. Yosef Sprinzak, the Speaker of the Knesset, once famously ended a visit to the Institute with the words, "Let us now return to Israel!"

Because of the traditional Jewish reverence for learning, the citizens of Rehovot recognized the Institute and its spirit as a national asset − even in the 1930s, Dr Weizmann had tried to rescue two Jewish Nobel Prize-winning scientists from Germany, but their trauma of brutal rejection and persecution by their country had stymied their capacity to adapt to new circumstances and they chose not to come. But in their hearts the citizens had mixed feelings about having a spectacularly neat asset in Rehovot, in such close proximity to the two *ma'abarot*. But the distance between the Institute and Israeli society at large would have existed even without such poignant timing. It was the unflinching support from abroad that helped the continuous development of the Institute in spite of the inability of the country to help it expand. In today's information age, Israelis take for granted the dominance of science and technology in their daily lives. Yet, as the scientists delve deeper into their explorations of life and travel further into space, the intellectual distance between them and lay people is still immense. Science must always remain a world apart in order to achieve progress − true scientists live in a sort of isolation, focused solely on their goals of discovery.

Rehovot had changed so much since my adolescence, when I travelled from Cairo to Jerusalem by train. In the early morning, before the climb to Jerusalem, I would take an appreciative look at

Rehovot, green with orange groves, the first touch of Zionist cultivation after the starkly parched desert sands and palm trees of the Egyptian coast of El Arish, and would while away the few minutes when the train stopped by staring at the opposite platform where crates made of thin wooden slats were piled all the way up to the corrugated iron roofs of open sheds. In the autumn they would be filled with citrus fruit individually wrapped in some chemically treated orange tissue paper for better preservation, ready for export, which in those days meant a ten-day journey by sea from Haifa via Gibraltar to England, which was the major citrus market. Moving back and forth on the platform as in a silent movie, there were muscular workers dressed in the standard uniform of the new socialist labourer – khaki shorts and royal blue cotton open-neck shirts.

At a pre-State concert of the Palestine Philharmonic, later the Israel Philharmonic and whose members were mainly German refugees brought up within the great musical traditions of Europe, the large audience of Histadrut members looked startlingly homogenous in their two colours. These standard clothes were manufactured by Ata in the Haifa Bay, the only modern mechanized textile factory started by the Möller brothers, two immigrants from Czechoslovakia, who had adapted their production line to socialist labour tenets: durable cotton for the household and sturdy work outfits. The workers and the kibbutzim were the major consumers of that very early industry.

A true oasis, the Philharmonic was invaluable in preserving a link to the European culture so much of our population missed. I remember walking down a street in Jerusalem's Rehavia neighbourhood before my marriage and hearing the same Beethoven Symphony emanating from house after house along the same street where everybody had tuned in their radios to our one and only general station that carried classical music.

14

And now into politics

Meyer Weisgal was an incredible personality. A fascinating raconteur, exuberant, amusing, frank and blunt, cruel in his wit, both cynical and sentimental, and often outrageously vulgar in his speech, with his big, bushy head of white hair he was unmistakable wherever he went. There was a sense of the theatrical world, from which he came, about him.

His home made a modest attempt at elegance in the very austere Israel of those times but the food, brought over from the San Martin faculty club, made no attempt to please. This was absolutely secondary, as it was everywhere else in the country. But when he and his wife Shirley entertained, the cross-section of Israelis and visitors from abroad was fascinating and lively. Some of the after-dinner entertainment was even unexpected as when, in a then very secular Israel, the powerful operatic voice of Jan Pearce, his houseguest, would soar into *hazanut*, or cantorial songs. The guest list would be composed of Israeli ministers, foreign financiers, eminent visiting scientists and Nobel Prize-winners, industrialists, millionaires, wives, mistresses, journalists and artists. Most of all, Meyer was a master fundraiser, a great implementer and the architect of the Weizmann Institute in its early decades.

As the servant of the scientific vision and Zionist policy of Weizmann, he knew everybody in the country and in Weizmann's particular world. Being American, he was very friendly with Paula Ben-Gurion and Golda Meir, who had both lived in the United States, and he had liberal entry into their homes where his Yiddish was not only acceptable in a Hebrew-conscious Israel, but its flavour much appreciated. He loved the language and spoke with a full range of its idioms and gestures, giving it a dimension that they could not reach. Mrs Weizmann, who was distant from the popular Jewish scene but knew what a valuable associate Weisgal had been for her husband, sometimes resented his possessiveness. If ever there was a conflict of views, I would see him grimace, looking uncannily like a Francis Bacon portrait, but he would never speak against her. He would then hurry to dismiss the matter with one of his colourful stories or risqué jokes, laughing heartily at his own bons mots.

Meyer knew Israeli politics at close range, having lived it all with Weizmann. Half admiring the well-seasoned politicians at the head of the State, half contemptuous of their personal manoeuvrings, he was amiable with friends and foes alike. He felt, where Abba was concerned, that the transition from diplomacy to domestic politics and the crossing over from his western culture to sabra roughness could have hidden dangers. It was important to protect and use his enormous capacities. The risk of failure when setting oneself on a political course with a mere four months' exposure to the electorate could hamper Abba's chances in Israel forever and diminish the Institute. The great coup of the appointment, instead of being a base from which to branch out politically, could be a very short-lived success.

We had timed our arrival in Israel for the beginning of July so as to be able to attend the Fourth of July American Embassy party where we would be able to see on one single occasion all the people who made up Israel's political life. Abba's most urgent task, however, was to present himself to the Israeli electorate – Israel was in the throes of its fourth national election – address meetings, be seen and of course be heard. At that time, an election campaign did not consist of impromptu appearances in crowded places just to shake hands, but mostly of mass meetings. While we were still in Washington, the inner caucuses of the ruling Labour Party, in a neck-and-neck race with the Weizmann Institute, had already worked out their own scenario. They thought Abba was too much of an asset to remain unused during the forthcoming election. Thus, on the dark runway of the small Lod Airport amidst flowers and flashbulbs, we had found ourselves greeted at 1 a.m. by an effusive contingent of senior Labour Party members. Their articulate and literary spokesman, Zalman Shazar (later the third President of the State), was ebullient. Moshe Sharett, who, as Israel's first Foreign Minister, had brought Abba into the two top jobs of Israeli diplomacy, was now seeing us out of them. The Mayor of Tel Aviv, Mordechai Namir, was also there, and although we were not due to be his constituents, he was a dominant figure in the Labour Party. The triumphant and astute Meyer Weisgal was glowing with visible pride from his talent snatching. Transcending his partiality to the Institute, he was pleased with the airport welcome, taking great delight in the fact that a political game was on and he was part of it once again. He was titillated by the fact he was running away with one of the Labour Party's trump cards and had decided to set up his own challenge to the Party. Meyer was not anti-Labour but was fed up with some of the Party's tactics and it was these he was challenging, from within the movement, not outside.

Throughout the flight to Israel, I kept thinking about our future and I was very apprehensive about Abba's capacity to adjust to the day-by-day Israeli scene after the broad sweep of America and the United Nations. The Israeli public knew him mostly as the distant but resonant figure that had made a powerful defence of Israel on the world scene through crises and wars. They were now eager to have their own image of him in their consciousness beyond the pictures and the stories in the press. They wanted to assess his mind, his Hebrew, his style for themselves, and get closer to him. He was the "unknown" star in the campaign.

During the ensuing months I sat on the wooden benches of many a front row at numerous outdoor meetings with my bunch of flowers in my lap. Much of the campaign had a rustic atmosphere. I remember how Abba once brought an outdoor mass audience to laughter and applause when, in the midst of the pastoral environment, a donkey brayed loudly and he said that he would prefer to hear opposition comments after his speech. I was not to have any special role in the election campaign. It was not part of the Israeli political pattern for a wife to be an active participant unless she herself had a position in the party. There were very few such women, but many others were involved with volunteer jobs at an organizational level. In the kibbutzim, where there was always strong political awareness, some women would sit and knit during political debates. Although many wives did not go out on the campaign trail with their husbands, I saw myself in a supportive role and accompanied Abba to many places. His struggle was our joint struggle.

There were prejudices too: he wore a tie, his suits were always pressed, he was too "English", his Hebrew was too good, and his assistant provided by the party kept repeating, "Why don't you speak to them in sentences of a subject, verb and object, full-stop?" And since most immigrants' Hebrew was rather imperfect, his assistant would add: "Why don't you use plain language with some of the customary grammatical errors everybody has got used to!" It was considered authentic macho sabra to use slang, or an occasional Arabic word and to speak Hebrew with errors. By some form of self-denial of the Jewish tradition, the Israeli was supposed to be even more authentic when showing off his disinterest in any purely scholarly occupation. As the campaign progressed, the audiences became larger. It was the age before television. Abba wrote to his family,

My own occupation has been addressing mass meetings. These have been so massive that I doubt whether there are really only two million people in Israel. Since nobody else is drawing these crowds, the country's attention has been arrested by this phenomenon. It disproves the theory that "the people" want to hear nonsense discussed – in bad Hebrew. They don't!

And since his family was worried about his political future, he added:

> The thereafter is not yet clear except that Golda [by then Israel's second Foreign Minister] has reiterated her "wish" to leave the Foreign Ministry and there is talk of making her vice premier [a veiled hint at Ben-Gurion's intentions].

Quite unlike today, it used to be an Israeli political tradition to present public office as an intolerable burden which politicians would reluctantly accept out of sheer altruism. Golda was a master in that exercise but some people in our political leadership had taken Golda's expression of reluctance seriously.

On 30 November 1959, during an unexpected hamsin, the Labour Party won the election by a massive margin and Abba was elected as a Member of Knesset on the Mapai ticket. I had a few pangs of the heart when, on the afternoon of election day, the Labour Party secretary in Rehovot called me to tell us that our young, part-time, Institute driver, Ze'ev, was packing opposition voters tightly into our private car and cheerfully transporting them back and forth to the polling stations for his own Liberal Party.

There has never been a clear victory in Israel for a single party at the ballot box, and even before an election is won, the politicians' wrangling and manoeuvring around the cabinet formation starts with great intensity and with sharpened vigilance from the press. The public, whose national hobby is politics, finds cabinet formation to be even more interesting than the election itself.

As soon as the election was won, Golda stated flatly that, contrary to rumours, she did not intend to relinquish her Ministry and that, in fact, she had never meant to do so! As a member of Ben-Gurion's inner team, she had sharply disagreed with him on various things, especially about accepting military equipment from Germany when America had put an embargo on arms to Israel. Ben-Gurion was never afraid of Abba's intellectual power or conceptual, analytical strength and he was too secure to feel envy. Golda, on the contrary, always felt threatened. On the other hand, she had populist intuitions and a way with ordinary citizens whom she made feel comfortable with her emotional reactions that were so very close to theirs. My own view was that Golda spoke for the ordinary citizen; Abba reasoned for him. Each gravitated towards a role, in her case defined by her temperament, in his case defined by his upbringing.

Ben-Gurion now had to choose, since his hopes of change had backfired. Golda continued to conceal a great mastery of political manoeuvring behind a façade of disinterested innocence. Ben-Gurion, however, maintained his position that Abba would be included in the new cabinet. It seemed important for him not to let Abba remain in the exclusive Weizmann domain.

In the jockeying between the two, Abba found himself going back and forth from Ben-Gurion to Golda, till one night during the deadlock we sat up until two in the morning discussing the confusion and uncertainty of the situation and the see-saw tactics. The next day, Abba sent Ben-Gurion a letter offering to withdraw from the political wrangling. This was his first political gambit. He was counting on the fact that Ben-Gurion would not wish to incur a lack of credibility in the eyes of the public and the world by renouncing Abba, as Abba's moves were now being watched in Israel and ever more closely abroad. It was also a test: how would an "immigrant" from the western world, of English upbringing, fare in the framework of Israeli political intrigue? In addition to Abba, the other young stars in the new electoral constellation were

Moshe Dayan, a sabra, and Shimon Peres, who had come to Israel at the age of ten. They were brought together during the campaign to create a new image of the Labour Party and were called the "Young Turks". Dayan had hoped to get the Defence portfolio, Abba had hoped for Foreign Affairs. But coalition needs, and the fact that Ben-Gurion was in no real hurry to give an upward push to impatient and able young men, led each of them to be a rung lower in the cabinet than they had hoped: Abba was appointed Minister without Portfolio; Dayan, Minister of Agriculture and Peres, Deputy Minister of Defence. Golda calmly stayed on as Foreign Minister.

I remember sitting in the gallery at the swearing-in ceremony in an old building (previously a bank) called "The Froumine House" on Jerusalem's King George Street. Although entering the cabinet was a great achievement, in our excitement the setting made the occasion look functional and prosaic. We joked between us, in a self-congratulatory spirit, that the scene was in stark contrast to what Abba would have become accustomed to if he had become a member of the British Parliament following Harold Laski's suggestion in 1945. Being escorted to the green leather benches of the House of Commons was quite different from the totally casual seating in the makeshift Knesset where the old columns of the original building in the middle of the assembly hall stood between Knesset members.

It would take seven years before the Israeli people would have the splendid Knesset of today, with its spectacular site on a flattened hill top, its panoramic view of western Jerusalem, its lower circular entrance for members, and its majestic square above for receiving world statesmen or for commemorative ceremonies and one single figurative expression in the assembly hall, a large lithograph of Theodor Herzl's bearded profile, printed on a thick slab of aluminum. And it would take still more time before it would develop any sense of decorum. We were young and we understood very well that the achievement lay in entering the decision-making body of Israel where older, seasoned politicians were treading. For us this was a dramatic personal event. Indeed it was an unusual achievement for Abba to become a cabinet minister within five months of his return. Once again he was going to hold two jobs since he did not relinquish the presidency of the Weizmann Institute as a dollar-a-year appointment. We also understood he would have to bide his time politically. In the meantime he had various assignments but they were mostly "ad hoc".

The government gave us an apartment in Jerusalem – two rooms, a bedroom and sitting-room and a part-time domestic helper who turned out to be a passionate member of the Herut opposition party and made her position clear on the first day she came to work. From the government storehouse they produced an old desk that Ben-Gurion had discarded as too small for the dignity of his office. The apartment had originally been divided in two to accommodate another base in the capital for another minister. The wall separating us was by no means soundproof. Our neighbour was Pinhas Sapir, the Minister of Commerce and Industry, a powerful and enterprising man totally dedicated to the creation of the infrastructure of the new State. With the seven hours' time difference, at midnight he would just begin to catch various investors or benefactors in the United States at what would be their 5 p.m., and he would yell at the top of his voice, because telephone lines were so bad and exasperating then. I did not keep house in Jerusalem. We preferred returning to our Rehovot home, to our children and our obligations there if we could finish early enough or were not too tired after some official dinner.

A couple of months after the ministerial appointment, some time in April 1960, Abba came to me saying that he had been asked to represent the Government of Israel at the 150th anniversary of Argentina's independence. I had been invited too and, in honour of our hosts and with the desire to show the Israeli flag with real panache, a plane would be put at the disposal of the delegation. We looked at each other wordlessly: the idea of a special plane was so ridiculous in terms of Israel's meagre economy and public criticism would be engendered. We assumed, therefore, that it must be a camouflage for some arms operation.

I decided not to join the delegation, because of the distance and the language – which I did not know, although Abba could show off his Castilian Spanish (completely self-taught during one of the UN years) – but would stay in Rehovot with the children. Then, the day before his departure on the famous plane, Ben-Gurion called Abba in and told him confidentially that the El Al flight was going to bring back Adolf Eichmann, the Nazi officer in charge of the extermination of Jews in Europe. Eichmann had been captured on the eve of the Argentinian festivities, when everybody's preoccupations had been around the ceremonies, parades and dinners. That night, in the darkness of our bedroom, Abba confided in me the true purpose of the trip. He literally whispered the story in my ears. I was so stunned by the daring of what he had said that I did not allow myself to discuss it one word further.

After his departure, I kept my radio on all the time. Abba was accompanied by General Meyer Zorea – a war hero travelling in the guise of a military aide to add to the decorum of the celebration in Buenos Aires – and other representatives. Suddenly, there was a radio communiqué which said the plane had made a forced landing at Recife. Recife? I wondered. I had been told Rio would be the stopover. What had gone wrong? Nothing had gone wrong. It was a masterly planned operation, as the whole world would soon know.

Once the news broke out like thunder in Buenos Aires, our official party, headed by Abba and the Ambassador, had already attended the ceremonies in dress tails and white tie at 11 in the morning. Abba had then slipped away from Argentina on a regular commercial flight to London, since no Argentinian airline had direct flights to Israel nor did we have regular landing rights, while El Al's special flight departed for Israel with Eichmann on board. Numerous news reporters from Israel and overseas telephoned our house in Rehovot, and since I was alone I had to handle them myself. Abba was incognito in London.

The press was preoccupied with the question of whether Abba had known beforehand. It was a typical diplomatic situation where the answer can never be a straight yes or no. One could not say that yes, Abba knew, so as not to affront the Argentinian Government's hospitality, however much they had given shelter to Nazis, because there was an impressive Jewish community there. Nor could one say no, as the Argentinian Government had given us special landing rights for the occasion and Israel wanted to develop a future relationship with Argentina. Also, it would have been insulting to Ben-Gurion, making it look as if he had put Abba in a tricky situation, which was not the case.

Following a trial in Jerusalem, Eichmann was sentenced to death for crimes against the Jewish people and crimes against humanity. He was executed on 31 May 1962.

15

"What about you, Eban?"

In 1961, two years after Abba entered the cabinet, a teachers' strike in Israel paralyzed the secondary school system for several months. The country lurched from crisis to crisis, week after week. We felt as if a great social breakdown was taking place. The Minister of Education and Culture, Zalman Aranne, had resigned, unable to cope with the strikes arising from the classic conflict between the Teachers' Union and the Finance Ministry. At a cabinet meeting, Ben-Gurion surveyed the long table of twenty colleagues and asked for a "volunteer". It was a strange method of selection, but Ben-Gurion was not a man of routine. The Ministry of Education had a negative image both for its bureaucracy and for its excessive centralization.

Ben-Gurion's call met with silence. Most members of the cabinet held posts that they would only exchange for one of the "prize" ministries – Defence, Foreign Affairs and Finance. Of the three young "stars" in the cabinet, Shimon Peres was Deputy Minister of Defence and not a cabinet member, and although Moshe Dayan was dissatisfied with his status as Agriculture Minister, he did not regard himself as a great educator. As a man of the soil, a *moshav** man, Dayan must have felt more comfortable with the smell of fields than the atmosphere of classrooms. Nor did he feel that the Education Ministry would offer more political power than his existing incumbency. Only Abba was in a position

* A *moshav* is an agricultural village based on a co-operative association of small-holdings.

to take up this new post. Ben-Gurion's eye fell on him, and he asked: "What about you, Eban?" to which he answered: "I'll accept the call."

Thus a new and important assignment fell to Abba within minutes. His heart must have skipped a beat, as he understood the sudden advancement with its complexities and challenges, including the second largest budget in the country and a vast constituency of tens of thousands of teachers and hundreds of thousands of students. I wrote to his family shortly afterwards:

> Everybody says what a hard and dreadful ministry it is, but maybe he can contribute much to it by new thinking and new methods… It gives him a sphere of work endless in scope. Schools now matter to us very much.

In 1961, in his second year as President of the Weizmann Institute, Abba convened an international conference in Rehovot on "The Role of Science and Technology in the Development of New States". The response of the scientific world was impressive. Meyer Weisgal co-operated with Abba in projecting the Institute on to the outside world. Invitations went out in Abba's name and he felt that he could again serve the international position of Israel. Giants of the scientific community attended, such as John Cockroft, (Lord Cockroft had split the atom with the great Lord (Ernest) Rutherford at Cambridge), Patrick Blackett, the Nobel Laureate in Physics, and Jerrold Zacharias, one-time director of Oak Ridge National Laboratory. The heads of international agencies including Paul Hoffman of the United Nations Development Fund, renowned experts in agriculture, health and economic planning were to follow in two more Rehovot Conferences on Agriculture and Economic Planning. Other Nobel Laureates, those who had made their names in prestigious laboratories in the western world, were now walking the paths of the Rehovot campus. Professor Kenneth Galbraith from Harvard and Professor (later Lord) Thomas Balog from Cambridge came to the Rehovot II Conference on Economics.

At the opening of the first Conference, Abba said:

> Mankind has a power that it never previously possessed, to control and use energy, to multiply industrial and agricultural production, to eliminate illiteracy and to draw the entire human race into the widening universe of knowledge. At the same time the expansion of national opportunities has liberated vast areas of mankind from colonial subjection, leading to the establishment of dozens of new sovereignties. These two revolutions, however, have not had much influence on each other. Most nations have not achieved access to the benefits of science and technology and few of them have created indigenous bodies of scientifically trained manpower. The two revolutions have led separate lives without the benefits that would have resulted from their co-operation.

The country was fascinated by our guests. Not since U Nu, the Socialist Prime Minister of Burma, who had been the first head of state to visit Israel, had there been such a flow of foreign dignitaries. They came from Ghana, Congo, Nepal, Sierra Leone, Thailand, Kenya, Ivory Coast, Brazil, the Dominican Republic and Singapore. Not one woman was in that group, such was the paucity of women leaders or eminent women scientists. All the same, Abba was thus enhancing Israel's foreign relations during his presidency at the Institute as well as illustrating the personal prestige that he had accumulated in his decade abroad as Ambassador to the UN and the USA. Golda Meir, in her autobiography some years later, described the Rehovot Conference as the starting point of Israel's successful attempt to win the friendship and understanding of new nations.

The Israeli public, somewhat puzzled by the erudite lectures and papers, found something heart-warming in the very arrival of so many eminent guests. It brought great animation to a proud and surprised Israel, so closed up within its small land. The United Nations responded to the challenge of the Rehovot Conference on Science and New States by reinforcing the co-operation between national leaders and scientific institutions. On the initiative of Dag Hammarskjöld, then United Nations Secretary-General, at a time when the appointment of Israelis to UN commissions was very rare, Abba was elected to be a member of a UN committee charged with the duty of supervising and encouraging co-operation between scientists and leaders of nations.

Abba's visionary proposals of collaboration between scientists and statesmen never developed its full potential. The Institute's project was discontinued in 1974 for budgetary and mostly political reasons following a change of government. I think that innovative non-governmental proposals often lead the way in a democratic society, opening new vistas and becoming adjuncts of national policy. In Israel, there are several multilateral projects of a similar spirit. They have the form of a pragmatic regional co-operation and are sponsored by independent institutions with impressive budgets, and there are scientific attachés in major embassies.

The pressures of our new society were such that we were never able to devote ourselves to one purpose alone. This pattern repeated itself throughout our lives. Whenever Abba did not hold two jobs simultaneously, we both went into a panic as if half-orphaned of inspiration and creativity or short of work. That year, 1961, he balanced a new ministry, a teachers' strike, an international conference and, for me came the additional responsibility of setting up the ministerial apartment in Jerusalem so that it would be more comfortable when we commuted from

Rehovot. The Ministry of Education brought us back to the grass-roots reality of Israel after the excitement of the Rehovot Conference wore off.

Our eminent caricaturist, Zeev, has portrayed Abba's entry into that ministry in an ominous cartoon entitled "The Courageous Knight", showing the ministry as a pre-historic cave at whose entrance glowers a dragon, complete with flames. Outside the cave lie the scattered bones of a devoured education minister (Abba's predecessor). The caricature was not totally out of accord with reality. The high-school teachers who had deposed the former minister had tasted blood and they were going to be just as implacable towards the new "intellectual minister" as they had been to his populist predecessor. These teachers were mostly university trained and felt that there should be a clear wage differential between themselves and the primary school teachers who had no more than seminary diplomas. The helpless minister bore the wrath of the parents, whose children were affected by the strike week after week. The youngsters were roaming the streets, sitting in cafés, mocking the peculiarities of their teachers and sleeping late, while their parents agonized over the prospect of their failing the examinations at the end of the year. A teachers' strike may sound innocuous, but it amounts to a social upheaval. The pattern of a fully active society where father, mother and child set out rhythmically at the customary hours of work and study was now disrupted. The great population aged twelve to seventeen was suddenly suspended in a vacuum, left to its own devices.

People expected much from Abba, seeing him as a symbol of a scholarly minister in a pioneering society and assuming that he would know what needed to be done. I wonder what they would have felt if they knew he translated Oedipus from classical Greek to English prose simply for mental exercise and his own pleasure! I felt that his English education would help to guide him in matters of curriculum and organizational structures. But England was a well-established society and Israel had more fundamental problems to contend with first. Abba became intensely preoccupied in fields far different from his tasks at the UN and the embassy. There were now days when he pored over documents formulated in a language far removed from what he was used to, papers carefully prepared for meetings with the Finance Ministry and the powerful Histadrut.

It took months to solve the issues with the secondary school teachers' association and the trade unions. Abba was able to work closely with the teachers' union because they respected his intellectual dimension and academic record and accepted his authority. By the spring of 1962 he felt that the strike must be ended even if that involved paying the teachers inflated salaries. This request exasperated Minister of Finance Pinchas Sapir, the man who rigorously watched over the modest purse of the land and kept a close and vigorous involvement in the infrastructure of every village, kibbutz or industry in the country. Abba nonetheless insisted and the salaries were increased, ending the strike. His efforts had pacified the relations between the two major teachers' organizations to such an extent that two years later, when the new Prime Minister, Levi Eshkol, appointed him Deputy Prime Minister, both organizations implored him to remain at the head of their ministry.

The Ministry of Education office was in an old Jerusalem building in the Abyssinian quarter, a few yards from the Armistice line that divided Jerusalem from Jordan after the War of Independence. I remember looking out of the window and seeing what an incredibly small space "no man's land" was. Opposite Abba's window stood Jordanian guards who occupied a balcony on the upper floor of a monastery, with rifles suspended from their shoulders and binoculars hung round their necks. They stared at us for hours on end, looking very bored. Children, undeterred by the enemy's proximity or the barbed wire, played in that border area.

Some while after Abba's appointment, I came up from Rehovot to see his new office. As they were redecorating, construction crews ignored the vaulted ceiling, lowered the height considerably and workers were beginning to construct a wooden ceiling instead. When I exclaimed, "Why? The arches and proportions are so beautiful, they belong to this kind of building," the architect, meaning to cheer me up, explained, "Ben-Gurion is a small man. The government doesn't like tall ceilings."

From those offices, Abba was able to institute great change and improvement in Israeli education. One subject he cared about very much was the recognition of universities outside Jerusalem. As the chairman of the Council on Higher Education, he sponsored the accreditation of Tel Aviv and Bar Ilan Universities, despite the resentment of the Hebrew University in Jerusalem, which believed that Jerusalem should have exclusive recognition as the centre of higher learning. Ben-Gurion himself agreed and was in accord that industrial development be centred in Haifa and commercial activity in Tel Aviv. My husband's contrary view was that whenever a community reached a population of several hundred thousand, it should have its own university and, he insisted, its own central library. Today there are huge numbers of students in Tel Aviv, a thriving university in Beersheba, and colleges spread throughout the country.

In addition to his great achievements for higher education, Abba's main task during his time as Minister of Education was to contend with the social and educational gap brought about by the waves of immigration in the 1950s. Except for religious institutions, the education system was centralized in the hands of the government which had hurriedly to create more classrooms throughout Israel and enlarge existing classes. Soon the classes became too crowded and had to be rearranged and brought down to forty students per class. Many more teachers were needed and *ulpanim* had to be created in co-operation with the Jewish Agency. (The *ulpan* is that unique Israeli institution for teaching Hebrew to immigrants through intensive immersion classes, a method still used today).

The social researchers at the Ministry of Education had taken surveys that indicated that in development areas with small towns and primitive institutions, the standard of literacy was abysmally low compared with the more sophisticated cities. The key was held by mothers who could not read to their children, putting them at a serious disadvantage by the ages of three or four. Ben-Gurion understood that Israel could easily become a society of "two nations" with disastrously different achievements in education and culture. Once Abba presented these issues at the cabinet table, the school system moved into top gear and education became a priority concern for the Prime Minister's office.

However, it was not until education became a subject of great concern to benefactors of Israel abroad, that other significant changes were made. The UJA Education Fund was established and the Rothschild Family Foundation, Yad Hanadiv, responded to Israel's plea about the education gap. When Victor Rothschild offered to create an outlet for educational television at Ramat Aviv on the outskirts of Tel Aviv, Abba was firm in his support of this idea but had to fight hard against Ben-Gurion, who contended that Israel could do without seeing people shooting each other on a television screen.

The vote for and against television was carried very narrowly in the Knesset. In fact, Abba realized that it was literally touch and go. He finally won the television battle by quoting the French Minister of Education and writer André Malraux, who explained that in France, millions more people had seen the plays of Racine and Molière on TV than in all the previous centuries combined. Ben-Gurion eventually recognized, as always, that modernity had to prevail, and ultimately the Educational TV station was established in the Judean hills, sponsored by the Rothschild Foundation.

Even at the time of the Six Day War in 1967, there was still no general television outlet in the country and some of us felt that we had done very well without hearing or seeing Ahmed Shukeiri, the military commander of the Palestine Liberation Organization (Yasser Arafat's predecessor as Chairman), standing on the ramparts of the old Turkish Citadel in East Jerusalem, threatening our people in West Jerusalem with destruction and pouring out venomous statements about our impending annihilation. It was only at the end of December 1973 – after the Yom Kippur War, our fourth war since independence, that Israelis were able to see their own representative debating on television against Arab ministers at the 1973 United Nations Geneva Peace Conference which Henry Kissinger initiated and Abba attended as head of our Mission.

It was also in his capacity as Minister of Culture that Abba received a very young Spanish-born tenor, Placido Domingo, who had landed his first foreign fixed contract as performer with the embryonic Israeli Opera. Domingo had come to plead for a doubling of their miserable budget. So unknown was he at the time that his name was not even mentioned in the press listing of the delegation. Whenever we met in later years he would laugh with us at those touching early times. There was so little money for "culture" then, and it would take another thirty years before the Israeli Opera had a public supporting body and would be housed in a dignified building.

A matter of personal concern for our family, as well as the country in general, was the subject of English language in schools. There were very few real English teachers at the time, and it seemed as though knowing the Latin alphabet alone would qualify you for the job. Israeli children could not pronounce "th" as anything other than "de" or "ze". Abba was expected to take a literary approach, teaching Israelis to struggle with *Hamlet* and *Macbeth,* and I remember how surprised officials in his Ministry were when he said that it was more important for the pupils to use colloquial idioms and make their English comprehensible on a daily level. They asked, "Do you want to make the English classrooms into Berlitz schools?" Abba replied, "Yes, if it will get them to speak English."

Whenever Abba looked back on his role as the head of the Ministry of Education and Culture, he felt a surge of satisfaction. His liberal views helped him to encourage a secular and creative approach in education. He gave his colleagues in the Ministry a feeling that general humanism would serve our modern society better than a religious domination of the curriculum and voiced it firmly in the Knesset Plenary and to the Educational Board. Setting the educational system on that course mattered to him very deeply: he believed in it and imparted it whole-heartedly. The fact that he himself was so thoroughly versed in the traditional Hebrew texts helped him to achieve this result, since colleagues recognized the total integrity of his beliefs. He felt that there should be an educational balance. Transcending the daily administrative technicalities, he believed that the young Israeli must never detach himself from his Jewish spiritual legacy – that to choose to be a secular person doesn't necessarily mean to be anti-religious. He strove to take a country composed of so many cultures and histories, and bring it to a modern, unified nation.

I have often felt that his biographers were so used to his reputation as a stellar diplomatic personality that they never fully stressed how, for Abba, these were years of great domestic challenges and fundamental contributions to the development of the state.

In 1963, after much painful criticism and many uncertainties about the security mishap in the Lavon Affair*, Ben-Gurion resigned and the Labour Party chose Levi Eshkol to be his successor. He appointed Abba Deputy Prime Minister. Abba still held the presidency of the Weizmann Institute and we continued to live in Rehovot. The Institute was, for years, the anchor that

---

* The Lavon Affair was one of the most damaging scandals in Israeli history. It centred on a failed exercise conducted by Israeli Intelligence in 1954 which involved planting bombs at Egyptian, American and British targets in Egypt. Pinhas Lavon, the Defence Minister, strenuously denied the accusation that he was behind the operation but later resigned his post.

would help keep us in politics. It remained for us what it was meant to be – a protection *for* and *from* politics, a means of freeing Abba for political thinking and for his elucidation of our regional and international events. He always hoped to return to foreign affairs, and the governors of the Institute still felt that Abba was a precious talent to safeguard for Israel's expression on the world platform, and for his conceptual leadership and vision in the Labour Party's politics. They continued to offer their invincible support amidst political manipulations which, in our emerging nation, were often valued more than conceptual force. The governors made certain that they would stand loyally in the background with him, as if in a waiting station.

16

The children and our home

Looking back, I am amazed at what little allowance we had in Rehovot for casual home life. Abba and I, first through years of embassy life and then political and official responsibilities in Israel, did not manage to bridge the gap between home and duty in the carefree way so many of today's young parents do, where children participate in everything in the house. As the youngest diplomats around in the 1950s at the UN and in Washington, we had been thrust so quickly, so unequivocally into the orbit of the preceding generation, with so many formal occasions. From the time our two children were babies, we had merged into the big and vital issues of statehood. Crises and obligations for years broke the continuity of home life. We celebrated birthdays rigorously and in Rehovot we stayed home most Friday nights, even though the children liked to rush out after dinner to play with their friends on the Institute lawns.

Throughout our eight years in Rehovot, Abba held the presidency of the Weizmann Institute concurrently with a cabinet post, and we were always travelling back and forth between Rehovot, Jerusalem and Tel Aviv on simple two lane roads. Abba attended cabinet meetings on Sunday – a working day in Israel – and the Knesset on other days. Wednesday afternoons and the weekends were kept for political consultations either at our home in Rehovot or in Tel Aviv, usually meetings with party members or the press.

Amidst all these comings and goings, we entertained constantly and mixed members of the Institute and government on all occasions. Our excellent Romanian cook, Tova, waited on our parties large and small, never deterred by the pressures on the house. She had served in a German officers' mess in the war, a job that saved her life. The number burned into her arm was a constant and silent reminder of her life story in those long summer months when the terrible heat made women wear short-sleeved dresses. Tova came to Israel before independence, on an illegal immigrants' ship that was intercepted by the British and sent to Cyprus in what were called "floating cages" for incarceration. Our driver, Yaacov Marcovich, a dare-you-all personality who had survived Bergen-Belsen as a child with his brother, drove Abba at a dazzling speed to upstage any other driver on the highway. Every day he would impart to Abba the wealth of information he had gleaned from other ministerial drivers, and very often from journalists too, while waiting for hours for meetings to end.

Eli and Gila, born abroad as children of diplomats, arrived in Rehovot into a milieu they knew only by hearsay, equipped with a rudimentary Hebrew and in the charge of their English nanny, Winifred Gates, who had agreed to come to Israel to help us settle in. Nanny Gates had been working for members of our extended family for eighteen years. Having to travel as much as we did, I was comforted by her watchful presence, since she was no stranger to the family. Nanny Gates was always ready for all contingencies and took our household's demands remarkably in her stride, especially considering that for her Israel was a strange country with a strange language and totally different modes of behaviour. She read the *Jewish Chronicle* because she knew some of the people featured in it, and always told me in advance the dates of Jewish holidays.

After a year in Rehovot, Nanny Gates decided to return to England. Eli and Gila were by then using Hebrew daily at school and at home, and she felt that their use of language left her out of much of what was going on in their lives. Between their childhood in the USA and their advanced Hebrew in Israel they were to grow up completely bi-lingual. In addition, with the protection provided by the Weizmann Institute campus, the children had become independent, each going his or her own way to play with friends within the grounds: her usefulness seemed to have worn out. But parallel to her role of nanny, she was always ready to assist me in our social obligations. She had been so supportive, standing by me, supervising preparations in the house where there was frequent entertaining. I'd bring her descriptions and stories about the people invited and she loved our "off the record" chats. The day she came to me to announce her desire to return to England, she cried and explained to me, ironically: "You don't know what it is like to be a minority!" Before she left, she gave me a poem about nannies, how they belong to all and to no one. I invited her to come back to Rehovot once more when we had to be away for quite a while and she was happy to know that she would see the children once again.

Many years later Eli and I spoke about the Rehovot years and Nanny. He remembered that both he and Gila suffered from the duality of their life in Rehovot. On the one hand, Israeli society demanded simplicity, informality, camaraderie and directness – an egalitarian society with its specific conventions. On the other hand, our home was filled with strict, neat formality. Nanny was a person set in her proper English ways. What she wanted from the children was not strange to Abba and to me but not right for Israel, where children were much freer and very direct and forceful in their form of expression. Our children also had to contend with the closeness that Israeli children felt, their homes in such close proximity to one another, set against the frequent absence of their own parents, so unlike their friends' families. I remember Anne Stone once asking Eli how he felt when we were gone. He answered, simply, "I miss the smell of Abba's cigars." And I once asked an angry Gila why she did not like her clothes, asking her, "What would you like?" and she answered "a dirty t-shirt."

The children were faced with two very different worlds: the world of school and the world of home. Eli felt that because we were not sabras, we were – each one of us – struggling on our own level to be accepted. Abba and I had our political and personal goals and the children their social goals. In a home filled with outsiders, Eli explained, there is a special value attached to success. Because you come from the outside world you must not fail, or more accurately, you must rise above the norm and prove that although you can never be a sabra, you can be an equal in your own right. The sense of being an outsider was one my children struggled with for a long time. Eli phrased it succinctly: "The head of the family chooses his career – it is his choice. But the children are thrust into the effects of that choice." In Eli's case the same thing happened to his children. Both my grandchildren, Yael and Omri, our sabras, born here in Israel, were taken by their father's musical career choice to America.

Having grown up in the Middle East, I was no stranger to many of the cosmopolitan, mixed characteristics of the region. The sense of being different became attenuated, and as it was my inclination to let the adjustment of the family take its gradual course, the children grew up, took roots and became "kind of sabras" themselves. Our home in Herzlia remains very much in their hearts, the place they follow, literally daily, from afar.

One of the conflicts we faced in our personal lives was Eli's Bar Mitzvah. He went through all the preparations, as all young Jewish boys do, and although we were not strictly religious, the day held great personal significance for us. But Eli came home from school one day very annoyed, for all over town there were posters announcing the event and inviting the public at large to attend. For him, the idea that this was to be a great public display was upsetting. In the end, the day was very moving for us all. Eli's school-friends placed themselves in the first row in solidarity and Eli recited his portion of the *"haftara"* (reading from the Prophets) very well. We survived the usual parental anxieties of the moment, and no sooner was the religious service over than there was a tremendous clatter in the sanctuary. Women in the gallery were throwing handfuls of sweets with tremendous zest and these were hitting the round, saucer-like metal tops of the modern chandeliers.

Although I was very moved and proud of my son, I had a sense of personal frustration. On the one hand it was a joy for me to see the women, who were so segregated in their upper gallery, make their presence felt. How I would have loved to sit together with my husband on that day instead of being perched up in a gallery, but in Orthodox synagogues this is prohibited. In moments of spiritual elevation one is thrown back into ancient customs but as a mother I felt left out. When I came down into the synagogue's courtyard, it was very touching for me to see Abba, tall in his prayer shawl and young Eli in his own new *talit*, standing together. How I wish I had a photographic memento of that special day.

As Eli faced the public eye, Gila had to face public expectations on another level. When her turn came to serve her two years in the army, she proved to be the least spoiled girl in her unit, although everybody expected the opposite. Her commanding officer told me she worked with maximum responsibility and great camaraderie. It was rather typical of Gila that when put in charge of drafting the reservists of her tank unit and noticing that one soldier was absent, she hitch-hiked (by lorry) to his home in a remote settlement in the Jordan Valley, right by the Jordanian frontier. She proudly brought back the missing reservist.

Abba and I were so sure after the proclamation of the State that it would be different for our children, but here we were with the old restlessness, even after the most extraordinary and spectacular achievements of the Israeli nation. Despite it all, the smallness of our space stands in stark contrast to our love of the land and its gem-like landscapes. Occasionally many felt a plain lack of opportunity here, even amidst our enthusiastic desire to develop and improve our society. For our children, who were brought here on the wave of their parents' dreams, the disparity is still there.

I feel that what Abba expressed in one of his writings, about a double process in Jewish life where our people at one and the same time feel a necessity to go back to their ancient roots and equally a necessity to throw themselves into the universal stream of modern life, remains valid, even today. It seems to me that Jewish life has always experienced these fluctuations of belonging and departing. The belongings are a continuous thread through generations and are undeniably strong. The partings have often occurred because of material or professional necessity and a desire to breathe the air of the wider world. Yet a strong affinity, a recognition of that original sense of belonging, always remains in one's mind and heart whether consciously or subconsciously. The nomadic instinct is a characteristic of Jewish life at all times, challenged by the undeniable pull of most Jews towards our ancient and unique land. We struggle to balance the privilege of living in Israel with the overwhelming complexities that seem to persist through generations. I think every immigrant has felt these divergent pulls in one form or another, at some time. For our family, the struggles were no different.

17

"Can't you think of a prettier subject?"

While Abba was absorbed in the problems of the Ministry of Education, in the spring of 1960 and at the request of Professor Isaac Berenblum, head of the first Cancer Research Department at the Weizmann Institute, I took on the role of President of the Israel Cancer Association, an obscure little organization formed in 1952, with an insignificant budget and no public projection whatsoever. Professor Berenblum and other doctors facing the issues of cancer, found that there was no public awareness of the vital necessity of early detection. Those with existing symptoms would not see a doctor "because they had no temperature" for instance, or other similar absurdities. Until this point there had been no public education such as that promulgated throughout the USA by the American Cancer Society in its first pamphlet, "Seven Signs of Cancer" which we were very soon going to adopt.

Shortly after taking on this assignment, I asked for an appointment with President Ben-Zvi, hoping for his patronage of our association. Both President Ben-Zvi and Mrs Ben-Zvi met my chairman, Professor Berenblum, Mirjam Klein, the secretary of the organization and me. Mrs Ben-Zvi, within sight of her husband, moved her head from left to right and turned down the request on his behalf. Known for her habit of making some of his decisions for him, she had always been the leader, the passionate exponent of political and social causes, while he was a more scholarly type. He, probably out of consideration for my husband's ministerial post, avoided a blunt refusal. I was quite aware that I had brought them into contact with a form of activity totally foreign to them. Early founders of the Haganah, the Ben-Zvis had been instrumental in the creation of some of the infrastructure of the Labour system in health and education before the establishment of the State and it was the force and power of the Labour movement that had made the State a viable national entity immediately upon the declaration of independence. My request was really going against the grain of their socialist beliefs, according to which the movement and the Party were to provide *all* the services for its people. I knew of a whole world where volunteer effort lent an additional dimension to a society but the Labour Party only acknowledged a national volunteer effort in security and defence. I was convinced that my "new" organization was vitally necessary to Israel. During our diplomatic service in Washington I had noticed how important the American Cancer Society was and was deeply inspired by this model of civic contribution. In our first year in the USA, I had made a point of contacting the Society – and learning!

Just as our meeting was breaking up, the President took me aside and asked me to explain more clearly why he was needed as patron. I took the opportunity to salvage what had seemed, just a few minutes before, an imminent defeat by assuring him of many precedents. Other heads of state were patrons of their cancer organizations, and I quoted Queen Juliana of Holland as an example. I added that I was not demanding anything incommensurate with his supreme place in the hierarchy of the nation.

Some time later President Ben-Zvi's ADC, Colonel Yossi Carmel, telephoned to say that the President had decided to accept my request. This gave me a sense of both success and encouragement. Year after year, during the remaining period of his presidency, both Ben-Zvis would receive us and representatives of our organization at the launching of our yearly fund-raising campaign. There was something refreshingly innocent in their lack of desire to distribute patronage between them. They had always collaborated very closely and this new cause was fully embraced by both of them. Since then, each President of the State has followed suit, launching every autumn, our national "Door-Knock" campaign, which still remains the largest single public education and fund-raising campaign in the country. One year, at my request, Ben-Gurion accepted the chairmanship of the campaign, as would do cabinet ministers and leaders of industry later.

The concept of operating on a national scale, with the added support of newspapers, radio and, some ten years later, television, for a cause that had no political implications for the country, was totally new in 1960s' Israel. Today, an infinitely more developed cancer association canvasses two million homes in one day, covering every city, village, kibbutz, place of business and industry. Every citizen is a participant in the fund-raising, and some forty-five thousand volunteers, of whom the majority are secondary school pupils under the tutelage of their school board, volunteer for most of the footwork. They are visible on every street and at every front door. Shortly after the initial successes that swept the country, I was told that not since the Jewish population's campaign in Palestine in support of its institutions and secret military training (*Kofer Hayishuv*) under the British Mandate, had there been such public involvement.

Although formed in 1952, by the time I joined in 1960, the organization comprised only two doctors, a public health counsellor and a part-time secretary, commiserating with each other about the dangers of delayed detection of cancer. There was no public consciousness of the Cancer Association's existence nor was there the slightest interest in the issues involved. The dramas and tragedies were borne by sad, silent and impotent families. Cancer was a taboo subject and if it had to be mentioned, it was called "that disease, God forbid". The subject was so off-limits, in fact, that when I had raised a substantial part of the money for the new departments of oncology at Tel Hashomer hospital (now called Sheba Medical Centre), I was told not to put our emblem on each donor's wing in order not to frighten patients. As a compromise, however, at my insistence, we did put a small emblem at the lower corner of each plaque.

The lack of interest was also due to the fact that at the time Israel was composed of such a young population that the subject of cancer was of remote interest. Statistics were incredibly rudimentary and only the general mortality figures of the country were listed in any formal way. At our initiative, a German refugee woman doctor started cancer mortality statistics. She sat in a bleak room at a small wooden table under a lone bulb hanging from the ceiling in some forgotten part of the Ministry of Health, filling in figures by hand, case by case. There was no specific break-down of the types of cancer or statistics on curability. All of these the Israel Cancer Association would help the government to finance, and years later initiate the processing of the figures by computer.

With just Mirjam Klein, I began our work from a ground-floor room rented from a doctor in Tel Aviv. There was one desk, one chair and one telephone. From that base we set out to canvass the whole country. Doors were opened to me everywhere – I was a sort of novelty – and this gave me a sense of excitement and the encouragement I needed to create an effective national organization.

The campaign was a product of "Early Israel": it was created speedily, and made possible only because of the spirit of those times, where originality and daring were in the forefront of the establishment of our social structures. I shuttled between Rehovot and Tel Aviv for endless meetings, and together Mirjam and I went to cities, government offices and non-governmental authorities, such as the Trade Unions Sick Fund, in which 85% of the country were registered for medical insurance. We visited hospitals, much to their surprise, to ascertain their needs, and thus laboriously established the initial contacts of the Israel Cancer Association with our public.

I also canvassed for the participation of the Israeli Arab population in Israel, starting with one meeting called by the wife of Mr Zuebi, the Arab Mayor of Nazareth. I remember the driver pulling up in the square in front of the Mayor's house and women, their heads covered with their hijabs, crowded into the windows staring at me and Mirjam. It must have seemed very strange to them to see two women coming to offer participation in a subject of no particular interest to them, unlike "*Tipat Halav*" for instance, that concerned itself with baby care, which they appreciated very much.

Shortly after I started my volunteer work, I went to the best known of the only two public relations firms that existed in Israel at the time: the concept was relatively new and certainly foreign. When I asked for technical help in the promotion of this new Israeli cause, Eliahu Tal, the head of the firm, said to me almost reproachfully, "Mrs Eban, can't you think of a 'prettier' subject to sponsor?" He thought for a moment and then shrugged his shoulders as if this was a woman's whim and what could he do but accept out of social courtesy?

Nevertheless, Tal harnessed his best energies to our cause and created the first literature and an emblem for the Israel Cancer Association. It was the first time that every home in Israel was called to face the subject of cancer and was made aware of this new organization that dared place itself in the centre of public consciousness. As we progressed it became clear that we were not merely creating a new "charity". Some complained that we would only create panic and anyway, who needed one more well-meaning organization? But I had arrived on the scene with the tremendous advantage of my husband's name. My part as an ambassadress, especially in Washington, also contributed to the public acceptance of the cause, and I was know in the press.

Our first national cancer campaign was to demonstrate a unique Israeli character. At a board meeting of the association, my colleague, John Furman, a Colonel in the British forces who emigrated from England after the Second World War, suggested that we should ask the army for help. At that time, in 1961, twelve years after the War of Independence and four years after the Sinai War, Israel still had to keep an army at full capacity. The army would be called to help the government and the Jewish Agency in civilian emergencies, such as settling floods of immigration by establishing absorption camps and developing new towns. Most spectacularly, the army had even helped on archeological digs, bringing heavy electrical projectors into the wilderness around the Dead Sea to illuminate some Nabatean finds. Soldiers were attached to such encampments for the sake of security.

As it would ordinarily take years to build any national organization, we agreed with John Furman and presented our case to the Chief of Staff of the Israel Defence Forces, Brigadier Zvi Tsur. To the outside world, this would have seemed an incredible request and it was incredible even in Israel, but it turned out to be a brilliant idea. How could we do it? Around our committee table, all eyes on me, it was decided I would be the one to present the idea. Slightly nervous, I presented myself a few days later at the main sentry booth of Army General Headquarters in Tel Aviv, riding in Abba's low-numbered ministerial car to prevent trouble parking.

I was met by an impressively mustachioed sergeant-major named Victor, regarded then as a national character because Israelis used to view ceremonial manifestation superciliously. In the very egalitarian early Israel, hierarchical army ranks were considered amusing and a touch pretentious. Everybody knew everybody in the commanding ranks by their first name, or knew of them from home, and salutes to commanders were the subjects of derision and jokes. For older people, the juxtaposition of the naive mentality of some immigrants with the new sabra assertiveness, brought out an avuncular pride.

Victor escorted me to the top floor reserved for the command of the Ministry of Defence but before he did so, in all seriousness, he clicked his heels in front of my disbelieving eyes and saluted. It made the ground tremble: it was well meaning but somewhat incongruous, and in stark contrast to the hospital of Tel Hashomer which I had just left, where life was much less decorous. The hospital departments were in derelict prefabricated huts, leftovers of the British occupation. Our cancer association was offered just three rooms to serve as the oncology department for the whole of Tel Aviv! To illustrate the conditions of the hospital then, the wife of the hospital director, Professor Chaim Sheba, had taken charge of the laundry, with its big mangles for smoothing the sheets, and was putting in long hours sewing curtains for the hospital's bare windows, all of it with one young assistant.

By the time I got to the Chief of Staff of the IDF, the ground had been prepared for me. Tsur (whom everyone called Chera), puzzled by my request to see him, had asked my brother-in-law, Chaim Herzog, then head of Military Intelligence, what it was all about, Chaim very lackadaisically said, "Why not listen to her first!" Chera, utterly surprised by my request, nevertheless said with aplomb, "I'll give you six months!" He then promised me three officers, each with a car – one for the north, one for the south, and one for the centre of the country. The three officers were at the end of their careers, due anyway to retire within six months. He added that an abandoned storage space could be used as our campaign headquarters: this turned out to be no more than the roof of some horrible, dilapidated, old building in a smelly, dirty part of Jaffa, where the army later installed a telephone – quite an asset, considering that the waiting list for a telephone in Israel then was months and sometimes years.

The officers' assignment was to visit and "conscript" every municipality in the country, putting our organization on the national map, which they really did. When officers turned up in their uniforms, everybody took notice: such a military presence suggested official approval. Our campaign was to begin in November and we worked like beavers the whole summer. On that roof in Jaffa, July and August were hell, the heat nearly unbearable, but we were a new element in the country and dared not fail. A woman lieutenant-colonel was assigned to help me on my rounds and to be my link with the officers. Sadly, she herself died of cancer a few years later. Before she fell ill, it was she who insisted that we include the Israeli Arab communities in our national campaign, and she would be pleased to know that they are very much a part of our organization today.

Having secured help from the army, I next went to the Chief of Police. Since the police were constantly patrolling the country in vans, we wanted them to use their usually empty vehicles to carry our publications and our receipt books to every community. They too accepted. So now we had personnel at no cost, and no expenses would be incurred for cars, fuel or time. Our fourth strategy was to see the Director of the Ministry of Education. We wanted him to send his own circular to the headmaster of every school asking for the co-operation of the Teachers' Union, permitting teachers to enrol and organize teams of students in every junior-high class in an exemplary civic project for youth. These young students would visit neighbourhoods in pairs, with a map of the streets and the specific buildings assigned to them, canvassing for donations and bringing cancer awareness literature to every home. It was very exciting and a totally new experience for the young.

Our very first assignment was to set up sixty-one breast cancer detection clinics, and later the novel programme of "Reach for Recovery." This is a programme for women who have undergone either a mastectomy or lumpectomy. Volunteers are trained to give support and information to family members. It is painful to remember how women, after a mastectomy, used to be told to fill up their bras with cotton wool. It was heartbreaking to see men who had had a laryngectomy hide away before our help existed, or be cast aside by a helpless family. When we had a larger office, one of our first projects was to gather them there and teach them to learn and use an approximation of speech. And now, following the fiftieth anniversary of the Israel Cancer Association, there isn't a single oncology department in the country that has not been helped by the Association.

There were so many achievements. We were partners with the medical institutions in putting up oncology wings, and promoting progressive ideas such as hospices, protective places where cancer patients can end their lives in dignity. During a private visit to London, I spent an intense morning with Dame Cicely Saunders who founded St Christopher's Hospice for terminal cancer patients, a revolutionary and compassionate programme. Soon after, in 1983, we initiated hospices in Israel. Our association supervised the planning and raising of money for contributing substantial parts of the total cost of eleven linear accelerators, as well as sponsoring the first projects of newly qualified post-graduate researchers, giving them their chance for initial professional recognition. We have never desisted from our role of public education and waving our flag at international conferences, especially of the International Cancer Union (UICC), of which our third Chairman, Professor Eliezer Robinson, would hold the presidency for one term – Professor Robinson continues to be a loyal and active Chairman of the Israel Cancer Association. Although I have retired, I continue to keep in touch with the Association and its most capable Director-General, Miri Ziv, who has become a close friend. Leon Recanati, whose mother Matilda was a deeply caring supporter of the Association from its inception, is Vice Chairman. We have been helped by wonderful benefactors abroad, including Dame Vivien Duffield who continues to assist the Sir Charles Clore Hostel (named after her father), that houses patients from outlying areas while they undergo radiotherapy or chemotherapy. Undoubtedly, however, our work could not have continued without the assistance of a tide of volunteers – the thousands of citizens of Israel.

In 1998, the year in which I resigned after thirty-eight years as President, I was presented with the Prime Minister's Award for Voluntary Service, and honoured by my colleagues with the title of Founding President. Vivien Duffield made a further generous donation to establish a Wellness department at the Israel Cancer Association headquarters in Tel Aviv and a Cancer Detection Clinic at the Rebecca Sieff Hospital in Safed: I am so proud that they both carry my name.

18

Mrs Weizmann and her house

I first went to the Rehovot home of Chaim and Vera Weizmann in 1946 when Abba, invited for lunch and a political discussion with Dr Weizmann, was told casually to bring his new bride. It was exciting for me to be invited by the two most charismatic personalities of Zionism. Dr Weizmann was seventy-two years old at the time, his wife Vera sixty-five. I was twenty-three and unfamiliar with these sorts of political luncheons.

Vera Weizmann will always remain in my memory as she was on the day of that first meeting: not tall, but stately, salt and pepper hair (as it would remain), face heavily powdered, lips painted a strong red and eyebrows thinly shaped in the style of Greta Garbo. When she looked up from under her large and heavy eyelids, Mrs Weizmann had an expression of world-weariness or haughtiness, but when she was delighted or amused, a charming smile broke out, illuminating her face and totally changing her. She was fastidiously attired that day as befit her reputation, and probably wearing her coiled gold watch-bracelet at its exact position high above her wrist, and her immovable strands of pearls. My first impression was that she seemed less snobbish than her reputation intimated.

Throughout the meal, Mrs Weizmann (one of the few Israeli women known in a very informal country as "Mrs"), never let the conversation take its full course but always broke in with some question of her own, causing us to veer off in another direction. At that time, the political discussions focused on the deteriorating relations between Jewish Palestine (the *Yishuv*) and the British Mandate authorities, caused mainly by the distressing consequences of the infamous 1939 White Paper. How would we save the hundreds of thousands of battered, destitute survivors of the Holocaust, who were desperately trying to reach Palestine? Our conversation centred on many British officials and Whitehall personalities, many of whose names I did not know. My husband had been invited to Rehovot on that day because, not yet demobilized from his war service in the British Army, he was already aligned in his heart and mind with Jewish settlement in Palestine. He knew the players as well as the game. As for me, with my background of Zionist parents and pioneer grandparents, identifying with our cause was a part of my very fibre.

At the end of the meal, we were led towards the tall glass doors of the dining room to be shown the panoramic view, densely green with orange groves beneath distant Judean Hills that made Israel appear even smaller than it was. Weizmann, whose eyesight was failing due to glaucoma and who was wearing dark glasses, led me paternally by the hand and then turned me around to the light "to see better," he said, fixing his eyes upon me rather than the view outside. I was being assessed, though I couldn't tell what sort of marks I was receiving. Flattered by his attention and yet in awe of these two dignitaries, I suddenly felt embarrassingly junior to the scene and proud that Abba, young as he was, seemed mature enough to have deserved the invitation.

Over the years of our official friendship, I heard Mrs Weizmann tell many fascinating stories about the early years before the State; the most poignant about Lord Balfour, the British Foreign Secretary who had signed the Declaration favouring the establishment of a Jewish homeland in Palestine, and Edmund Allenby, the British General who took Jerusalem from the Turks in 1917. One year later, on an unbearably hot and dusty hamsin day in July, Allenby, who had been invited by Weizmann to the cornerstone-laying ceremony of the Hebrew University, exclaimed, "Dr Weizmann, you are a very intelligent man. Do you believe that any damn Jew will come to this bloody country?" Weizmann's reply was, "Come back in ten years!"

As the President's wife, Mrs Weizmann evoked both curiosity and a measure of reserve in Israel. She was often criticized for upholding the classical, conservative pattern of diplomatic and political life, and not adopting a more informal manner, in accordance with the nation's austerity. Her table, with its old English silver and specially made porcelain, was superb, as was her food: the divinely domed soufflés and the lamb flown in from Paris weekly by El Al – a gesture made to the obligations of the presidential mansion. In season, she served a shaped dessert made from ruby-like Santa Rosa plum pulp, topped with curlicues of fresh cream, the creation glowing like a jewel as light from the glass doors fell upon it as it was passed around.

Mrs Weizmann maintained a great deal of vanity as a hostess. One morning Reti, her secretary, gave me an unexpected call at 11 a.m. in a great flap and with many apologies. "*Voilà*," she said, "one of the ladies has just dropped out of today's luncheon party. Could you make yourself free for one o'clock?" I could and I did, and was thus surprised to see that the dessert served was one from parties Abba and I threw, and for which Mrs Weizmann had asked the recipe with what was, of course, almost a command. When "my" dessert was marshalled in on a silver platter, it aroused admiring exclamations and was a culinary triumph. Mrs Weizmann never attributed it to me – nor did I mention anything, of course.

Her regal nature was known outside the Weizmann house, the governors of the Institute taking great pride in her and calling her their "grande dame", in appreciation of her innate sense of style. But not everyone was as enamoured. The people of Israel resented the fact that she was functioning as the First Lady of the Land without knowing any Hebrew, whereas she assumed that her loyalty to "The Cause" and her concern for her husband were self-explanatory and sufficient. However, that she valued the pioneer society in Mandate Palestine is clearly demonstrated by her foundation with Rebecca Sieff (later Lady Sieff), Edith Eder, Romana Goodman and Henrietta Irwell, of the Women's International Zionist Organisation (WIZO) at the time she was a practising doctor in Manchester. Mrs Weizmann had played a critical role, however fortuitous, in saving her husband for the Jewish people and she had shared all the painful Zionist moments with him. She always appeared to be much stronger than he, as evidenced by how he would often be sick after a political crisis, and she seemed to provide him with the emotional balance he needed to perform his important duties of state. Her Hebrew language skills seemed secondary to all this support.

Born in Russia, in Rostov-on-Don, beyond the Pale of Settlement which suggests a privileged background, Vera Weizmann, *neé* Chatzman, remained deeply attached to that heritage. The philosopher Sir Isaiah Berlin, a close friend of the Weizmanns, told me how Mrs Weizmann would sit at the Passover Seder table, many years later, and read the Haggadah in Russian. Like many of the bourgeoisie of pre-revolutionary Russia, she was also fluent in French, having learned it as a child. Taking their lead from the Court during the Czarist regime, educated people would often speak French at home amongst themselves and with friends, preferring it to their "native" Russian. Following her medical studies in Switzerland, she also spoke German well. Vera went to Manchester in 1906 after she married Chaim Weizmann who was already working there as a chemist, and was destined to develop processes vital to the British war effort. Gradually English became the language she spoke the most, and she was very much at ease with it by the time I met her, except for her Russian mannerism of dropping the definite article.

Mrs Weizmann possessed a great deal of worldly knowledge, first from her bourgeois upbringing and later from her experience as a political hostess in London where, in the world of great houses, glittering political salons and brilliant conversationalists, she had created for her husband a respectable and appropriately formal environment; an embassy-like home where he, as the unofficial ambassador of his people, could expound, debate and explore his Zionist projects with the leaders and opinion-makers of Britain. She knew and admired the English way of public life and, rigidly, would not budge from it, an attitude that was bound to lead to a kind of silent confrontation between the style of her values and those of what was basically a pioneer society.

The prestige of her central place in society seemed to go against the grain of the Jews of Palestine, most of whom were penniless, idealistic immigrants or refugees. Mrs Weizmann's compatriots judged her to be intelligent, disciplined, exacting, well-mannered and well-read, but always concluded their view of her with the standard cliché that she was "snobbish". She exasperated them by her detachment, showing a lack of desire or an inability to balance the national scene, with its urgent collective concerns and overwhelming human issues, against the international one, and even more so by her superb showmanship. Most of the Russian and Eastern European immigrant politicians had journeyed to Palestine in the 1920s and 1930s to be workers of the land, leaving behind their homes for what they felt was an historically-compelling destination and her life had been notably easier than theirs. She had splendid talent in "staging" her husband, but within the daily running of political affairs in Palestine, Weizmann's colleagues would have dearly welcomed some simple, informal friendliness from her. She was very far from personifying the kind of unassuming political wife the Israelis used to view and describe with great praise as "modest" and steeped in domesticity.

Some years later, when Abba and I lived at the Weizmann Institute, I felt sorry for Mrs Weizmann, already widowed for seven years by the time that we moved there. Although she always had friends from abroad, like Flora Solomon, staying with her (together they spoke their Russian English, had fun, gossiped and told colourful stories about pre-revolutionary Moscow), her remaining son and grandchild were never there on her birthday, and I wondered if the absence of any family members saddened her.

One year, thinking to bring some animation to Mrs Weizmann on her birthday, I gathered Eli and Gila together and we went up to her home, nicknamed "The White House". The children were dressed festively, each carrying a brightly-coloured posy. Eli hid on the floor of the car lest any of his schoolmates see him decked out in the suit and bow tie I'd asked him to wear (a leftover from our Washington days); six-year-old Gila, on the other hand, seemed pleased to be out of her shorts and tricot shirt and down from her tree house, and had turned herself out very party-like, with ribbons in her hair and a dress smocked by Nanny. On our arrival, Gila presented her flowers to Mrs Weizmann, who hugged her and put the bouquet down on her table. Gila, upset by the shortness of the ceremony, promptly snatched it back, brought it straight to Mrs Weizmann's face and ordered firmly, "Smell it!"

In 1976, ten years after Mrs Weizmann's death, we were invited to a memorial ceremony at the Weizmann Institute. Abba was Foreign Minister by then, and very busy in Jerusalem, so I went alone. Some 200 people had gathered that spring morning on the lawns of the Weizmann House in Rehovot: this former residence of the first President of Israel was about to be opened as an historic landmark. The ceremony was the last to encapsulate the Weizmann era forever; the leading characters, Israel's approximation of a king and queen, had long since passed on, and the courtiers were now in possession of the scene.

Friends and dignitaries came from far and near. Meyer Weisgal, who was by then President of the Institute and who had known every festive and poignant moment of the house, was quite overcome with emotion, and had to choke back his tears as he delivered his speech. Following the ceremony, we all gradually dispersed throughout the house, some of us nostalgic, some curious and still others merely dutiful in their presence. The double-panelled entrance doors were wide open on this inauguration day. I remembered them as always being closed, a black-uniformed maid peeping through the round openings and steel bars to identify the visitor. Sometimes Reti, her secretary, came out to greet the guests; at other times it was Yehoshua Harlap, Chaim Weizmann's personal driver and helper. The antiquated, bulletproof Lincoln, with its old-fashioned white tyres, offered by the manufacturer when Weizmann became President in 1949, was on display on a platform and under a metal canopy, just off the U-shaped driveway. The Weizmann House gleamed in its new whiteness. The old grandfather clock stood in the entrance, still chiming on the hour, now tens of thousands of hours away from its departed owners. I remembered the precision of the place when, at 6 p.m. while it chimed, Elsa or one of the other maids would come up to draw the curtains in the study and bring an ice bucket for drinks. In the bedroom of the "Chief," as Weizmann was affectionately called by those close to him, the bedside clock had been set to stay forever frozen at the hour of his death. Surrounded by all the things that comprised their home, we knew so clearly that they were gone and their era over. At the end of the long entrance room stood the bust of Weizmann by Sir Jacob Epstein, visible from the three main official rooms, seeming to watch me with an impassive expression as I moved from room to room.

The house, built in 1937 by the German-refugee Bauhaus architect Eric Mendelsohn, was the talk and spectacle of Palestine in those days, having challenged Israel's best craftsmanship. With its off-white marble floors and dark bronze staircase that emerged from its circular marble base in a Futurist swirl and ran a full three storeys high, it was like nothing else in the country. Inside, every bit of furniture had been imported from England in the 1930s, re-creating a sophisticated capital in stark contrast to the small, agrarian "colony" of Rehovot in which it stood. Blanche Dugdale,

Balfour's niece and biographer and a close friend of the Weizmann's, wrote: "Here was the noblest modern house I have ever seen... perfectly expressive of its owners. Like them, it is a national possession, and I believe is so looked upon by all Palestinian Jewry."

As I stood in one of the hallways and looked at the flowers, obviously bought locally and haphazardly placed in tall vases for the occasion, I couldn't but recall the exquisite tableaux of the Weizmann era. Each room had been graced with the loving creations of Mrs Weizmann's Yemenite gardener who, with an innate sense of composition and nimble fingers, used to put together the most subtle shades of flower, those from the house's garden being supplemented with some from the Institute. Looking out into the garden, I remembered the summers Vera Weizmann asked me to come and swim in their pool on very hot hamsin days; theirs was perhaps the first private pool in Palestine. While not big enough for real exercise, it offered delicious relief from the merciless Mediterranean sun, and the novelty of hearing the rhythmic noise of one's strokes in the total silence of the place.

In winter, there was always a fire in the library. Tidily lined science and history books ran the length of the room under windows that looked like portholes. Tea was served with English ritual while Mrs Weizmann would discuss current issues and the stands taken by cabinet ministers or Knesset members who made the news, especially when their rivalries obscured their principles. She was always avid for political news and not indifferent to snippets of gossip. I remember sitting there very primly in the soft glow of apricot-coloured lampshades edged with ludicrous little pompons. Bambi, the small pug Dolly de Rothschild had sent her one birthday, would be on her lap. The armchairs were fat, upholstered, English objects, lovely to sink into in winter but insufferable in summer, at a time when there was no air-conditioning. Weizmann's striking portrait, by the English academician, Sir Oswald Birley, hung over the fireplace, setting the tone, his head majestically facing the room's occupants.

In those days, Mrs Weizmann followed the news from the *Kol Israel* English-language broadcasts. There was always a book on her round mahogany side table, marked at the place she wanted to discuss. Her conversation was like a performance played against a list of points she kept methodically in her mind, both to derive maximum benefit from a conversation and, probably, to help her memory along. Her copy of the *Jerusalem Post* (called *The Palestine Post* before 1948) would be conveniently nearby, and those of us who read the Hebrew press, where the political scoops emanating from cabinet meeting leaks were often ahead of the English, would loyally fill her in.

In all of her discussions in these later years, Vera Weizmann tried not to carry over her husband's ambivalent attitude towards Ben-Gurion, perhaps understanding that the Weizmann Institute, whose research funds were supplemented by a substantial yearly grant from the government, had a better chance of political survival that way. I remember when Ben-Gurion went to the USA in 1961 for the first time in eleven years, to meet President Kennedy. Cabinet members and dignitaries were lined up in order of precedence along the customary red carpet at Lod Airport to wish him well on his trip. Mrs Weizmann, in a demonstrative gesture, had taken the trouble at her advanced age to arrive at Lod at what was an early hour for her – 10 a.m. – to attend the ceremony. Ben-Gurion, flattered and beaming upon discovering her at the very top of the line after all the ministers and dignitaries, threw his arms up and exclaimed loudly in English, "You!"

As for Paula Ben-Gurion, Mrs Weizmann forever held her in unreserved contempt: she considered her to be blunt, tactless and envious, and spoke with derision of all the hours Paula spent gossiping on the phone. Beyond the political issues that had forced them together, Vera Weizmann and Paula Ben-Gurion had very little in common. Paula resented the extraordinary capacity of the

Weizmann couple to create, without office, a vast web of contacts and followers. She, unlike Ben-Gurion, resented the style that was attached to the Weizmann name, and Weizmann's special position within the international world. Mrs Weizmann, on the other hand, though fortified by pride, knew that from the time the State was proclaimed by the Provisional Council, the ultimate power resided with Ben-Gurion and her husband had become merely a symbolic figure.

But for all their animosity, Vera Weizmann and Paula Ben-Gurion did have one thing in common: each had left her profession – Mrs Weizmann as a doctor, Paula as a nurse – for the demands of their husbands' political lives. As Mrs Weizmann told the story, she had received her medical degree in Geneva and then passed a second exam allowing her to practice in England. When her husband felt he was making no headway in his scientific career in Manchester and wanted to move, she had put her foot down firmly against settling in Germany – she simply could not bear the idea of a third exam. I once discussed with her the submissive role that women accept by making such a decision. She simply replied, "This is important ... and yet it is also unimportant," which in the context of our conversation, I took to mean that while the issue was important, the sacrifice was not. I have always remembered that sentence and the pause between the two adjectives, as if she was balancing in her mind one against the other, telescoping her own life in a flash.

I asked an attendant if I could see the red-leather guest book with its gold-edged pages, once kept open at all times, and it was found in a drawer. Leafing through the pages, I saw the signatures of Queen Elizabeth of the Belgians, heads of foreign countries, three prime ministers of Israel, African leaders, Nobel Prize-winners, ambassadors and all the British High Commissioners, from first to last. There were the signatures of famous composers and musicians: Arturo Toscanini and Jascha Heifetz, Leonard Bernstein and Isaac Stern, who had rushed to Israel after every war to boost our morale. Zubin Mehta's signature brought back the memory of his performance in Bethlehem's Manger Square with the Israel Philharmonic Orchestra after the Six Day War; how he had waited patiently for the muezzin to finish his call to prayers and for the church bells to ring at Vespers before beginning. How soothing their performance had been for us, following so soon after the deafening sounds of mortar shells!

At the close of the day, I made a final visit to the library. There were autographed photographs on side tables, of the people Weizmann had approached on behalf of Zionism and who consequently became supporters and friends of the Zionist Movement. On one of the tables was a photo of the goatee-bearded Jan Smuts, a Field Marshal and twice Prime Minister of South Africa who, at Mrs Weizmann's request, became the world patron of Youth Aliyah, an organization that rescued thousands of children from Germany and throughout Europe before the Second World War broke out. There were signed photos of President Truman and one of Albert Einstein who had been quite flirtatious in his younger years and amusedly autographed his photo, "To our witty queen, with affection and respect."

They were mostly small photos, so unless visitors were told the details of the Weizmann story these, like little private icons, could be thought of as merely the results of courteous exchanges. Not many people know that Weizmann held two thousand talks before achieving the Balfour Declaration, a simple, one page document, or that this document was not hammered out in the stately rooms of Downing Street but rather in an underground shelter beneath the Prime Minister's office during the First World War. The photos provide a record of the immense involvement the Weizmanns had with the world.

Set apart from this galaxy and on a small table, stood a photo of their son Michael in a bomber's jacket. Michael was an RAF pilot during the Second World War and had been reported "missing" after an anti-U-boat mission in the Bay of Biscay. Abba had known him in Cambridge and had asked him to join the Zionist Society, but Michael deferred, explaining, "We have too much of it at home." It is said that Michael had a premonition he would not return from his mission, and wrote letters home criticizing the inadequate preparedness of the Royal Air Force and its tendency to overwork its pilots. Next to his photo was Mrs Weizmann's own official portrait, in which she looked more like a character out of a Russian novel than a political figure. Wearing a mink hat almost as dominant in the composition as her face, she looks out with a sad, sad smile; looking closely one can see the pair of flyer's wings she has pinned to that hat. One never commented on either portrait, chilled by the significance of her loss.

Finally, I looked at the famous picture from Mrs Weizmann's last official trip to Washington to meet President Truman, who had restored the Negev to Israel in the 1947 Partition Plan and recognized the State of Israel in specific response to a letter received from Weizmann on 12 May 1948. These incredible political achievements of Chaim Weizmann have still not received their full credit in Israel. The photo shows Truman looking at Vera Weizmann tenderly, while Abba, then Israeli Ambassador to the UN, stands behind them looking young and slim. As I stood there, taking in that photograph so many years later, I was startled by David Samuel, who had shown Tsilla and me round Oxford many years before. He asked how I felt about the occasion, saying for his part he would call it an "Ode to Death". I confided my puzzled impression: in all the celebratory speeches that day about the house and its role in history, nobody had even uttered the name "Vera Weizmann".

19

Rachel Ben-Zvi and her shack

A place I love to visit from time to time was once the official residence of the second President, Yitzhak Ben-Zvi and his wife Rachel. Proclaimed a National Trust by a Knesset edict, the people of Israel call it with whimsical affection: *HaTsrif*, "The Shack".

Consisting of a large, greyish-blue, wooden building and an adjoining small stone house, the two structures sit together in the shade of old trees in the midst of what is now an indifferently kept garden in Jerusalem's old residential quarter of Rehavia. The larger building was used for receptions. In front of three large glass doors, potted plants were dispersed on both the tiled floor and the shelves on two sides of the room. This staging was meant to be reminiscent of a previous, much-publicized Ben-Zvi home, a small, battered, wooden construction in what was to become a well-to-do neighbourhood. Built next to its own plant nursery, the first of its kind in Jerusalem, this rudimentary notion of a home became important in its later political symbolism, and it was here that the Ben-Zvi's two sons, Eli and Amram grew up.

The space around the old presidential residence is narrow and closed-in, almost suffocating, and the defiance of the accepted architectural standards of such a significant building is still startling. The furniture lining the reception room is of the style I define as "Early Israel". Armchairs are upholstered in the only colours then available in the country: beige, copper and dark green. Three huge beams painted a vibrant royal blue support the hall's ceiling and this odd mixture of colours shock and surprise the visitor.

One rarely sees tourists on these premises now called *Yad Ben-Zvi* or The Ben-Zvi Memorial, but the bookshop there is well frequented by those Israelis who, fascinated by their history and folklore, are eagerly searching for documentation of their local roots. Next to the bookshop, in the original, small, stone building, one discovers Ben-Zvi's library which houses his own collected material, much of it about the less-researched diasporas. It is as if the smaller the diaspora, the greater the chance that it would engage his interest. Ben-Zvi's own books are kept behind glass. Brochures and leaflets about him and Rachel are displayed on open shelves, and a disorderly mass of papers that has been neither filed nor shelved is piled high on whatever piece of furniture seemed capable of withstanding the weight of it all.

Today's bookshop exists in what was once the dining room of the presidential home, but there was nothing to preserve of its previous function besides the long, massive, light-oak dining table that was moved to the library. Researchers now sit silently around it, concentrating intently on the biographical material on Ben-Zvi and his epoch or on the precious ethnic material accumulated there.

Rachel Ben-Zvi, who ruled over this small intimate world, was an intransigent feminist, utterly intolerant of any horizons except those of Zionism and more specifically of the Labour movement. I remember once commenting that some of the early Arab houses in the hills of Jerusalem, poor as they were, seemed to me to fit organically in the landscape, a characteristic that Israelis, in their search of architectural immediacy with the land, had often praised. She fell upon me as if I had been a traitor to the national values. I felt it would have been utterly impossible to question her views on *any* subject: nothing was open for discussion. Her world was intransigently polarized into Jews and Arabs, and since Arabs were the enemy, they had to be wrong about everything – even the simple, human, creative innocence of a home. She seemed to me to have closed in on liberties of the mind like a clock dial with its arms folded on midnight.

Rachel and her two sisters were born in the village of Malin in the Ukraine. Imprisoned for a year as an anarchist Rachel, after her liberation, immediately made her way to the Black Sea port of Odessa and journeyed to Palestine, which she defined as "my country". She arrived in a land that was still under Ottoman rule in 1908 and was followed later by her sisters. Rachel was full of messianic visions of a utopia, wherein its central figure, the Jewish worker, would enjoy a life of social justice and creativity. Not a minute was to be wasted by contemplating any possible difficulties.

The previous year, her husband-to-be had arrived from Poltava, another small Ukrainian village but a centre to which the Russian authorities sent rebellious intellectuals to be kept at a great distance from Moscow. Yitzhak Ben-Zvi's family was familiar with prisons. His father, Zvi Shimshelevich, later shortened to Shimshi, had been imprisoned in Siberia but escaped to Palestine after sixteen years. His sister, brother and aunt had been imprisoned in 1906 when a search by the Russian police revealed a cache of weapons belonging to *Hashomer*, the Jewish self-defence organization that Ben-Zvi founded and headed. The authorities, who never protested at the killing of Jews, did not accept the assurance that the arms caches were primarily for self-defence against pogroms.

For Rachel, meeting Yitzhak Ben-Zvi in Palestine must have been like looking at a moral mirror-image of herself. Each of them had decided to strive for an improved social order. Back in Russia they had been revolted by the oppressive Czarist regime, the social injustice, the blood baths of violent pogroms. The idea of freedom and social equality, coupled with the vision of a secular independence from their families set in traditional ways, had become so compelling that nothing would stop them. As the families they left behind were still debating whether to be socialists or Zionists, they reconciled both and became Labour Zionists, a movement that grew to become the party of Ben-Gurion and Ben-Zvi.

On arriving in Palestine, Rachel gave herself a new name: "Yanait", a derivative of her father's Hebrew name. By adding one letter to her name, the Hebrew letter *Chet*, one created an unkindly pun about her, Ya*ch*nait, a slang word for a totally ungraceful woman. It would be used by members of her close circle to deride her dowdy appearance and eccentric ways. She would be known for the rest of her life both as Rachel Ben-Zvi and as Yanait, never simply as Rachel, unlike Paula Ben-Gurion, who always asked to be addressed only by her first name, or Vera Weizmann who would forever be *Mrs* Weizmann. Rachel would leave a strong mark in what might otherwise have been in the early years of her century, entirely a man's world.

Within a few years of her arrival, unable to accept the bare hills of Jerusalem, Rachel Ben-Zvi went to Nancy in France to study agronomy and bring back its usefulness to settlement life. She had already participated in Zionist congresses in Europe, having first attended at the age of nineteen. Always an impatient extremist, the original ideas she expounded – such as a port for Tel Aviv – were appreciated but judged totally unfeasible at the time. When her passionate lobbies for the settlement of the Northern Negev went unheeded, she began going on missions to the Labour-affiliated women's groups in the USA. She had been one of the founders of "Pioneer Women" and on her first trip on their behalf, speaking no English, she addressed them in Yiddish. She succeeded in raising only enough money for the construction of a well for the agricultural high school she had established, such was the penury of American Jewry at that time. Rachel became a strong figure in what was known as the Second Aliyah, or Second Immigration, to Palestine: a distinct wave of immigration that occurred from 1904 to 1914 and to which both Ben-Zvis belonged. This group had consciously decided fully to live the socialist ideal and because of their impassioned activism, the political fate of early settlement was literally in their hands. It is extraordinary to think today that a core of no more than 1,000 to 1,200 people of that Second Aliyah were going to determine the shape of the Jewish society of Palestine for many years to come. Their ideologies were so firmly defined that they obliterated the view of anything unrelated to their disciplined and institutionalized orbit of life or to the vital interests of settlement and development. Unlike the immigrants who, on their arrival, went to reinforce the early colonies of Petah Tikva, Rehovot or in Emek Yizrael, the Jezreel Valley in Southern Galilee, the Ben-Zvis chose Jerusalem and went to work as teachers, founding the first Hebrew high school there, a *Gymnasium*, as it used to be called in Germany and Russia. They lived together in Jerusalem in some abandoned ruin, unmarried, to the dismay of their families (they married ten years later in 1918). Equal partners, pooling their resources with two art students of the Bezalel craft school, they formed a small *communa*: a common project in those days.

Acceptance into a *communa* was not automatic. There was at first great scrutiny about a prospective member's capacity to measure up to the enormous difficulties and it was only after clearance on these grounds that the collective vote on admission would follow. It was an awesome process that rejected the ordinary citizen in order to strengthen the inner force and assertive choice of the early settlement. *Hashomer* was an even more selective group: smaller, but more combative. They moved from place to place in the Palestinian wilderness, guarding the workers and the land from Arab theft or from slackness when vigilance was essential, until they hit on the idea of working and settling permanently in the same place. This, for instance, is how Degania, the first collective community to call itself a kibbutz, would be established.

There was a uniqueness about this pioneering movement because, revolutionary as it was, it derived its resourcefulness from a humanistic dimension. Deeply rooted in Jewish tradition, these pioneers could have become internationalists, but their specific religious background had propelled them in a particular direction. Yanait herself was an eighth-generation descendant from a rabbinical family and all the men in the movement knew the scriptures and the prayers. They had completed their Orthodox Jewish education dutifully, having been offered no alternative, but with a heightened perception of their world they were no longer content with learning Jewish history from a distance. They wanted a physical and spiritual repossession of it. Theirs was a double calling.

After working hours, members would have long meetings debating the security, political and social issues of the Jewish population in Palestine. They were intransigent in their formulation, to themselves and to others, of their tempered-steel ideology: only by hard labour on the land would they consider themselves entitled to the land. In order to "belong", they had to attune themselves to a rigidly disciplined way of life, proving themselves capable of facing the harsh physical and emotional demands that came with collective existence. It was only an ideologically dedicated core that could transcend the health hazards, the security risks, the climate, the harshness of daily life, the nightly separation from infants and children who slept in a communal nursery, the anonymous clothes and the lack of privacy. Such a tall order of privations demanded from the settler total abnegation of an earlier life and a constant consciousness of one's communal purpose for the realization of the ideal they had sworn themselves to.

Rachel Ben-Zvi's singular mindset extended far beyond politics and entered the realm of the personal as well. She lacked any interest in all forms of aesthetics, whether small expressions of femininity or the simpler graces of domestic life. It was inconceivable to her that anybody should preoccupy themselves that way. Golda Meir had similar attitudes but knew the outer world better and she once recounted her own experience of that pioneer world so pared of all frivolity. Golda, on holiday at Rachel Ben-Zvi's kibbutz, had decorated the tables with colourful paper napkins and was criticized for such "bourgeois nonsense". The appellation *bourgeois* was the harshest possible criticism, immediately evoking a betrayal of socialist values. Zionism progressed well with single-minded dedication. Perhaps because conditions in those early years were so tough, and the number of people willing to accept violent hardships so few in relation to the Jewish population, it was thought that diverting oneself one iota from the supremacy of sacrifice, would lead to not lasting in the tightly-knit pioneer milieu. In creating a new society, the best support one could give was physical strength, determination and selflessness. The Ben-Zvis never failed there.

Yitzhak Ben-Zvi was a Mapai Member of the first Knesset, while Rachel, having always had a good rapport with young people, continued with the great educational enterprise she had set up in 1920. The Talpiot girls' boarding school was the epitome of the concepts common to that generation: the return to the land, the emphasis on cultivation, the need to defend whatever one had settled, equal expectations from women, however harsh the circumstances, and the usage of Hebrew as a daily spoken language. It was no mean inventory but Rachel Ben-Zvi succeeded in fulfilling all the "commandments".

Yitzhak Ben-Zvi and David Ben-Gurion met for the first time in Palestine, as young, new immigrants. They studied at the same time in different institutions in Constantinople (Istanbul) and began a political friendship that would span over fifty years. They shone on the early political scene, serving together on every single political or defence committee of Jewish Palestine, both very active on the issue of the political rights of Jewish people to buy and cultivate land.

The ubiquitous Rachel and Ben-Zvi would work closely with Ben-Gurion, who was the leader at every stage. In 1910, when all three were in their late twenties, they issued a newspaper entitled *Achdut* (Unity), the first Hebrew socialist periodical, that became *Davar* in 1925, the Labour Party's newspaper for half a century until its closure in 1996. In spite of its seriousness, *Achdut* had a colourful beginning. When, at its creation, it was confiscated by the Turks, Rachel Ben-Zvi went underground and produced a clandestine edition that used to surface unexpectedly as if from nowhere – once actually from Safed, one of the centres of Jewish mysticism.

Their first local political test presented itself on the issue of "Ottomanization" in the First World War: enlisting Jews in Palestine to serve in the Turkish Army! I have been asked so many times how is it that I was born in Egypt of Palestine-born parents and while my answer is always "Ottomanization", usually people haven't the faintest idea what it was about. In the First World War, the Turks (for four centuries the rulers of Palestine) were expecting an Allied invasion of Palestine. As such, anyone who had not accepted Turkish nationality was asked to leave Palestine and given the choice of going either to Damascus or Egypt. This is how my mother's family was expelled to Egypt, her father, my grandfather Mikhel, had acquired British nationality from his years in South Africa and my maternal uncle, David, had volunteered to serve in the British Army. In Turkish terms they were on the enemy side.

Rachel, Ben-Zvi and Ben-Gurion saw the situation differently. In a matter of days they had amassed hundreds of signatures in which the local people committed to stay in the Land but under negotiated conditions. If war did come to the Palestinian part of the Turkish Empire, they would not be sent to serve elsewhere, but only in Palestine. They had cast their lot with the local Turkish authority set on designing a protective strategy for whatever meagre settlements existed then. It was a very daring political manoeuvre.

I first met Rachel Ben-Zvi one year before her husband's presidency which would be the culmination of their dense political careers. She was sixty-six, the State was three years old and I had been an ambassador's wife for one year. Abba and I, with our eight-month-old baby Eli, were on a brief vacation in London on our way to Israel. But grandma Alida Eban, with what possible other reason than "*A la recherche du temps perdu*", wanted to keep Eli for herself a while and had already contacted a nurse to take care of him after Abba and I continued to Israel.

I was looking forward to seeing my parents and I was also eager to catch up with developments in the country – especially the role women were playing in the building and defending of Israel – and so I asked to visit Rachel's much celebrated school for girls in Talpiot. I remember her so well from that first meeting, with her round spectacles with their thin metal frames that had replaced the pince-nez of her early pictures. Her face was ravaged and grooved by life-long exposure to the violent sun of Palestine, the marks of work and wear only adding to the great dignity of her presence. Her voice was soft, almost childlike, and in surprising contrast to the way she communicated, and her proud, splendid bearing.

The young girls who came to Rachel's school stayed for a two-year training period. They looked tanned and strong: a new breed who would emerge as experienced horticulturalists, proficient in the usage of arms – almost mini-Yanaits, inculcated with her idealistic motives and values. Her model school was a stark white building. At its entrance, like sentries on guard, stood two cypress trees, but beyond this picturesque illusion and the experimental patches of cultivation, it was a completely isolated place. Sadly, the school was destroyed in the Six Day War.

The set-up was nice and modern, and a far cry from the ordeals of the women Rachel had led back in the 1920s and 1930s when, I am told, the girls had started work at dawn, singing as they walked the few kilometres from their piece of soil, wearing loose dresses and kerchiefs on their heads, a spade or shovel on their shoulders, the flesh of their fingers hardened. Defiant and ambitious, with Rachel amongst them, they pushed wheelbarrows filled with earth for planting trees in the large tin cans in which kerosene used to be imported, or, as documented in old photographs, stood close to one another in a long line and passed buckets full of water from one to the other – in the absence of irrigation the only way to water the saplings they were growing.

If the terrain was on a hill, Rachel Ben-Zvi and her workers would sit on the ground, break the stones and do the terracing. It is illustrative of her priorities that actual settling on the land came first at any cost – a cost that was too often brutal. Mrs Weizmann, still a practising doctor in Manchester at that time, on a visit to Palestine in the 1920s with her friends Rebecca Sieff and Edith Eder, described the school in her memoirs, *The Impossible Takes Longer*:

> ...very impressed by the hard work done in rebuilding Palestine by the devoted chalutzot, a new name at that time for our pioneering working women. But we were appalled by the arduous physical conditions of their lives for the sake of equality with men. We thought these enthusiastic, idealistic women were mortgaging their future motherhood and even risking their health. They were working ten or twelve hours a day, breaking rocks and stones for road-making and repairing, carrying heavy loads, performing super-human tasks. Their bare, simple homes were neglected. Their cooking was haphazard at best... Pre-natal care had not been heard of and the fate of unborn generations was left to chance. Even the most elementary essentials were lacking. Only one central purpose guided them: building, building, building! Nothing else mattered except the future of the new Jewish society.

Vera Weizmann's medical anxieties about the health risks that might affect the next generation were too short a view of things. The succeeding generation turned out to be a sturdy breed. The hurt would come differently.

Eli, the youngest of the two Ben-Zvi sons, had at a very young age gone to Kibbutz Keshet near Mount Tabor in Lower Galilee, without finishing his secondary education, as brazen as his mother had been when she ran off to Palestine. He could not have pleased his parents more, for there, on the land, was where the young belonged. From the top of Mount Tabor there were great sweeps of view: the endless Mediterranean Sea and the snow-covered peaks of Mount Hermon – the physical aspect of the country was an inspiration. The task of digging into the land, of starting on virgin soil by oneself and creating growth, was exciting to Eli, the young *chalutz* (pioneer), and to his friends. All the Ben-Zvis seemed made of the same mettle.

In 1947, after the Arabs rejected the United Nation's 29 November Partition Resolution on Palestine and war was declared on Jewish Palestine, much of the manpower of the kibbutz was dispersed in their attempt to get as organized as possible for war. Only a few had been left to collect the harvest when Arabs from the region descended on the kibbutz, hiding in wait for their prey. The defence was overwhelmed and Eli, aged twenty-four, and his friends were shot in the beloved fields they had created.

I have always tended to associate Eli Ben-Zvi's awareness that fate might call on him prematurely as it did on Chaim and Vera Weizmann's son Michael, the pilot who was killed in action in the Second World War.

After President Weizmann died on 9 November 1952, the Ben-Zvis were given national recognition and Yitzhak Ben-Zvi was elected by the Knesset to be the second President of the State.

Ben-Gurion had pulled up his scholarly old friend, associate and supporter, who never competed with him or questioned his pre-eminence. By submitting his name for the presidency, Ben-Gurion could both pay a debt of loyalty and be sure that Ben-Zvi, a faithful and disciplined member of the Mapai Party, would not operate on his own as Weizmann had.

My later encounters with Rachel Ben-Zvi were all official. I would see her at ceremonies at the Knesset, at the Weizmann Institute on Weizmann Day, or year after year at the great military parades on Independence Day. For political reasons, following the victories of the Six Day War in 1967, these became smaller, with no demonstrations of heavy armaments, and soon they were discontinued altogether, replaced by parades with social and military symbolism. Rachel Ben-Zvi would always appear in sombre dresses closed all the way to the neck, a Simone de Beauvoir-like turban of muted colour crowning her head. She was the dowager of the State.

My fondest memory of her will always be the way she handled her first official dilemma as Israel's First Lady. Immediately on their elevation to the presidency, the Ben-Zvis were confronted with a problem not typical of their usual concerns: where would they live? Weizmann had used his own spacious home in Rehovot as a ready-made presidential residence after he was elected, but now an official residence would have to be created, since Mrs Weizmann would naturally continue to occupy her own home. Ben-Zvi let his wife take over handling the situation and the nation, stressed by severe austerity, wondered: "How should this be tackled?"

She decided that the trappings of the presidency should be commensurate with the asperities of the times and the austerity of the early 1950s, which had included as an example, the absorption of approximately 100,000 Iraqi immigrants in a single year. The strain on both the people and the economy had been quite excruciating, despite the genuine elation and joyful reassurance caused by the increase in our ranks and the great spirit of altruism throughout the land.

Rachel first thought that the residence should be in the Negev, but she was talked out of it. Both the public and the decision-makers deemed it historically appropriate that the President of Israel's official dwelling should be in Jerusalem. That being the case, Rachel was determined that it be a sort of replica of their first home, a *tsrif* — a shack once again, but on a larger scale, as necessitated by the new exalted circumstances. The new shack would have the character, simplicity and truth of their life; it would be their trademark, and would have the correct symbolism at a time when our society was still in the making. As long as the country was still absorbing the survivors of the camps, keeping thousands of new immigrants in tents and in *ma'abarot*, the presidential residence would be a great message of solidarity.

They stubbornly held on to their demand, to the distress of government officials in charge of the project. The architects certainly had different ideas. The Weizmann Institute and the Hebrew University had long since begun pioneering in modern architecture, but this was not for the Ben-Zvis. A huge wooden shack was built in the very same quarter that had housed their original "home" with its adjoining plant nursery in Jerusalem's Rehavia. When finished, the presidential home had an incongruous rustic Scandinavian character, despite the dark blue presidential standard with a white menorah in the main reception room.

Inside, the walls were panelled with natural pinewood which had ironically been imported for its look of austerity though Rachel, with her one-track mind, showed no concern for what it had entailed. An impressive carpet, hand-woven by Yemenite women on a special loom created for the purpose, and of a size never seen before, displayed themes of local character: elongated cypress trees, stylized women with amphoras on their heads, crimson pomegranates and olive branches. One of Rachel's sisters,

Batya Lichansky, was a sculptress and as they were both aware of a new Russian interest in the vibrant colours and simplified shapes of folk art, they decided to give a lively and imaginative endorsement to local motifs. To Batya Lichansky we owe a larger than life-size, powerfully chiselled, bronze head of Yitzhak Ben-Zvi.

There were glass display cases containing antiquities and medallions, and the newly created emblems of army units. Mrs Ben-Zvi, as I always called her when we were together, once took me around to see it all. The display on which she lingered was rather odd amongst the array of archaeology and history, consisting as it did of twigs topped by tufts of white cotton resting on glass shelves. Cotton cultivation was a brand new and successful enterprise in Israel. The cotton became such a momentous addition to our meagre resources that a new term – "our white gold" – seemed to appear from out of nowhere and catch on like wildfire.

State occasions made no pretence at being elegant or polished. The china was the coarse white faience used daily in local cafés and workers' restaurants. Since this was the only porcelain manufactured locally, Rachel Ben-Zvi decided it would be the official choice. The napkins were of robust white cotton with a self-coloured pattern of little checks, and since these, too, were the only kind manufactured locally, they would be the official table linen. The service of the black-uniformed waitresses was in the pleasant and conventional style, but the food was terrible – I remember one State luncheon in particular when we were offered a main course of over-cooked, tasteless chicken legs, dreadful enough to occasion comments from the departing guests.

The smooth, well-mannered and always extremely polite Chief of Protocol, Fritz Simon, threw his arms up in despair at Rachel's high-handed official posture, but she had tremendous aplomb and did not care: her stance was probably also meant as an indirect reproach of that distant lady, Vera Weizmann, who was absolutely set in her English ways and her superior discipline and manners.

Both Rachel and Ben-Zvi recorded all the events of their lives, mostly in their books. His are more scholarly; hers more poetical and always on some high emotional pitch. She wrote *Telling my Journey*, full of fascinating descriptions of their early excursions in a bare, uncultivated Palestine, with Ben-Zvi carrying on his shoulder his old Turkish gun which he called his bulldog. She described a trip to the Dead Sea in a frantic search for the sources of the pathetically small Arnon, a rivulet that terminates at the Dead Sea. She even wrote a booklet about this excursion where they literally endangered themselves and friends in a life-threatening storm because of her determination to get to "her" Arnon, a name she remembered from her youth in Russia, when she had asked her Hebrew teacher in the Ukraine whether it was as big as the Dnieper! On every trip they picked up reeds and the leaves of small bushes and weeds, discovering an unknown vegetation that had never before been studied, catalogued or defined. This was new terrain for scientific pursuit and they went with botanists, bringing back plant specimens and shells by the bagful as they explored the land.

But it was the eastern Mediterranean that evoked Rachel's insatiable curiosity and inspired her spellbound explorations. She was indefatigable, trekking through the desolate Ottoman and Mandate Palestine and making seven trips to the desert wastes of Transjordan (today's Jordan), to Egypt, Lebanon and Syria, and later to Yemen, all accessible before Israel's War of Independence. Whether by foot, donkey, mule, horseback or lorry, any method of travel was acceptable and comfort was never an issue with her. These new experiences yielded an ecstatic sense of belonging which she expressed in words of a passionate and proprietary right about every single landscape or physical sight connected with our ancient history.

Rachel's writings oscillate between the poetic or ecstatic in her love of the landscape, and the sad or poignant, as in her story entitled *The Sister*, a tale about her other sister who, as a nurse, had bravely treated people with typhus in the Old City of Jerusalem, later dying herself of tuberculosis. The book also serves as an autobiography of her younger years, describing the three girls' youth in Malin.

The Ben-Zvis' Hebrew writings are full of Latinisms mixed into a pure biblical style which jars today, almost to the point of irritation, as we have become so used to modern, creative Hebrew. Words like *idealismus, realizatia, contributia, problema, revolutia, liquidatia, substantia* and *platforma* might look charming and quaint in their old political contexts, but they disturb the flow of the fascinating narrations and descriptions that make up the Ben-Zvis' journals. These terms have all been replaced by modern words, created or chosen by a Hebrew Language Committee (which later became the Academy of the Hebrew Language) and are very much part of daily usage. In addition, one must be knowledgeable in the Hebrew calendar in order to place Rachel's and Ben-Zvi's writings in their time. Not one book makes a concession to western civilization's calendar by using both ways of describing the years of writing; they acknowledge only the Hebrew calendar.

They were going by the lunar calendar when they offered the presidential home to be used on the first of each month by one of the infinitely diverse communities who were slowly making up the new nation. One by one, month by month, came groups from Morocco, Egypt, Yemen, Algeria, Tunisia, Lebanon, Bukhara, Britain and all of Europe, but mostly the oriental communities. The Ben-Zvis called them "The Tribes of Israel". They came to tell about their countries of origin, to describe their form of Judaism: the intonation of their prayers, their crafts, the women's costumes, their wedding or birth ceremonies. Some, like the Jews of Cyrenaica, a province of Libya, had been cave-dwellers. President Ben-Zvi once called my father to ask if he could help him locate some of the Cairo *Genizah* (the centuries-old documents of the Jewish community there). He was indeed able to assist.

The Ben-Zvis were a great unifying force in the country. As the various communities came to them, so did they, in their spirit of sincere human and national concern, travel to visit them in their tents; they trekked along gravel paths, across mud puddles and down uncharted roads to visit immigrants located in wastelands. They also wished to perpetuate what they hoped would remain in history a literary symbol of the beginning, and because they were such daring, stubborn visionaries, courageous and sacrificial, the people and events of those times become more touching in their purity of purpose and naivety with every passing year. Theirs is a perfect and moving founders' legacy. They created a secular, national culture in Palestine after centuries when the connection of the land with its people had been exclusively in the religious domain. Rachel, in particular, was especially conscious of the special experiences of those years of exploration and ingathering, of defence and construction. She felt a strong need to leave a record as documentation of the pioneers' lives and of the years preceding the establishment of the State of Israel. She must have known that future generations would want to know about the very early years of our nation.

Towards the end of her life, Rachel was to become one of the founders of the Movement for a Greater Israel, that was for nationalizing all the territories acquired in the Six Day War. She tried to get my husband to become a member of the Movement, although his political thinking was different. Many Labour leaders and leading authors, such as the Nobel Laureate Shai Agnon who wrote about Eastern European Jewry, the beloved poet Natan Alterman, and Chaim Hazaz, who studied the Yemenites, joined the Movement.

20

Paula

When we first knew the Ben-Gurions as young and junior associates in the Labour Party, Paula never referred to her husband by his first name, David, but as "Ben-Gurion". It was the prevailing fashion in these early years of the State, for wives of leaders to call their husbands by their family name in public. Rachel Ben-Zvi referred to her husband as "Ben-Zvi" until she exchanged this characteristic socialist appellation in favour of the exalted title "The President". I myself had gone through a process of indoctrination as a young bride, having once phoned the Jewish Agency and asked for "Mr Eban", only to have the operator at the other end reply, "What's all this about *Mister*?" After shedding "Mr", I never said "my husband" which would have sounded so bourgeois, but spoke of him as "Eban" when talking to a member of the Labour Party.

Paula even more frequently referred to her husband by his initials in English – B.G. – even when speaking in Hebrew. It deceptively implied a sense of familiarity, but everybody knew that there could never be an ounce of familiarity, warmth or humour in a conversation with Ben-Gurion. The sabras preferred the Hebrew pronunciation of Ben-Gurion's entire name, with the accent on the last three letters or, later, "*Hazaken*" meaning "the Old Man". But at home and abroad there was only one acceptable way to refer to his wife, and that was "Paula". The only exception made to this rule was by Menachem Begin, the head of the Herut opposition party, precursor to the present-day Likud, who was expected to greet her solemnly as Mrs Ben-Gurion and kiss her hand. The one time he failed to take notice of her in the Knesset in his usual "Polish gentleman's manner," she called him to order.

Hebrew was not Paula's favourite form of expression. Born Paula Munweis in Russia and brought to the United States at the age of eighteen, she had learned English, but marrying Ben-Gurion in New York nearly a decade later in 1917, meant learning Hebrew. From then on, right to the end of her days, you would find her speaking English, Hebrew and Yiddish – all within one impatient conversation.

Throughout the country there was a patronizing affection for Paula's linguistic peculiarities. One of them was to repeatedly inject the words "*kootch-mootch*" into every conversation. I could not decide what to make of it at first, but eventually I began to understand that "*kootch-mootch*" was not some cheerful, juvenile alliteration, but rather a defence mechanism that appeared when Paula could not cope linguistically with the intricacies of a subject. She held on to these all-purpose non-words with steadfastness, at times using them to convey a convenient dismissal of any subject she did not know how to pursue, while at other times seemingly guided by some unconscious instinct not to give an answer that could be ascribed to her. As a result, the conversational flow was often disjointed.

It was sufficient merely to pronounce her name to evoke a laugh – and everyone had their own story about her. Danny Kaye told us how she had listened patiently to his enthusiastic conversation about Israel for some time and then burst out: "*Nu*, say something funny! You are supposed to be a comedian." She was the talk of ministers and the joke of officials who had daily dealings with the Ben-Gurions. Her incautious remarks moved in ripples from the centre of power to the extremities of the country.

Paula had a mordant humour, and liked grating the minds of politicians with blunt remarks about other politicians. Her comments were usually a reflection of the esteem or lack of esteem in which B.G. held the people surrounding him. Her desire to debunk politicians for their self-importance was, I think, partly sadistic and partly a way to achieve an impious dominance over her politically saturated environment.

After the War of Independence, the country had become very much like one big family. Everybody's business was known by everybody else, and Paula exploited this fully. One of our diplomats, a short, grey-haired man, strongly myopic and pompous, was assailed immediately by Paula as she opened the door to him with the question, clearly audible in the room where I was sitting, "Why aren't you married *yet*?" She had no hesitation later on in asking the same question of Dag Hammerskjöld, the Secretary-General of the United Nations, when he came to Israel.

Paula had her own ways of operating politically; hearing from Ben-Gurion about the issues that preoccupied him, she would immediately move them to the personal level. She was quite capable of directly calling a member of the Labour Party opposed to B.G.'s policy, and pleading for her husband's point of view, exclaiming crossly: "How could you do this to Ben-Gurion!" Indiscreet Paula understood that political tactics demanded watertight imperviousness. Her well-known indiscretions were never on the national level, except once when, sitting at her Knesset table in the MKs' lounge, she predicted (or knew already) that the religious party would drop out of the government.

Sometimes her antics would inspire affection. Meyer Weisgal once told us in great amusement that Paula had woken him up one morning before 7 a.m. and asked in the most astonished tone of voice: "Why are you up so early?" She just could not bear to wait to find out what Meyer had brought her from abroad. Presents were a special treat in Israel's times of austerity, and she loved them – the silver presentations and the embroidered table linens. I remember her opening cupboards to show them to me, and how the smell of mothballs would waft into the room. She valued the gifts more for possession than for actual use; perhaps these few elegant items linked her imagination to a graceful world very remote from her own life and her exhausting struggles.

For the political leadership of the Labour Party, Paula was the personification of George Orwell's Big Brother. She went to any length to eliminate what she feared might become an intrusion on Ben-Gurion's monolithic status in the country. Abba, when Minister of Education, once opened the school year with what general opinion described as a very endearing speech on the morning radio, addressing both parents and children, an audience which is equivalent to the whole country. Paula called me immediately afterwards and said: "Eban must understand that only Ben-Gurion can speak to the whole nation," and hung up. I dutifully reported these words.

Achievements – diplomatic, economic, and educational – were always a "first" in the early 1950s, and always very exciting. There was the first Chief of Staff after the underground years of the Haganah; the first cabinet in 1949 and, after the Declaration of Independence, the first Knesset; the first Israeli airline; the first Israeli stamps; the first torpedo boats; the first Ambassador accredited to the new state (the Soviet Ambassador, upstaging the US by a mere three days). There was the time Ben-Gurion, accompanied by Paula, went to the US in 1952, as the first Prime Minister of Israel. The purpose of his visit was to launch the first State of Israel Bonds. Abba had preceded B.G.'s visit by appearing at a preparatory conference in Washington. I remember how the participants, inspired by his presentation of Israel's economic and political situation, got up as one and shouted as if at the end of an exciting concert, "Bravo, Bravo!" Abba was dazed. He had not expected that kind of reaction. I was very moved that he had connected so deeply with the Jewish political and financial leaders in attendance. Later I thought secretly of our good fortune that Paula had not been anywhere near the place to offer her objections or attempt to restrain Abba. Ben-Gurion, on the other hand, would probably have appreciated the speech and been proud of his Ambassador, as he had on other occasions.

On their arrival, we met them at La Guardia. From the minute they stepped off our recently established national airline, an atmosphere of great elation pervaded New York. We entered the city in an impressive motorcade together with flags and sirens. I sat in the second car, with both Paula Ben-Gurion and Jeanette Lurie. The Mayor, Vincent Impellitteri, along with Ben-Gurion and Abba, rode in the first. That evening, the Ben-Gurions were the central figures of a mammoth gathering at Madison Square Garden where Abba introduced the Prime Minister. The overflowing crowds roared with adulation and a titanic wave of affection rose from them and pounded on us all. Ben-Gurion's dramatic presence, his entourage, the huge American and Israeli flags side by side – all these tangible proofs of American recognition were reflected in the people's ecstatic reception.

The next day we would all witness first hand the great American demonstration for heroes. The cars rolled along from Wall Street to the centre of New York in a snow-like storm of white ticker-tape and confetti. The elongated view of skyscrapers dominated the scene and the big city was eerily silent as all traffic was stopped for the official party's passage. All along the way we saw masses of people smiling, rejoicing, waving their individual blue and white flags, calling, shouting and at times singing out their good wishes or simply murmuring "Ben-Gurion!" in a quiet voice. What a unique privilege that was.

During the visit, Paula asked to go shopping. Garfinckel's, the highly elegant department store of that time, was duly alerted and we went to look for dresses. Within a minute, Paula called me to her changing room. I found her standing there, unbelievably, in knee-length bloomers and a Victorian bra buttoned with hook and eye from under her shoulder blades to her waist. (Apparently, in their hotel apartment there was daily and nightly a big to-do about who from the embassy female staff would be available to get her in and out of that armature which she called only by its Russian name: *liftchick*.) As the saleslady was asked to prepare some choices, I hurriedly took off my slip in the adjoining changing room, threw it across the partition and told her she *must* put it on, which she did with touching obedience, although it was amazing how little she had cared.

Before she left Washington, I held a ladies' luncheon in Paula's honour at which she gave me one of the early creations of our small Israeli industries. It was a small, silver-plated dish, proudly stamped "Made in Israel", and at the centre, standing out like three beats of a drum, the initials PBG. This gift would always stand to remind me of an independent character who was mostly weighed down by endless domestic cares and, at times, by her own personal unhappiness.

As a young wife home on leave from our ambassadorial duties in Washington and New York, I used to call on Paula, and later more frequently when we were living in Israel. The first time I was invited to their home, I was struck that the Ben-Gurions used the same thrifty wall decoration as my grandparents had in their house in Motza. For the sake of economy, rooms in early Israel used to be painted up to the level of an average person's height in oil paint, and above that, in whitewash with a darker separating line. Paula would take me to her small, pale-blue kitchen, where a tiny wooden table, also painted blue and uncomfortably placed against the wall, would seat her and Ben-Gurion for their meals. Ben-Gurion would nearly always sit alone, Paula giving him the space to worry about matters of state while she stood by ready to serve him. While we chatted, Paula would spoon some tea into a steel strainer, rinse the tea under the tap, place the strainer over a glass and pour boiling water over it. What was by now a glass of tea too hot to hold was hurriedly put into an individual metal holder with a handle. It was the nation's common way of serving tea at the time.

There was no central heating in homes then so in winter a small kerosene stove with its distinctive smell would be burning in one corner of their living room, while the fireplace that was never used gave a look of sunken sadness to an alcove at the opposite end of the rectangular main room. As we occupied the small lounge unit in the centre of the room, I tried my best to appear like an old-timer in the land, enjoying Russian-style tea while Paula took homemade biscuits out of a large, round tin. Opening the tin precariously against her bosom, she announced that these prestigious confections had been baked for Ben-Gurion's Bible group composed of writers, scholars and historians. On meeting nights she would serve them tea herself while they discussed specifically chosen portions of the Bible, which meant nothing to her.

Paula's biscuits were more than legendary: they were officially documented. When the papers of the American Foreign Secretary John Foster Dulles were shown to us during Abba's visiting professorship at the Institute of Advanced Studies in Princeton, a conversation about the biscuits was selected and brought out as proof of the talk's complete accuracy. Apparently, during the Secretary's visit to Israel in 1953 as part of a tour to acquaint himself with the Middle East, Dulles came for a talk and tea with Ben-Gurion. He liked Paula's biscuits very much and asked her if they had been baked in her home. Taken aback by his interest, Paula answered: "I guess they were baked in some home or another."

Close to the political life of Israel, I could not help being aware of the vast difference between the conditions in which Weizmann conducted his diplomacy and politics and those provided by Paula Ben-Gurion's home, with her limited education and eccentric personality. Yet everything around had been geared to serve only one purpose – the advancement of Ben-Gurion's career – and both he and his colourful, sharp-tongued wife fared very well under the presidential regimes of both Chaim Weizmann and Yitzhak Ben-Zvi. Protocol-wise, they were second in rank, but as the first Prime Minister, it was Ben-Gurion who concentrated all the real political powers.

Paula saw her own role in a very particular light. She was first and foremost, caretaker of Ben-Gurion's home and health. While Paula planted herself firmly in everyday reality, Ben-Gurion seemed to exist on some remote planet. He was single-mindedly oblivious to details of his environment and sometimes even of people. Once he asked Abba to return home from America for urgent consultation. When Abba arrived at the appointed day and time Ben-Gurion, in his staccato manner of speech and with utter surprise, questioned him amiably: "What brings you here?"

Paula literally waited on Ben-Gurion, preparing his food herself and laying out his clothes on his martial-looking steel bed, the type used for immigrants and known in the country as a Jewish Agency bed. She watched over his daily nap from 2 – 4 p.m. with such aggressive vigilance that even events of great national importance could not deter her from guarding his routine. When an aide rushed to tell them that he had just heard on the radio that President Truman had officially recognized the State of Israel, Paula curtly said that she could not disturb her husband's sleep. Again, when Moshe Dayan, then the Israeli Chief of Staff, appeared at her front door, wanting to see the Prime Minister (who was also Defence Minister) without delay – the issue at stake was the "simple" matter of the Sinai War in 1956 – she shrugged off his intrusion and said she had no intention of waking Ben-Gurion. Everbody who came to see Ben-Gurion encountered Paula on the ground floor of their Tel Aviv house – today a protected building on what is now Sderot (Boulevard) Ben-Gurion – before going up a few narrow wooden steps to his study and library which occupied most of the top floor. As his sentinel, she made sure she picked up from each departing visitor some comment about the meeting that had taken place with B.G. which she could later report back to him.

Between such vigilant bouts of protection, Paula spent many devoted hours on the telephone, keeping herself updated. Her conversations, with me at least, usually took the form of questions, and I remember how she would go straight to the heart of the matter, and then hang up abruptly. Paula had strong intuitions and an amazing gift for "reading" people. When a member of the defence establishment, who had been close to Ben-Gurion on security matters, was discovered to be a Russian spy, Paula said to me, "I kept asking Ben-Gurion, where does this man's high living come from?"

I will always remember the first time when, as a gesture of friendship, Paula took me to see B.G.'s impressive library – a suite of three large, door-less spaces – and allowed me to roam around for a few minutes. She waited for me at the entrance of the library as if standing in religious awe of the place. Paula followed with reverence Ben-Gurion's intellectual explorations: Buddhism and Ancient Greek, the latter of which he had learned in a London air-raid shelter during the Blitz after Doris May, Weizmann's loyal Oxford-educated secretary who was a graduate in Classics, had taught him the Greek alphabet and bought him a dictionary. Ben-Gurion's interest in Buddhism had been occasioned by the visit of the Prime Minister of Burma, U Nu. Ben-Gurion later stayed with him for a week in a Buddhist monastery.

During the Sinai War, Ben-Gurion fell quite ill. Diagnosed with flu, he ran a very high temperature. Nevertheless, he remained in complete charge of the war, which he conducted from his bedside. Since Israel was bombing the Egyptians alongside our French and British Allies, one could not exclude the likelihood that the Egyptians would bomb us in retaliation. When I visited Paula after the war, on a home leave visit, we discussed the great miracle that had left Tel Aviv unscathed. I remember that special conversation and how we shared a moment of horror, thinking what might have been. It was one of the few times we talked in complete accord. Almost eleven years later one could not approach Paula on the subject of the Six Day War. Ben-Gurion was not at the helm anymore and could not face the fact that his successor, Levi Eshkol, could possibly know how to deal with such a crisis.

When you were with Paula you would notice how agile she was; she was of average build with dark brown hair and a determined chin. She wore trousers and pullovers in winter, which was not at all common for women in government circles, but associated with spartan kibbutz life. In summer, her floral dresses were rather matronly; she would make her impression by what she said and not by how she looked although she was proud that after three children she had a perfectly flat tummy, and did not hesitate to show it to me. When first I knew her, she had a quizzical smile and a piercing look, though in her later years, following a cataract operation, that was masked somewhat by the thick glasses she wore. The way she went about this surgical ordeal was typical of her style.

Waiting for Ben-Gurion to go to Burma in response to U Nu's invitation, she swore her husband's aide to secrecy and he, in turn, obtained a promise from the press (one could still accomplish such a feat then) that out of consideration for Ben-Gurion, they would not print a word about the operation until his return. Paula then took herself to hospital for the full week that cataract operations required then: the head was kept immobile between two small sandbags on either side of the neck for seven days. My mother came from Egypt to Palestine for the same operation and also spent an equivalent time in the hospital between her two sandbags. Far away in Burma, Ben-Gurion knew nothing of Paula's protective plot. There was great moral allure in her total managerial independence about whatever concerned her health and self at all times and under all circumstances. The nation, identifying with the burdens of its leader, later strongly and admiringly approved of her inimitable way. When I went to visit and congratulate her on her wonderful behaviour (and great showmanship, though this I did not say), she shrugged her shoulders and stated self-deprecatingly: "I did not want him to be bothered."

She had not always behaved with such proud altruism in her younger years. Ben-Gurion, before the State, had often gone abroad on political missions for the Histadrut or to represent the Labour Party at the great Zionist Congresses in the various capitals of Europe, at times staying away for weeks on end. When America became especially important to Israel after the Second World War, he stayed in Washington for six months because Weizmann and Sharett had decided to open an office there and Ben-Gurion was determined that it would not be staffed with Weizmannites!

Paula's feelings of abandonment occasioned the violent unleashing of despair. Even her scientist daughter, Renana, mentioned this in her only personal interview to *Yedioth's* New Year magazine, in September 2004. Ben-Gurion had often left Paula to fend with oppressive financial worries; rotating their debts, piastre-pinching,* borrowing, coping with the children's sicknesses, some of which were exaggerated to increase the dramatic effect of her self-sacrifice and solitude. She had been left with the burden of being a single parent, despite the very nice letters Ben-Gurion frequently penned to his children, expressing concern for their health and interest in their homework and exams. This reality was quite different from the superior life Ben-Gurion had promised her at the beginning of their marriage. Soon after the wedding, he had volunteered for the army and was away for two years fighting during the First World War. Paula had entreated him not to join up, citing as an example other equally pregnant women whose husbands did not leave their wives to fend for themselves. She would later write to him: "I see you prefer Palestine to your family."

"If I stayed with you now," wrote Ben-Gurion in reply, "...all our life together would be ordinary, petty, and pointless. This is not the kind of life I want to live with you. Be strong in body and spirit, for a great future bright with light and happiness is in store for you." And indeed, Paula was part of the excitement of those

---

* 100 piastres equalled one lira, the first Israeli currency.

incredible years of the founding of the State, and she was in the central orbit of historical issues. Yet Ben-Gurion's collected *Letters to Paula* seem more like a self-conscious documentation of his pre-State life for posterity, than the endearing letters of a husband to his devoted wife. Many of them were immediately made available to the Party, in rare cases even before the children were given them which really smacked of extreme socialist rule. One can't help thinking how Ben-Gurion and Paula were really owned by the Socialist Party's worship of the State, which unfailingly came before any other consideration.

There are also her sad and savage letters to him, a documentation of a life of emotional uncertainty as a woman, of harassing material misery as a housewife, of illiteracy and of deep loneliness. As the top political wife in the country, these emotions could be shared only with Geula, her eldest daughter who was her friend and confidante. Of course in the years we knew them, all seemed solidly established in their life, and her devotion looked as if it had been serenely there forever.

In the early years of the State, there was a small seaside hotel in Tel Aviv called the Kaete-Dan, where James McDonald stayed. The first US Ambassador to Israel, he shared the same three-storey building with the Soviet Ambassador, each having one floor, their two flags flying at opposite corners of the small building. People reported that the Russian always seemed, as if by accident, to come out of the elevator on the wrong floor! The place looked more like a solidly run European *pension de famille* but for its hours of *café dansant* every afternoon and night, when some of the more extroverted citizenry would shed their problems and tensions to rally on the terrace, swaying to the tango music of "*Artzenu Haktan-tonet*" (our own tiny country) repeated ad infinitum within the daily spectacle of glorious Mediterranean sunsets. "*Artzenu Haktan-tonet*" was sung throughout the country, the words bringing out an intimacy that enveloped all imperfections with kindness, a consciousness of one's destiny that had placed one there, and the sense of everyone's individual importance in that land. The borders between national and personal emotions were blurred.

A mere few streets away, in their two-storey house, the Prime Minister and Paula gave every citizen the feeling that they were the great overseers of the country, setting an example of simplicity and modesty. Minimalism had been part of their adolescent upbringing, and later of the circumstances of their socialist ideology. Palestine was derelict, poor and primitive when they arrived successively, he in 1917 and she in 1919. "I have no bread," Ben-Gurion wrote in a letter during those early days in Palestine, "but I have a dream." Hardship was once again part of their life and austerity had now branched into political necessity. The regime was egalitarian and everybody lived on a shoestring. In Paula's home, threats and dangers loomed larger than in any other Israeli's. She had a strong understanding of the national condition, and was always in unison with the people. She presented herself on the daily scene, equal to any ordinary worker, and was equal in performing the humblest chores.

Ambassador McDonald was a tall, lanky man of Scottish descent who had headed various United Nations humanitarian agencies and was far more familiar with the issue of refugees than with the technical procedures of diplomacy. His memoirs were later found to contain amiable descriptions of his own working conditions when he was accredited to the new State, and here is one such description about a working lunch:

> One December day I went there for lunch with the Prime Minister – with Mrs Ben-Gurion as cook. The house was as cold as a barn....The only source of warmth – and this theoretical – was an ancient portable heater, the survivor of a decade of wear and at the moment busily emanating strong oil fumes in every direction. When the Prime

Minister arrived, we went into the dining room, which had a temperature more appropriate for a refrigerator. The three of us sat down with a fugitive shiver or two and sought to forget the cold by doing justice to the ample food Paula had prepared for us.

Later Ben-Gurion and I carried the heater to a corner and, sliding our chairs to it as near as safety permitted, discussed a number of problems. It was a scene which I suspect is not often duplicated in the capitals of the world: a nation's Prime Minister with his luncheon guest, the American Ambassador, discussing matters of state, while the wife of the Prime Minister vigorously does the dishes in the kitchen.

With the wear and tear of her life, Paula's expression changed; her face became harder and more bitter, her voice almost raucous. She was increasingly impatient, sad and disapproving when in the concluding years of his political career Ben-Gurion became obsessed with the Lavon Affair (see p. 197).

She felt he carried the obsession too far, and that the incident had stuck to their life like glue. Ben-Gurion wanted a judicial body to judge who had given the instruction for the mishap, while for security reasons a ministerial body of seven was appointed instead. Even after he retired from the premiership in 1963, he attempted to pursue the case privately with two lawyers who volunteered their services, but nothing came of his efforts. It was a very drawn out case with deep implications for years to come. Paula was rarely seen then. With the conflict still preoccupying the country, one day I asked to visit her, as I had done over the years, but she refused. These were terrible years for them and Ben-Gurion, whose power base in the country had been built so assiduously over so many years, was now skidding. It was such an anti-climax after so many achievements and such fame.

I have always felt that Ben-Gurion was the only one who could have led the War of Independence after the Arabs refused to accept the United Nations Partition Resolution of 29 November 1947 and went on the attack. Weizmann, whose political and diplomatic skills were great and who had achieved so much diplomatically with the Balfour Declaration, without all the sustaining machinery of a state, could never have taken on the role of Commander-in-Chief, sending the Haganah to war in 1948. It needed Ben-Gurion's determination, unquestioned leadership, strongly established following and capacity to make daring decisions and take action.

I remember Paula's concern for Ben-Gurion at the Knesset session during the fierce and emotional debates about German reparations. Ben-Gurion had the capacity to transcend the political immediacy around him and move to a rational sphere with surprising detachment, untouched by the trails of emotion he left behind. The debates took place in the original Knesset building in the heart of Jerusalem, a makeshift state of affairs that lasted until the new Knesset building was erected in 1963. I remember how, on 7 January 1953, Paula sat herself in one of the ground-floor boxes reserved for ministerial aides and secretaries so as not to be conspicuous. She hid behind a side curtain, holding it back sufficiently to be able to see Ben-Gurion perform. His policy in favour of reconciliation with Germany was violently attacked from all sides. There were demonstrations; the people threw bottles and rocks, smashing the Knesset windows and injuring hundreds of policemen. The hysterical crowd tried to force its way into the building: it seemed as if a Jewish revolution was on. Ben-Gurion called the army in to disperse the crowd.

Inside, a great restlessness could also be felt; the Knesset membership had its Holocaust survivors as well. The heckling and shouts were terrible, the opposition party vitriolic. Menachem Begin, himself a survivor of the Holocaust and whose family had been annihilated in Poland, almost spat out his words, calling the acceptance of reparations, "the ultimate abomination since the creation of the State". Paula, like many of us, identified emotionally with the revulsion and resentment at the idea of "reparations" seemingly being balanced against six million lives. But for her, Ben-Gurion had to win. After two days of intensive debate, a vote was taken and Ben Gurion's government won by sixty-one votes to fifty.

Sde Boker, the shack in the Negev to which Ben-Gurion semi-retired while still returning often to Tel Aviv, served as a vision and an example. Although his descents to Sde Boker had been motivated by two of his resignations in 1953 and 1963, he also wanted to show the way to a conscious policy of populating the Negev. For Paula, however, it was a real hardship. There was no enchantment for her in the desert and little consolation in the dramatic landscape. She missed her children: her son Amos, her beloved daughter Geula, and her pride, the biologist Renana, whom she and Ben-Gurion, in a joint parental effort, had nursed and saved from meningitis as a child, and of course her grandchildren. She missed her two Tel Aviv friends, Esther, the renowned painter Reuven Rubin's wife, and Lola Beer, the most prominent couturier of Israel, both of whom provided her with most of her life-sustaining gossip; and she missed the political personalities coming and going, the foreign visitors and the world celebrities. Many would come in loving pilgrimage to Sde Boker but it was not the same.

The subsequent dynamism in the country was to prove that Ben-Gurion's apprehension about populating the south was well founded then, but the Negev that Weizmann had won for Israel in Washington has developed spectacularly. I remember the first housing project in Beersheeba, when some sort of contraption would churn up concrete and pour it into rectangular wooden frames erected on the sand to make a street of little two-storey houses in a few days to settle new immigrants. We were two of Ben-Gurion's official guests at the inauguration ceremony when water and electricity were brought to Eilat. We stood on the empty coast in what was whimsically called the "Governor's Mansion" – four steel poles covered in a brown Bedouin-woven wool cloth.

Besides retaining our deep admiration for our unique B.G. like the whole nation, Abba and I always remembered the unmistakable style of our last visit. Invited for lunch, we sat on wooden benches in the kibbutz dining hall of Sde Boker and ate some mushy kibbutz food that Paula shared with us. She then very demonstrably opened a basket with fresh food and colourful desserts, which she had brought down from Tel Aviv. "Only for B.G.," she emphatically announced while we, the guests, settled down to our rubbery, dried-out, egg-powder omelette.

21

The Ministry of Foreign Affairs
and the Six Day War

In the summer of 1966, a few months after Abba's nomination as Foreign Minister, and after the children finished their school year, we moved from Rehovot to Jerusalem. After eight years at the Weizmann Institute, the departure was hard. For the children it meant parting from friends and the very verdant premises of the Institute where they could play so freely. However, the change meant going towards Aubrey's realization of a long-delayed ambition. Since Meyer Weisgal was in the USA and many of the scientists were away on holiday, there was no official farewell.

Our new home was the official residence of the Foreign Minister in Jerusalem. This two-storey, stone house, located in Rehavia in the old part of modern Jerusalem, was then and is now the State's only other official residence besides the Presidential Mansion. We were already familiar with the house from our predecessors, Moshe Sharett, the first Foreign Minister, and his family, and Golda Meir, the second. Its exterior was as chilling as all Jerusalem's stone buildings. Balfour Street, which bordered the house on one side, had such a narrow pavement that if two people crossed on it, one of them had to step down on to the road.

During the time of Ben-Gurion, as well as that of his twice successor Levi Eshkol, prime ministers often conducted state affairs from the modest homes in which they had lived before assuming their exalted positions. Both residences and the scale on which one entertained were much smaller and more intimate then, but as a gesture to Israel's international relations, the house in Rehavia was bought for the Foreign Ministry shortly after the War of Independence and remained the Minister's domicile till Yitzhak and Leah Rabin took it over as their official residence when he became Prime Minister and thus it remains.

We inherited the house in an uncared-for condition. Considering that it was built in the early 1930s, it was an amazingly modern home. The living room's huge glass doors looked out on to an uncluttered inner courtyard with a single jacaranda tree. When in flower, its spread of mauve blueness gave the place a merciful patch of colour which allayed the austerity of the courtyard and afforded us much pleasure.

Golda, as Prime Minister, had understandably not shown a special interest in the running of the place and the administrative officer of the Foreign Ministry had asked that the house be given a thorough renovation, or at least have its rooms repainted, but since there were already rumours that Abba might be Golda's successor as Foreign Minister, she avoided getting involved, saying "Let Suzy worry about it," which I did when our time came.

Some months after we moved into our new home, on 23 May 1967, we were still asleep when the telephone rang at 5 a.m. I picked it up and Yitzhak Rabin, then the military Chief of Staff, asked me to transmit important information to my husband. This sort of thing – a wake-up call at an odd hour, followed by an abrupt statement – had happened to us before. The assassinations of UN Middle East Mediator, Count Bernadotte, in 1948 and the King of Iraq in 1958 had both been conveyed to us in this manner (as would that of the Egyptian President, Anwar Sadat, in 1981). Listening to my husband's voice and to the unclear sounds coming from the other end of the phone, my instinct told me that soon we would be utterly engaged; I was already familiar with periods of activity in which there is space for nothing else but the task in hand. We waited anxiously for the 6 a.m. news and heard that

President Nasser was threatening to impose a blockade of the Tiran Straits. We were shocked but not totally surprised. In the eight days since Israel's Independence Day on 15 May, the enmity between Egypt and Israel, which had abated to some extent in the ten years since the cease-fire agreement of 1957, had been taking an aggressive turn.

The Tiran Straits between the Sinai and Arabian peninsulas separating the Gulf of Aqaba from the Red Sea had not been the subject of anxiety since the conclusion of the difficult and protracted Dulles-Eban negotiations of 1956-7, which followed the Sinai Campaign about "free and innocent passage" of Israeli cargo under foreign flags. Protected by the internationally recognized "freedom of transit, commerce and navigation", our presence in Sinai had assured our communication with Africa and Asia. But on that morning of 23 May, there was an attempt to upset the carefully achieved "guarantees" that Israel had obtained through negotiations which affirmed that the Straits of Tiran were an international waterway and that, ultimately, should they be blocked, Israel had the right to use self-defence.

In 1956, President Dwight D. Eisenhower had been unequivocally determined to get Israel to pull back from Sinai following its surprising thrust into that peninsula, made with the approval and assistance of both France and Britain. It had been a very daring and adventurous operation in which each participant nation had had its own reckoning with Nasser's Egypt after he nationalized the Suez Canal. The French were instigated because of an Arab rebellion in Algeria supported by Nasser, the British because they had been forced out of Egypt, and together with the French had lost control of the Suez Canal, and the Israelis because fedayeen, the Arab terror gangs of those years, were penetrating Israel from the Sinai and the Gaza Strip. The Soviet Union, in a tendentious collaboration with the US, had readily approved of President Eisenhower's castigations and enforcement of a pull-back. These were forcefully expressed in the threatening notes from Eisenhower and the Soviet Prime Minister, Nikolai Bulganin. Now, suddenly, the issue was being forced back into our consciousness. Apprehension filled our bedroom in those early morning hours. It felt as if some dreadful apparition had stepped in front of us.

In search of an explanation, my mind rushed to the wings of this new instantaneous theatre. There had been no wrangling with the Egyptians or the UNEF (United Nations Emergency Force) over any issue concerning Tiran. There had been no symptoms of friction in the long-standing and smooth-running arrangements of UNEF surveillance which was placed in the Sinai after the 1956 war. Not a move, no stray bullets, not a whispered complaint. It seemed too arbitrary for such a menace to be hurled at Israel from the desolate coastline of Tiran, too dangerous to be true, too true not to be ghastly. But there it really was and from then on we were to live with this issue, day and night, for an interminable three weeks.

A few minutes after Yitzhak Rabin's call, the Prime Minister, then Levi Eshkol, rang to say he was convening the ministers of his National Security Committee at 9 a.m. In order to give Abba two hours for consultations, I woke our help early to get the day started, beginning with the preparation of a 7 a.m. breakfast for the eight people in his immediate team. The usual procedure would be followed: briefing of the foreign ambassadors in Israel and the Israeli ambassadors abroad and at the United Nations, and dealing with the political domestic scene and the press at home and abroad.

By 9 a.m. Abba had left, the children had gone to school and his advisors had hurried to their telephones, desks and cables. The house, taut with so much new activity only minutes before, was left with an array of empty coffee cups and full ashtrays, completely still and looking at me like a big, forlorn child needing attention. Such was the atmosphere of those days – on the one hand, a sense of domestic normality, and on the other, brewing political crisis and looming war.

Since the beginning of 1967, the Syrian border had been the focus of constant tension. The Egyptian front had not worried us, but since January, the Syrians had been party to thirty-six incidents conducted by the terrorists of El Fatah in Israel's territory, including the laying of mines within five miles of the Israeli border. One knew the army would deal with it, and yet the country being so small, every incursion seemed personal. There was always an immediate and complete national identification with every incident. We knew very well that these attacks were planned in conjunction with the Syrian authorities, and had retaliated against one such incident on 7 April, in an air engagement that was emblematic of the future in its numerical proportions in that the Syrians lost six MiGs while we lost no planes. Randolph Churchill, here on a brief visit for the dedication of the Winston Churchill Memorial Forest near Nazareth, was at our official residence for tea when the news was telephoned through. He seemed a most fitting guest for the occasion! All the same, the Syrians continued their actions well into May.

On 11 May, at the request of the Northern Command, Abba had been taken by army helicopter to tour the north and view the harassed settlements of that frontier. I accompanied him that day, curious to see the area for myself. We went to various points along the border to look at the different targets. Above Kibbutz Dan, near Kiryat Shmona, in that final stretch of Israeli land, a lone soldier (a reservist from Tel Aviv) stood in camouflage and utter solitude, save one telephone, surveying the scene through field-glasses from his position at the end of a long, empty, serpentine trench. There was a horizontal slit, no wider than three inches, which he used both for ventilation and to see through. The soldier had to stand immobile for hours at a time and the silence seemed to me unbearable. When I asked him what sort of indications of trouble preceded any sabotage or shooting, he told me that there was usually a herd grazing right in front of his trench on the "other side", and whenever that herd was withdrawn, some trouble was to be expected. He admitted that besides the few incidents known of in advance, most shootings started suddenly, and there were always stray bullets on both sides.

At Kibbutz Dan, we were shown the children's shelter – cots of steel kept underground – which made me think of Israeli children everywhere, meant to grow up in security but actually brought up in an atmosphere of constant alertness and danger. A protective concrete wall built in the kibbutz and slanted to face the usual angle of enemy fire was riddled with bullet holes. There were two blue-flagged OPs (observation posts) in that area for UNTSO (United Nations Truce Supervision Organization), set up in 1948 to guard the armistice lines that had been established with Egypt, Lebanon, Syria and Jordan, after the Israeli War of Independence: in no way was it comparable to the UN Emergency Force strung along the Egyptian Sinai border that was over three thousand "observers" strong.

We had been told before, and our visit of 11 May was meant to confirm to us, that the whole length of that northern frontier with Syria was watched over by an Israeli force of a mere 126 men, so as not to be provocative in any way. Just beyond Kibbutz Dan, on these last few metres near Arab territory, we had gazed at the landscape ahead of us, and there on the right was Syria and on the left Lebanon. We were able to see for ourselves just how easily infiltrations were staged. Lebanon (as would be proven in the coming war) was not interested in incidents with Israel. Rather, at the point where Israel, Syria and Lebanon converged, it was simple for the Syrians to pass infiltrators into Lebanon and let them penetrate into Israel from that direction, so that frontier incidents would appear to have originated from Lebanon. This became a common occurrence over the years, and even after Israel has pulled out of the "security zone". The Israeli army was originally set up as a defence force to protect the borders of the State and, by and large, this remained the case until the Six Day War: they were anywhere in the country except on that frontier.

Although the Soviets and Syria accused Israel of concentrating troops on their frontier, I was consistently told the number remained 126. On one occasion we asked the Soviet military attaché to choose any position along the front for inspection. He picked various spots at random, and when he found no concentrations of troops he still could not believe it and must have gone home simply thinking that we were experts at hiding people!

Independence Day parades are always occasions for political utterances meant not only for home consumption but also for enemy ears. Starting in 1950 they were once held every year in a different city and in 1967, it was Jerusalem's turn, but because of the 1949 Armistice Agreement, the parade had to be limited. I remember the discussions beforehand and the recommendations that it should be held without heavy armament so as not to provoke the Arab population. Therefore, in the end, only mortars and command cars rolled past the presidential stand. MK Israel Galili, a member of the cabinet, called the editors of the Israeli press and asked them not to over-play either the Tiran Straits threats or the opposition Rafi Party's* decision to mock the mini-parade by displaying cardboard dummies of tanks as a criticism of the Eshkol government's decision to abide by the Armistice Agreement. All this did not save Israel from a Jordanian complaint that we were violating the Armistice Agreement.

In order to compensate the public for the mini-parade, it was decided to hold a tattoo at the Hebrew University. At the rehearsal, a poem by Israel's national poet, Natan Alterman, was read. The last verse warned the Arabs not to attack Israel again because they would be likely to meet the same fate as in 1948 but this was deleted for the actual event.

Yitzhak Rabin, further informed about signs of troop movements in Egypt, and Levi Eshkol made a very firm statement.

* Founded by Ben-Gurion on his retirement Rafi was labour-orientated, hawkish on defence and liberal on social affairs.

It followed one Rabin had given the previous week containing only a vaguely masked warning to the very radical Syrian regime about their endless intrusions which eroded Israel's daily security. The whole country listened to both speeches on the radio (there was no television in the country then), and were reassured that our leadership was not remaining passive. But what the public perhaps did not realize was that those statements would prompt the Arab world to seek a response from Nasser, widely considered the overall Arab leader.

During the parade, a note from Mossad was slipped into Levi Eshkol's hand and another into Abba's. That same night there was a festive Independence Day concert at which Artur Rubinstein played, and the Israeli Army was put on an initial alert. Nasser was soon to materialize the aggressiveness of his speech but it still seemed a show of bravado for our benefit. We hoped against hope that he would realize how risky such an embroilment would be and reconsider, though we all sensed strongly that somehow it would not play itself out that way.

The next day, Nasser began filling up the Sinai with troops he had hurriedly brought back from Yemen, while Egyptian combat units and artillery vehicles rumbled through the streets of Cairo, tying up traffic for hours. They were heading north, and north meant towards us. He was going "to show the world" and strengthen his hand in the Arab world, but in fact he created terrible logistical problems for his army which was spreading further and further away from its base.

I remember thinking, after the war, about when and what was the turning point in the situation, and it seemed to me that Nasser's staged act had engendered a new reality in its overreaching intention. At the time, he might still have been ambivalent about the war since, only a week before, he had sent a cable to Arab students in London in which he repeated his oft-stated belief that the time was not yet ripe for a war with Israel. As things developed, however, he would become trapped in the expanding momentum of his wishful scenario. His pride and the obligations of his rhetoric would soon propel him to a point of no return. How else could he have spread his resources so unreasonably thin, conducting two wars simultaneously: the one in Yemen, with 70,000 troops – a third of Egypt's standing army – and accompanying equipment, and the other against Israel? The calculations of an emotional, populist leader superseded what might have been expected from a reasoning politician.

On that same day, 16 May, we had a luncheon at our residence for all the ambassadors and their wives whose countries we had visited on an official tour two months earlier: Thailand, the Philippines, Japan, Burma, Australia and New Zealand. In the evening, I travelled to Tel Aviv to attend a fashion show for the Israel Cancer Association. In New York, the Secretary-General of the UN, U Thant, was wrangling over the United Nations Emergency Force (UNEF) at Gaza and events were soon to go from bad to worse. Abba, after lunch, had gone to a cabinet meeting. We were used to intermittent regional changes in our work; for years these were very much part of the daily worry of diplomacy and of what Israelis called with a sense of resigned docility, "our Israeli reality".

As I continued with whatever obligations I had, I could not filter out the overwhelming mood of concern in the country. I often wonder at the way events conjoin in the mind of a politician's wife. You sit at a typical foreign minister's luncheon, talking about Thailand, Cambodia and Australia, while your tense husband has just hurriedly mentioned something to you before the guests arrive, that is either another current news item from the ministry or something of major national concern, and though you know not which, you have been trained to be ever on the alert. You look at the foreign ambassadors and wonder how informed or uninformed these emissaries of such far-away lands are, working here with such small Missions (as was the case before the Six Day War). Does everybody know and yet not talk about the latest

Israel-Arab news? Of course they do. Observing Abba, through a mixture of instinct and experience, I could immediately sense the depth of the danger, and was consumed with the question: Did the present symptoms mean war – again – for Israel?

At the fashion show, the French and Swiss wives of ambassadors sat next to me and I listened to them as was demanded, but my mind was elsewhere. I wondered what moves were being decided at the cabinet meeting. I sent a message to the orchestra members not to play so noisily, and instead they played even louder. Deciding to relax a bit, the show began to be fun. I liked the style of the young French designers, throwing convention to the wind as one of the models came out with bare breasts bouncing under a dress made entirely of beads – not exactly a common view in austere Israel. Long-legged, sophisticated models were still rare in the country. The Swiss ambassadress spotted her country's flag on the left hand glove of an outfit. "Only on one hand?" she exclaimed. Just a few hours earlier, the cabinet had formally received the first report of the massive concentration of Egyptian troops.

When I think back to those three weeks of crisis in May and June 1967, I am still amazed at how we continued with our more mundane engagements. In mid-May, we gave a luncheon and attended Levi Eshkol's dinner for the Prime Minister of Finland, Rafael Paasio and Mme Paasio, who were on a state visit to Israel. I can recall the wife of our Chief of Protocol mentioning to me how pretty the flowers looked, knowing that I had undertaken a project to promote the sale of Israeli flowers abroad, and my comment back to her that I felt as though the evening was our "swan song" of diplomatic hospitality. She looked surprised, and the next day the Finnish Prime Minister and his wife cancelled the rest of their visit and flew home.

How incongruous it all was! The cabinet and Nasser, the loud band, the bouncing models and the risqué fashions, the ranks of "proper" ladies loyal to the cancer cause, and of course those dreadful hotel pastries. Everything revolved simultaneously in my mind: the political, the public, the humanitarian, the social, the personal, the culinary. These were the concerns of an official woman's life. These were the events in my life on Tuesday 16 May, just one week before the announcement of the blockade of the Tiran Straits. Exactly three weeks later, we would be in the middle of a war.

The role that the UN played throughout this entire dramatic episode must never be forgotten. On that same long day, a day of outward social gaiety and internal anxiety for me, the Egyptian Chief of Staff, General Muhammad Fawzi, wrote to the Indian commander of the UNEF, informing him that he had given instructions to the armed forces of the UAR (United Arab Republic, composed of Syria and Egypt) to be ready for action against Israel "at the moment it [Israel] might carry out any aggressive action against any Arab country". He added that his troops were concentrated in Sinai, explaining: "For the sake of complete security of all UN troops which instal observation posts (OPs) along our borders, I request that you issue your orders to withdraw all these troops immediately." Such a request would have left Egypt in sole control of Sharm El-Sheikh, and to make doubly sure, he asked to be informed of its fulfilment. It was an incredible request and Israel, fully visualizing the situation, became even more worried.

Certainly no UNEF commander is an ultimate authority for moving his contingent of men. Fawzi's demand occasioned questions about the source of the instruction and the authority of the UNEF. Wouldn't they have to be subjected first to political decisions? The Indian Commander, General Indar Jit Rikhye, as is fitting in such a situation, informed U Thant. But on 17 May, the Egyptians, without waiting for U Thant's answer, began taking over UN OPs from Yugoslav hands on the border so that UN forces "would not be harmed if hostilities break out".

Why this strange sense of urgency? Was all our trouble not with Syria? Were Egyptians now taking over from Syria? Was this a move to wage war against us? Nasser claimed *we* were going to start the war, but if that was the case, I wondered, why should they have worried for the safety of the UNEF? If Israel was really going to be the attacker, wouldn't it have been useful to let her fall foul of UN surveillance, on the old Armistice line? As the Egyptian aggression was gaining momentum, the tension and anxiety in Israel were working themselves up to fever pitch. Abba was running from the Foreign Ministry to cabinet meetings, to the security and defence committee of the Knesset, to the small security cabinet, to the Prime Minister's home, to meetings with the Prime Minister's advisors, sometimes in Jerusalem and other times in Tel Aviv's Ministry of Defence where it had always remained.

At a cabinet meeting on 23 May, MK Chaim Shapira, the Minister of Internal Affairs, and a member of the National Religious Party, suggested that since Abba had negotiated the freedom of passage in the Tiran Straits with a previous American government, he should go to the US to assess the American government's attitude on this issue as well. After all, when we had pulled back from Sinai in 1957, it had been the US, backed by the UN, that had guaranteed our right to self-defence in the event that the Straits became blocked. Levi Eshkol agreed with Chaim Shapira's idea and gave Abba his full support as he would throughout the coming days. Eshkol and Abba each knew their own role and place and exercised them with great integrity in the very personal, manipulative atmosphere around them. In spite of the fears and restlessness in the whole population, Eshkol never lost sight of the fact that as Prime Minister he had the obligation to transcend the pressures put upon him for an immediate military response.

The cabinet voted in favour of checking reactions in Washington. The army command, however, considered the diplomatic option a dangerous delay in light of the frenzy of those days. My husband was convinced that the political leaders' sense of timing had to work on two levels – the diplomatic and the military – and Eshkol, a down-to-earth realist, had a similarly reasoned and all-encompassing view of state matters. In their fear and anxiety, a nervous public would not grasp the value of these attributes until after the war. A completely understandable panic and deep stress seized the nation during the cautious weighing up of two options and earnest efforts at balancing them.

Timing was as vital on our side as on the enemy's. If you converted time into space, everything was a matter of inches. Abba had argued for checking the international positions before taking definitive actions by stating, "We must resist, but whether we must resist alone or with the support or understanding of others, this is now the question." The ministerial session of 23 May ended with Israel's leaders agreeing to give diplomacy its chance and leave the military decision temporarily in suspense. On the necessity of using diplomacy, Abba had made his point by remembering 1956 and 1957 when, after the Sinai War, we had lost the political advantages of our victory. "Israel might win the war, but lose its victory," he said, a point of view that would guide him all along.

At 3 a.m. on 24 May, at the end of a long cabinet meeting with the Prime Minister, Abba was to set out to check the validity of those 1957 guarantees. Accompanied by Moshe Raviv, his Foreign Ministry Political Advisor, he left for Paris in an empty El Al Boeing that was due to pick up some military material there. He hoped to meet President de Gaulle but didn't have an appointment when he left and our embassy was still organising it on his arrival. Next would come his talk with the British Prime Minister, Harold Wilson, in London and only then would he fly to Washington. For my part, at home with the children, all I could do was listen to the radio, my main source of information, and wait for updates from members of his immediate staff, especially the Deputy Director-General of the Foreign Ministry, Arthur Lurie. I would have no direct contact with Abba for the length of his mission.

At the instruction of the cabinet, Abba was to explore first what the French, our ally in the Sinai War of 1956, were prepared to do for us, but the talk with de Gaulle turned out to be a real set-back. France, who had sold us the Mirage jet fighters in April 1962 that established the quality of Israel's air defence and who had been our ally for nearly twenty years, now seemed to be utterly against us. For Abba, the response was a shock. Before he even sat down for their talk, de Gaulle in a pontifical tone had said, "*Ne faîtes pas la guerre*," or "Don't be the first to shoot!" Two hours later, at Abba's stopover in London, Harold Wilson, who had said he would be available at any hour, was sympathetic but gave no advice. After all, the Egyptians had overturned British rule and taken over the Suez Canal in the Officers' Revolution of 1952. There was no love lost between the two countries. The USA was now left as the key, the hope, the chief guarantor, the supreme power that could counteract the mischief of the Russians who were acting as if by remote control in the area. The Russians had already moved some ships from the Dardanelles towards the Mediterranean. Units of the Sixth Fleet were also instructed to move eastwards. Everything was now pinned on the USA and on Abba's talk with President Johnson and the US Secretary of State, Dean Rusk, both of whom he knew from his time as Ambassador.

After President Johnson's return from a day's visit to Canada, and after he had received his briefing, Abba, Abe Harman the Israeli Ambassador in Washington and Eppie Evron, the embassy's minister who had preceded Abba, sat with the President and his team for two and a half hours. It was important for them to assess the American frame of mind. There was no question in Washington that Israel was an injured party. During those deliberations, the Secretary of Defence, Robert McNamara, received information confirming that the State Department considered Egypt's moves to be acts of aggression.

At their end, the Pentagon had conducted simulation exercises which proved that in all cases Israel would win a war with Egypt.

President Johnson felt that the answer to Nasser should be a multilateral action. He wanted to send an international naval force of maritime countries through the Straits. As the talks progressed, he asked Israel to postpone its decision by forty-eight hours. In their hearts, the Israelis present wondered whether they should comply – after all, it was their lives at stake – but these words were from the President himself. As they prepared to part after the long talk, walking together towards the elevator, President Johnson turned to Abba and said: "I must emphasize the necessity for Israel not to make itself responsible for the initiation of hostilities. Israel will not be alone unless it decides to do it alone. We cannot imagine that it will make this decision."

Nevertheless, despite these sentiments and the fact that the President is titular Commander-in-Chief of the USA's armed forces in whose hands rest all final decisions, a few days later President Johnson admitted that he could not pull together the international naval force (called the Armada) that he had suggested, without the approval of Congress. The situation was getting markedly worse. It looked as if Congress, still reeling from the war in Vietnam, was not in a rush to get the USA involved. What we did not know at the time (nor have I ever found it mentioned in any book I've read on that war) was that the State Department had approached eighty-six countries to join the planned international naval force. I learned of this impressive attempt only at an Israeli-Palestinian Symposium on the Middle East held at George Washington University in memory of my husband in September 2003. Retired Ambassador Joseph Sisco revealed this number, apparently for the first time. I was surprised that the Israeli Foreign Ministry had never mentioned that fact and wrote to Professor Nathan Brown, an Arabist and head of the Middle East Department at GWU, who confirmed that eighty countries had been approached, but only Canada and Holland had responded positively.

On the way to deliberations at the White House on 26 May, an urgent coded communication arrived from home. Advisors in

Levi Eshkol's office had sent Abba a cable to be used in his imminent talks with President Johnson. The first part stated that the danger now was not from Syria, but very specifically from Egypt. The second part, however, asked Abba to demand "...a US commitment that an attack on Israel would be considered as an attack on the USA". Coming from the Prime Minister's office, it was natural that there was nothing tentative about the message but how could Abba ask President Johnson for such a commitment? Constitutionally, only NATO could claim such a right. Abba was simply astounded and shocked by the reckless exercise of power emanating from the closest advisors to Israel's highest political authority. He said later, "Here we were seen in the Pentagon simulation in the position of a strong nation, winning whether attacking or being attacked, and suddenly I am asked to portray a weak and helpless nation!" The American information was also that the Egyptians were not meaning to attack *then*.

I like to think that members of our Foreign Ministry would never have dared send such an unprofessional cable, but this came directly from the Prime Minister's office and was actually sent twice, the second time a few hours later with the exact same text. Surely they could not have failed to know that the President had no such authority without Congress, but nevertheless, there it was. It took a while to handle. Abba had no alternative but to have the cable read out at the meeting. Retroactively, this whole manipulation and intellectual affront can only be recorded as a symptom of strained nerves in Jerusalem, of real fear, excessive lack of sleep, the frightening weight of responsibility and a most irresponsible political request. For Abba it was a disparaging act. People at home were pulling the carpet out from under him.

Meanwhile, for those of us in Israel, the twenty-one days from 15 May to 5 June (the official declaration of war) continued to be lived in unrelenting intensity. The public's anxiety, fears and restlessness seemed to penetrate into our home, through our very walls. I hardly went out of the house so that I could be available for Abba when he was able to call, and also to avoid being asked questions to which I would not have known the answers. The crisis was the focus of the entire nation and particularly the troops waiting in the desert, as it loomed continuously larger by the day and more dangerous by the hour. This period carries its own name in Hebrew: *hamtana,* the waiting period.

I think that, more than anyone in the government, Abba continued to be obsessed with memories of the sterile conclusion of the Sinai War when, in a united front, the USA and the USSR had demanded that we pull back from the Sinai peninsula, leaving Israel with little guarantee that the same situation would not happen again. He had lived the situation first hand. Would America recognize now, a decade later, her specific commitment to Israel's free passage in the Tiran Straits, as established with UN sanction by the Dulles-Eban talks?

It was not only a bilateral matter between Egypt and Israel. There was the UN and what de Gaulle had described as the "Four Great Powers" of the USA, the USSR, France and Britain. Each was to have a role directly related to our crisis. But the number "four" brought a sarcastic remark from President Johnson who asked, "Who are the other three?"

In Israel, the one and only question that consumed everybody throughout this waiting period was: would we have to initiate the war to avoid Nasser's further build-up in the Sinai? When President de Gaulle had said, "Don't shoot first until the Egyptians declare war," Abba had answered: "The blockade of Tiran *is* the first act of war." But de Gaulle did not recognize it as such and surprisingly declared France's failing us in a totally unexpected and dramatic statement: "1967 is not 1957."

The army was now fully mobilized, having called up reservists and stationed active soldiers, and moved from a defensive to an attacking posture. Military commanders, especially Ezer Weizman, then Deputy Chief of Staff, signalled to the Prime Minister that they were ready and that we should not wait any longer. Some confronted him, especially Ezer Weizman, wanting to go to war immediately. On the other hand, Yitzhak Rabin came to our home on 22 May to evaluate the situation. When Abba asked him: "What do you need most now?" he declared: "Time, time, time." They had similar thinking then. The option of military response had been left in suspension during Abba's talks in Paris, London and Washington; it had been said that only with additional military preparations (as per Rabin's request) and his verifications in Washington of the past international guarantees, would Israel's cabinet make its final decision by a vote on the war. These were nerve-racking days for the public and even more so for the political leadership.

The political side was soon to take over. It became at best brutally competitive and at worst ruthless. There would be many personal tribulations on the way to final unity and the vote. Eshkol had been urged by his advisors to address the nation in order to reassure it; however, unprepared and not seeming well, he had stuttered while reading his speech. As a result, in what seemed a real mutiny, he was removed from his post as Defence Minister, which he had held concurrently with the premiership. Then Rabin collapsed and the public was told that he was suffering from nicotine poisoning. Ezer Weizman took over his post for the day and a half of Rabin's recovery. Meanwhile Moshe Dayan, a member of the opposition party Rafi, who had had nothing to do with the preparations for war until now, came across as a usurper as he took over the Ministry of Defence four days before the war. Bringing him into the cabinet boosted the military and public morale, as people held in their minds the image of the defiant, triumphant Dayan they had known in the past. Ben-Gurion and Shimon Peres, their minds stuck in scenarios of previous conflicts, opposed war which they believed Levi Eshkol could not conduct and win. Abba was attacked for wasting time on checking guarantees and Abe Harman was criticized for having rushed from Washington to Jerusalem, only to report what was already known

– that there was no progress on the American idea of an international naval force sailing through the Tiran Straits.

General Meyer Amit, head of Mossad, was sent to Washington by Levi Eshkol to meet his counter-part in the CIA on 31 May and 1 June in a last attempt to gauge as precisely as possible the American position. It was a useful move for both countries. The USA could not maintain that Israel had surprised it and Israel understood that the USA would not prevent her from making her own decision.

At the opening of the summer session of the Knesset, Justice Landau of the Supreme Court said to me in anger: "How long are you [in the Hebrew plural] going to wait? Indefinitely? You must specify a dateline." I assumed, of course, that he meant me to pass the message on to Abba.

The opposition was very active. Menachem Begin, heading his Revisionist Herut party, at first said that Ben-Gurion, the leader of Rafi, should return as Prime Minister while Eshkol assume the position of Deputy Prime Minister. Although Ben-Gurion did not say so himself, Peres suggested on his behalf that such an arrangement would be considered acceptable; Peres and Ben-Gurion both openly expressed their contempt for the government. Then Begin suggested another option – that Ben-Gurion should be Defence Minister, which Eshkol strongly opposed, stating: "The two horses, Eshkol and Ben-Gurion, can't pull together." The Rafi Party itself, surprisingly, did not suggest Ben-Gurion for any ministerial job, but suggested Dayan as Defence Minister in a coalition government.

There were other moments, such as when former hero of the War of Independence and Minister of Labour, Yigal Allon, won the majority of our own Labour Party (Mapai) to be nominated Defence Minister, and there were even discussions as to who would replace him as Labour Minister in order to keep the balance of party votes. But, of course, Dayan won in the end.

It felt as if cards with ministers' portraits were being shuffled in the corridors of power. Finally, Begin was brought into the cabinet as Minister without Portfolio, Dayan was appointed the Minister of Defence and Eshkol continued as Prime Minister. Abba remained the Minister of Foreign Affairs, although at one point it was suggested that a few ministers should head the delegation to the UN with him. Abba balked and said: "How would it be if the war was conducted by a few chiefs of staff?" and he won.

The whole world had been watching Abba's moves on the international scene. I found myself pulled in two directions: a worried wife, sharing the scene from the inside, and a member of the anxious public, watching the moves from the outside. I knew and understood rationally what he wanted to achieve but his brinkmanship worried me, although from his professional point of view this was how a Foreign Minister was supposed to act. He tested the potential of diplomatic efforts and their validity to the ultimate in a way that should it have proven incorrect, would have resulted in a totally ruthless political reckoning. The danger to him loomed large in my heart and I had the most fearful anxieties as had our children who, young as they were, sensed it all.

Yet throughout, I stayed with Abba's perceptions, trusting his long span of experience in the world of power games. Of course I knew that a politician's history of splendid service does not necessarily prove him right, but while everybody else was occupied with the present, Abba both looked back on the earlier context of a situation and ahead at all possible eventualities. I don't think his contemporaries wanted to extend Israel in that way at that time. Except for close colleagues who were technically involved with every one of his steps, it was the immediate present that mattered, but Abba stuck to his focus on the long term. I never once wavered in my belief that objectively he was doing the right thing. Commitments this time had to be the vanguard of political opportunities. It was terrifying to understand his responsibility in inducing the nation to walk such a tightrope. I also feared for his safety, his strength and his staying power, but felt

I had to remain outwardly as cool as possible. It was important that our home not seem dotted with worried exclamation marks, and should keep a co-ordinated inner strength. I saw how Abba lived in the poignant solitude of his decisions. These were hours in which the collective and individual future was at risk.

In the end, his steps and determination assured the position on which Israel would build its international policy, leading to the much-used and controversial UN Security Council Resolution 242 which called for withdrawal of Israeli armed forces from territories occupied in recent conflict. But by 1 June Abba came to realize that there was nothing further to expect from the diplomatic option. Our friend the USA, and the world, were leaving us to our own capabilities. We would now have to do everything by ourselves. On 4 June, along with the entire cabinet, he voted for the pre-emptive attack of 5 June.

Before he flew to the US to attend a UN Security Council meeting in New York, Abba knew that the Israeli Air Force had performed extraordinarily well – up to 400 Egyptian planes had been destroyed: therefore Israel had to prevent pressures for an immediate cease-fire while Egypt was being misled by Nasser and his generals about *her* so-called victory. We parted on the front steps of our official residence, the police guard opened the gate and Abba walked down to his car. I was still standing at the top of the steps, bidding him farewell, when shrapnel whizzed between us from the direction of the Old City. The police guard exclaimed: "What is that?" Abba got in the car, and I hurried inside to gather the children into the bomb shelter. The battle of Jerusalem was already on. That night, accompanied by Moshe Raviv, Abba travelled to the airport through side roads as the main highway was being shelled.

With Abba gone, like all the women who were alone with their young children, I would spend the next few days in our shelter with Eli, Gila, our devoted housekeeper, Chana Sternbach, and her young son Udi. I remember the children joking about the huge glass doors of the living room on which they had helped to glue gauze panels. A few days earlier, when a BBC reporter was due to interview him at home (it could not be in his office where there was so much tell-tale activity), Abba had remarked that glass doors covered like this would give an indication that we were already preparing for war, and so we stripped them for the interview and afterwards redid it all. There was always a degree of humour in these life-threatening scenarios. A friend of ours, a Canadian doctor, was enlisted by Jerusalem's Hadassah hospital for the duration of the war. As she left home, bullets already pelting all over the city, her husband shouted after her: "Drive carefully!"

How terrifying those days were and how anxiously we awaited every radio bulletin. When there seemed to be a lull in the fighting, the children and I came out of the shelter and rushed to the patio to pick up the still hot, hard-edged shrapnel, of which Eli has kept an impressive collection. My brother-in-law, Chaim Herzog, then a reserve general in Military Intelligence, was appointed the government's official spokesperson, and assigned to give the military assessment on the radio every day. He did a great deal to maintain the nation's morale; informative and calming, he gave us a sense of national confidence with such pronouncements as, "If I had to choose between being an Egyptian pilot or staying in my home in Tel Aviv, I would feel safer staying in my home."

At the time of Abba's great and moving speech to an overflowing United Nations Security Council in New York, everybody turned on their radio to listen. In New York and across the United States, and in many other countries as well, entertainment programmes had been cancelled in order to broadcast the session and the speech, while in Israel I struggled to get a reasonable reception. A friend called me later from New York and said that it was better for me not to have been there, that I wouldn't have been able to bear the anxiety and the indescribable tension for Abba. She said: "He, as the sole spokesman of Israel at that United Nations session, bore the total responsibility for presenting Israel's case." But I so much wanted to have been in that Security Council hall during those highly charged moments that I held on to the window sill, half-listening and half-praying. It was important to me that I had managed to call him an hour before his presentation to say that Jerusalem's East and West were now reunited. He absorbed that news and rushed back to his notes.

On the last leg of his flight to New York, where he had assumed he would be starting work on his speech, the steward had delivered an urgent message from the captain's cockpit. Israel's Ambassador to the UN, Gideon Rafael, informed Abba that he would have no time to go to the hotel – where he planned to complete his speech – after landing but would have to go directly to the Security Council as everybody was already there, waiting for him. Ambassador Rafael had already been informed of the Israeli Air Force operation on the opening morning of the war. However, the Egyptians were unaware of their defeat, believing instead the tall tales about their own victories. Thus neither side was in a hurry to press for a cease-fire, a situation Abba was able to exploit in order to gain vital time for Israel.

Abba's plane was only two hours away from New York. On board, the team scrambled to get him organized: the curtained cubicle reserved for the stewardesses was put at his disposal and everyone scrounged for bits of writing paper. These would be the only notes he would have when making his speech at the UN.

At home, I tried to imagine the pre-speech atmosphere. In my mind's eye I could "see" Abba thinking. The speech started with a dramatic announcement: "I have just come from Jerusalem. Israel, by its own efforts, has passed from serious danger to successful and glorious resistance." Thus was the first official intimation to the world that we had won the battle of Jerusalem. Abba proceeded with a duel with the Russians, represented by Alexei Kosygin. The Soviets and the Arabs had demanded that Israel be forced back to where she had been on 4 June. As Abba's biographer, Robert St John wrote:

> The spectacle of one of the smallest countries in the world pointing an accusing finger at one of the greatest powers of world history sent a wave of surprise through the UN Assembly hall. It was a moment of great triumph. Never had the plight of Jews in general and Israelis in particular been articulated so compellingly to an immense, world-wide audience. It was as though all his life, until now, had been a preparation for the hour and twenty-five minutes at the podium where he used all his talents to plead with the rest of the world for justice.

When Abba finished, there were expressions of exaltation, love, sympathy and admiration for him and for Israel. President Johnson said that his speech had been worth several divisions in the way it would rally public opinion in support of our cause. One of the greatest hours of Abba's life, it had been an amazing performance: his speech had emerged from pain and dilemma, and little did people know how truly extraordinary it was considering the shortness of time and the chaotic conditions of its preparations. After he left the UN to check in at our Mission, however, there was no sign from Israel of the emotional storm he had just stirred. Absorbed in its own tension, Israel was steps behind. There was a time gap, an emotional gap and an intellectual gap. I later wrote to a friend in America:

> I heard over Voice of America part of Abba's speech as he answered Kosygin. I listened intently, was with him, as was most of the country, except Rafi, who were resentful of the turn of the tide that had taken place for Abba. *Ha'aretz*, our leading morning paper, simply ignored the speech. It never mentioned it or even printed part of it or

gave it a line, or told of the world reaction to it. There is the hour for arms and the hour for the battle of words.

Soon, the Israeli Mission to the UN was swamped with thousands of letters and endless telephone calls. They had to hire special staff to cope with the response and over the following days, as Abba's speech reverberated across the world, the media was full of news on Israel. Both politicians and regular citizens felt a moral and intellectual elevation and marvelled at the power of his arguments.

Abba came back from New York on my birthday, 9 June, for further consultations. As he stepped down from the plane in the deserted airport, with absolutely no press reception, he surprised me by whispering, "Many happy returns of the day." I was elated to know that even with all the commotion, he had remembered.

We made for the Dan Hotel in Tel Aviv where again there was not a soul around. The big lobby was dark and empty with only one miserable fluorescent light. We went up to our suite where Yaacov, Abba's driver and ever-loyal helper, had miraculously organized a bottle of champagne from the empty hotel kitchen in honour of my birthday. I asked the hotel to take it back. "Not now," I said, not wanting to celebrate when the country was still at war despite our victories. Abba said to me, "What are we going to do with all those territories? We will have to give them back after some frontier adjustments which will be necessary for security!" I answered: "I won't enter the apartment if you say this! How can you tell this now to mothers and wives who have just lost a son or a husband?"

Abba soon left for a cabinet meeting, where the discussion would not only be about the territories but, more urgently, McGeorge Bundy's query. Bundy, one of President Johnson's team until 1966, had telephoned Abba before he left New York for Israel. The question, clearly emanating from above, was: "Wouldn't it be strange if the Syrians, who had brought the war upon us, were to remain unpunished?" Johnson's political team was divided between those for an attack on Syria and those against. We had the same situation in Israel between Moshe Dayan, who was against and General David "Dado" Elazar, Chief of the Northern Command, who was desperately eager to settle his own account with the Syrians. The cabinet was divided as well, but eventually Eshkol and Rabin decided on an attack. A cease-fire with Syria had been declared a day before, but since the Syrians continued to fire, General Elazar felt that we could still take over the Golan Heights. And he did, parachuting his troops behind the enemy lines to achieve victory.

With the battle of Jerusalem over, we were free to move about the city, and I went first to visit the wounded at Hadassah Hospital with Rachel Gordon, Abba's secretary, and later to Tel Aviv to see the wounded son of one of our house workers. In marked difference to my hospital visits on behalf of the Israel Cancer Association, it was strange to see only young patients in hospital beds. With such beautifully built bodies, some so cruelly and irrevocably damaged, they were surrounded by their families, who were grateful for the simple fact that they were alive, despite severe injuries.

A few days later I went for what was to be a most dramatic visit to Ammunition Hill, now in our hands after years in Jordanian-occupied Jerusalem. It was from there that most of the Jordanian mortar shells had been fired on Jerusalem. We had heard in our shelter the deep thuds as they hit the ground around us during the three-day battle. The stories of bravery at Ammunition Hill made one shudder; Jordan's Arab Legionnaires were fierce combatants and the human cost had been terrible. A member of the Foreign Ministry's staff, a huge, solid man who had been part of the fighting on that frontline, took me to the site, recalling for me the frightening moments, the rhythmic noise of the constant fire and the trembling fear of even the bravest of men. He recalled how, at a distance of a mere few inches, soldiers next to him had fallen. "It was," he said, "sheer hell." But they had held out.

No one who was there at the time will ever forget the moment when we heard over the radio: "The Temple Mount is in our hands!" Israeli troops had penetrated the encircling wall of the Old City. How mixed the feelings of our nation were then. How saddened we were by the heavy losses, how exalted by the victory. How we all called our family and friends, in mourning or in ecstasy, depending. I went alone to visit a bereaved mother from the Foreign Ministry, and with Abba to console a member of my mother's family – David Mouchine and his wife Doris, whose son Oren had been killed in Khan Yunis in the Gaza Strip. As we were leaving, David seized my husband by his lapels and angrily said to him: "Don't you dare give back territories!"

Then came the day we were allowed to enter the Old City. It seemed as if the whole of Israel was streaming towards the Holy City like sleepwalkers. Rows and rows of people, ten-wide, entered the Jaffa Gate. Silent, stunned Arabs crouched in their tiny shops staring at us just as we stared at them; it was eerie. Our new freedom across the city was elating: the 1948 separation had been effaced.

The Jewish people, who had once again experienced fear of annihilation, were now conquerors. Had we ever been conquerors before, I asked myself? My historical memory seemed to fail me. Weren't we always subjects of some greater or more powerful authority, sometimes merging solidly and constructively into an existing civilization and sometimes simply tolerated or worse?

Even those of us who were torn by the deliberations, the dangers and the isolation of Israel, had merged into a nation movingly united. We had lived for weeks on our collective nervous energy. It was as if some mystical event had come to pass, an event beyond human understanding, painful even in its success and its devastating scale. There was much introspection, especially amongst the young fighters who had been brought up on a concept of social morality, the respect for human dignity and who had had to confront new images of themselves, the Israeli condition and the torments of killing.*

There were the immediate practical matters of daily living to attend to. Milk and bread had not been available for days. Volunteers went out to distribute the mail that had accumulated in the central post office, working late into the night. I remember the sense of safety that reigned in what had so recently been a claustrophobic city. Some two or three days later, Eli and I went to the first concert in Jerusalem, initiated by the violinist Isaac Stern. Isaac flew over in a spectacular gesture of solidarity and performed with the Israel Philharmonic Orchestra. During the interval Eli and I were on the receiving end of overwhelming and ecstatic appreciation of Abba's performance at the UN, our countrymen finally aware of his speech after families and friends had called from New York and elsewhere.

A short while after the war, I joined Abba on his second visit to the north, this time to the Golan Heights. We were received in Kuneitra, Syria's former command post. I noticed a few massive, carved and heavily gilded armchairs covered in a dark red, floral European silk. It brought me full swing back to the Levant. We then heard rumours of Syrian soldiers chained to their positions and of many who had not fought but run away. That night I slept in Tel Aviv, and the next morning when I opened our hotel bedroom curtains I was literally startled by the view of throngs of people bathing in the sea as if it were a regular Saturday morning. You would never have thought there had been a war.

Curiosity soon got the better of me, and grabbing a friend from Rehovot, I drove through the West Bank. The landscape was so unspoiled, it was breathtaking. On another day we went to the casbah in Nablus. I was told not to go alone, so asked for a Ministry car and driver. We entered the casbah very carefully, not

* A paperback entitled *Dialogues of Warriors* would later create a national stir as soldiers, seeking moral answers in a world of cruel necessities, gave voice to the turmoil within them.

knowing what to expect. People looked down at us from small, upper-floor windows as we passed through the narrow, main market street, more fit for a donkey than a Foreign Ministry limousine. The onlookers, mostly women, were passive, and we felt the ambivalence of being a conqueror. The incomplete silence was oppressive. We too, in the car, remained silent.

The "territories" were now the subject of the world's attention and what would be the post-war settlement. Israel now had a much better negotiating position than would have been the case had we rushed into war. The Six Day War had bestowed upon us a new international status. We now had to face a wide range of political problems and many moral dilemmas.

22

The social and the political

A Minister's wife does not need to have an additional official role at her husband's side nor any special prominence. As far as the country is concerned she can take on any job and appear or not appear at official functions.

Since the wife is a definite partner of this high-ranking government position, however, I knew that I would have to fulfil many social responsibilities. Both diplomatic wives and the homes they maintain are, on every level, part of the public relations projection of a country. Foreign Affairs is very demanding in terms of personal contacts, communication and public appearances. However, I always felt that the diplomat's wife, while fulfilling her supportive role, could also use the opportunity for a creative or useful public role in order to benefit a humanitarian or cultural cause of her country. In my case, I would continue as President of the Israel Cancer Association. In addition I served on the Tel Aviv Mayor's Cultural Committee for several years, dealing with works of art sponsored by the City's Art Committee. We enriched a previously bare Tel Aviv with sculptures by Kenneth Noland, George Segal, Menashe Kadishman and Yitzhak Danziger. I enjoyed that assignment a great deal, in part because I had met Noland in New York through Joanne du Pont, was a friend of Kadishman, and George Segal and his wife Helen became our life-long friends.

The Committee covered the artists' air fares and accommodation but did not pay them a fee. Noland shipped his wooden sculpture from New York instead of creating it in situ and asked to use the time allotted to the project to see the country, especially Jerusalem. Segal chose to work locally and in 1973 he created a "Sacrifice of Abraham" after first shipping his white plaster and tools. At the time white plaster was seen as a daring medium. Little did I know how poignant the subject would be when, within months, the Yom Kippur War was thrust on us. Kadishman made the three huge corten circles for the city's Mann Auditorium, to this day home of the Israel Philharmonic and the scene of many cultural events. Danziger presented his art work in the form of a three-part, white curved wall standing up in the beautiful, green HaYarkon Park.

During those years I sponsored the first piece of conceptual art in Israel called *The Jerusalem River Project*. In dry, arid Jerusalem the artist, Joshua Neustein, chose a sloping, bare, rocky hillside in North Talpiot. From the top of the slanting surface to the nearby small valley, some thirty microphones were installed, one at the edge of each step and the sound of water was played from a disc at the top of the valley. The illusion of water gave a wonderful sense of excitement and as I stood at the bottom of the valley I felt the urge to run barefoot through it! This fantastic experience opened a gate to many similar creations.

Art had its place too in helping the very young State in its superhuman task of absorbing immigrants by the hundreds of thousands from East and West. I volunteered to serve on the local committee for Jerusalem's greatly disadvantaged neighbourhood of Katamon Chet and managed to have the Housing Authority add one room for each large family while I supplied the women with sewing machines. This poor, crowded neighbourhood, literally on the Jordanian frontier before the Six Day War, was crying out for help, and the extra-curricular attachment lasted for several years, unpublicized at my request.

After the Six Day War, we had some singularly exciting moments in our house. The NASA physicist, Professor Eric Steig, on a visit to Israel, offered to show us the film of the first landing on the moon. Gila was particularly excited and invited some of her school friends. At around this time there was a World Symposium of Jewish Journalists. We became their hosts after they asked to meet us and they descended on us with a tremendous onrush. When they left Martha, our Hungarian cook, told me with a shrug, "Never mind what I prepared for them, what they really wanted was to eat Mr Eban."

After the Yom Kippur War in 1973, there were endless working lunches for the Kissinger team about the cease-fire first with Egypt and later with Syria. Nancy Kissinger, his new bride, used to fly with Henry's shuttle party to Damascus; no matter how important matters were, she never agreed to stay overnight in Damascus and they both preferred to return to the King David Hotel in Jerusalem after every talk.

On one occasion I was in our Herzlia home with my children. Nitza, Abba's personal secretary, called me from the Foreign Ministry in Jerusalem at 10 a.m. and said casually, "I hope you will arrive in time for today's farewell luncheon for the Japanese Ambassador at your Jerusalem residence; it's set to begin at 1.30. I retorted, "Good God, nobody ever told me a word about it," hung up the phone and started giving instructions right away. Martha was called urgently. The huge freezer I had imported for the house blessedly saved the day and by 1.30 food, flowers and service were all lined up in the proper assemblage and with total credibility. Martha, who in her youth had been a ballet dancer and had once demonstrated for me and Grace, my secretary, the *grand écart* on our kitchen floor, performed something no less acrobatic in preparing that day's lunch!

There is yet another meal I shall never forget: a late supper party we gave after a Yehudi Menuhin concert for some forty guests. Menuhin, seated to my right, kept looking at a Chagall ink drawing on the wall facing him. The drawing portrayed a fiddler, beard and fiddle in one long black composition, and a circle with two lovers' heads in the centre on the white paper sheet. During the dessert, Menuhin very sweetly asked me if I would agree to sell him this drawing. Rather startled by the request, I explained that I had bought it as a young bride in Paris in 1949 and couldn't bear to part with it. He was not willing to drop the issue and I was even more embarrassed when he suggested he was willing to pay any price I cared to. I asked him, "Why are you so eager about it?" and he answered, "See, the fiddler has seven fingers. Think what I could do with seven fingers!"

I should not leave out the dinner we had for the British Foreign Secretary at the time, George Brown. Earlier he had had a long talk with Abba in the study while people were demonstrating in the street outside about the civil war in Biafra. George Brown downed drink after drink and by the time he reached the dining-table he was absolutely plastered. He gradually became abusive to his Ambassador who simply got up from the table and ordered Mr Brown to follow him to the King David Hotel while Mrs Brown retired to the drawing room, sat on a sofa and cried. Of course there was a letter of apology the next day: the event and the apology were common features of George Brown's life.

We travelled frequently. In 1970 we went to Holland, Belgium and Luxembourg and although such trips were really hard work, I rarely enjoyed a visit more. The Dutch knew both our ancient and modern history and it was a relief not to have to explain things from the beginning. To our surprise there was even a Hebrew quotation in one of the official rooms in the Queen's palace. I still have a photo of our mission marching in, all of us with heads looking upwards to read the surprising inscription.

The Foreign Minister, Joseph Luns, was utterly charming as ever. While Abba had known him for a long time, it was different to meet him and the other officials in their own environment. Queen Juliana received us with great warmth, indeed the depth of sincerity of her feelings about the Jewish people was well known. The Dutch gave us a beautiful farewell at the station where we were seen off from the Queen's *Salon d'Honneur*, and Abba reviewed a Guard of Honour on the platform. We got on the train and stood in the doorway as if in a picture frame and, as the train glided out very slowly, everybody stood to attention while the Israeli national anthem, the *Hatikvah*, was played. It was a very beautiful moment and so different from ceremonies at airports. I was told that protocol demanded that the train must start to move before the *Hatikvah* is played – if the synchronization is faulty and the anthem starts one moment too early, then the train cannot move. A plane escorted our train to the Belgian frontier.

Our Belgium visit was also a success and of great political importance since Brussels is at the centre of the European Community. Notwithstanding the French opposition on the grounds that Israel was not geographically part of Europe, Abba's diplomacy and the European experts of our Ministry eventually succeeded in having Israel named an Associate of the European Union in November 1995. Abba was a great admirer of Jean Monnet, one of the unifiers of Europe. Mme Harmel, the wife of the Belgian Foreign Minister, Pierre Harmel, took me to visit the Institute Courbet at Ornans across the border in France. I found her a very warm and outgoing person, and within minutes we were great friends.

I believe I managed to uphold our "national honour" at the glamorous dinner the Foreign Ministry prepared for us. M and Mme Harmel headed one of the two long tables, and the other was co-hosted by the Senate President and his wife. The Senate President, who is next in rank after the King, sat next to me after dinner and remarked on what a beautiful dress I was wearing. It was my "White House" dress and when I thanked him for the compliment he added, "But you know, not everybody could wear it." Surprised, I said, "Do you really think so?" He paused a moment, then went on: "Well, not Mrs Meir, for instance." I was startled by this type of compliment, and replied by pointing to my head and saying that perhaps Mrs Meir had a few things there that

I lacked. He laughed and said, "I wondered how you would get out of that one."

The next morning I visited the Hebrew school in Brussels where the children in each class met me with a different sentence they had learned in Hebrew. Extremely moved, I then said a few words of greeting to the whole school.

Everywhere I went I was accompanied by two security guards, one from the country we visited and one from Israel. The fellow who looked after me in Belgium, although young, acted in a very paternal and protective manner, and I particularly remember one moment during a women's tea at the home of some well-known collector. I was going through three floors of art and paintings when suddenly on the top floor he spotted an open bathroom door, away from the crowd. Out of the blue he said to me, "Mrs Eban, this is your moment!"

As we left Brussels, British security officers got on our plane and our protection in London continued to be very tight until Abba left for Germany, the first visit made by an Israeli minister to that country. He was so reluctant to go and upset when he left. We decided not to make it the kind of social event we had in the two previous countries and Abba met his counter-parts to discuss restitution payments. Everything went without a hitch except for a threat made on his life. This turned out to be a false alarm, but because of it the Germans wouldn't allow him to visit the German-born Israeli actress Hanna Meron, still in hospital after losing a leg in the savage attack by the PLO at Munich Airport in 1970.

Abba called me every evening and I remember remarking how circumstances had changed; not long ago one German would have been able to kill hundreds of Jews whereas now, hundreds of them were watching over one Jew. During Abba's visit, the German translation of his book *My People* came out and I think that the presence of this book in that land was a further significant step along the road to reconciliation.

Busy with my daily occupations at home, I reflected how, in the preceding decades, many women had become Heads of Mission, entrusted with the top responsibility. They had gradually established a more progressive and egalitarian social concept regarding their own capabilities to serve in the Foreign Service. Although I felt that I *did* receive recognition for my part as wife of the Minister of Foreign Affairs, I knew a few wives of foreign diplomats and some in our own service who were unhappy that the work they put in to help their husbands' positions did not receive adequate recognition. On the other hand, regulations prevented them from taking on external jobs while on post. I was also surprised by the imbalance created by the fact that in all our official trips we encountered more women ministers, prime ministers and presidents in the world than director-generals of ministries. I think it is because a director-general is responsible to the minister *at all hours* of the day or night, especially during emergencies, and because he controls every department of the ministry, he sometimes cautiously and tactfully influences the minister as well.

Besides the problems of co-operation within the Ministry, there were always sensitivities about political loyalties of colleagues in the Diplomatic Service. The classic conflicts between the Ministry of Foreign Affairs and the Ministry of Defence, or even with the Prime Minister's office, had always existed and there was no guide for the perplexed. When state matters demanded specific internal positions, Abba sometimes wondered where some Foreign Ministry colleagues stood on the perceptions of *his* policy. For example, were they in favour of his views on not nationalizing *all* the territories but only stressing the need for corrective lines essential for security purposes? Where did they stand on the issues concerning the measure of a reprisal after a terrorist act, or when Israel was asked not to launch a reprisal at all, the reasoning usually given being concern for public opinion abroad? Had his colleagues' attachments landed their reasoning totally in the

Defence Ministry's conception, which at times leaned virtually to the right? Had there ever been an Israeli Foreign Minister who had not experienced this tension between the Foreign and Defence ministries? Abba and I discussed these internal political features when we were alone, as well as the way they sometimes affected personal relationships with colleagues.

Living at close range with many of the pressures and the balancing of power as I have, I think that the wife of a politician is the one with whom, after consulting with his immediate colleagues, he will often share his feelings and worries with no inhibitions. It is an undefined role but it has its existential space in the couple's relationship and their work.

Understanding ahead of his time the necessities of creating a professional workforce if one was to create a new state, Abba had written a memorandum in 1944, in a Palestine still at war and still under British Mandate, about the new concept of a Jewish diplomat. This document encompassed a fresh challenge: how would we function on the world scene in Zionism fulfilled? If hard physical labour and working the land was a new constituent of the personality and make-up of the Jews in Zionist Palestine, for Abba, the young exponent of the new Zionist diplomacy, its spirit and purpose had to be recreated in a no less innovative way. The old ad-hoc representation would have to make way for a new individual with a new configuration of his personality. He would have to be knowledgeable in his sovereign country's issues, in the history and politics of the area and in foreign languages; that is he would have to be *professionally* equipped in the representation of his people: the Zionist diplomat later to become the Israeli diplomat.

In the relatively short history of our Ministry of Foreign Affairs, I remember the various Director-Generals, from the first, German-born, Oxford-educated Walter Eytan, who responded to Sharett's vision of a school for training diplomats in the service of a Jewish State, even before there was a State. This school was established in the framework of the Jewish Agency, the dedicated political body that represented our people during the British Mandate.

Walter Eytan was extremely selective in creating the infrastructure and function of the Ministry. Everything was so new – from UN sponsorship and the technicalities of the Armistice Agreements after the War of Independence, to the fact that we had never negotiated except with the British government and the Arabs of Palestine. Together with Yigal Yadin who was to take over as Chief of Staff from Yaakov Dori on 9 November 1949, Walter Eytan led the Israeli delegation to Armistice Talks on the island of Rhodes. Besides UN sponsorship there was another novelty: an American mediator, Dr Ralph Bunche with whom Abba had worked in his early days at the UN.

When Abba succeeded Golda Meir as Foreign Minister, he inherited her Director-General, Arye Levavi, the perfect civil servant. Levavi kept a balanced view of political events and was less emotional than Golda. Abba appreciated Levavi's loyal co-operation. Levavi watched both the world and domestic press reports, searching for repercussions relating to Israel's foreign affairs. During the Six Day War, Levavi lined up his cautious self against the desperate decisions demanded at that time and oversaw the daily running of the Ministry. He resigned after the war.

The third Director-General and Abba's choice in 1969, Gideon Rafael, originally from Germany, was a dynamic man. He immigrated to what was then Palestine with Youth Aliyah, and became part of Moshe Sharett's team in the Jewish Agency. Able, hard working and well-seasoned in diplomatic and intelligence matters, Gideon very strongly coveted the position of Director-General under Abba. With no academic training but rather an innate political ability, Gideon was both constructive and manipulative, and quickly established a strictly centralized regime which was too personalized for the liking of many. Everything and everybody had to go through him first. In the daily running of the departments he blocked direct access of heads of department to the Foreign Minister. His method was useful as a time-saver for the Minister but it created a certain resentment of him in the Ministry. Gideon, set on power, did not care.

As a way of sifting the extremely urgent from the "only" vital, Abba found the shield of a Director-General useful and the system efficiently centralized. A Director-General could contribute his own expertise and thinking on specific matters, make suggestions, test possibilities and feel free and welcome to do so.

In the elections held after the Yom Kippur War, on 31 December 1973, Labour just managed to retain power but the real "protest" election came in 1977, the second after the disastrous Yom Kippur War. Menachem Begin's Herut/Likud Party finally defeated Mapai, part of the Labour Alliance (Ma'arach), which had been in office continuously since 1948. Moshe Dayan took the meagre two mandates on which his newly created party had won and crossed over to Begin's party, thus becoming the new Foreign Minister. Of course many of us were shocked, and Dayan dealt with the pressures from his immediate colleagues by doing away with the Minister's weekly consultation with heads of department. In the Ministry's ranks it was thought that Abba's system had been better after all. On the other hand, Dayan and Abba had a similar view about posting troops ten kilometres from the Suez Canal.

These were now discussed again after the country's complete surprise at a self-serving Foreign Minister who orchestrated his act under the permissiveness of "charisma". But had this mutual view prevailed prior to the Yom Kippur War, it could have done much to save lives. The Israeli public is well seasoned politically; they sense the personal game and relish it, aware of all the tensions and rivalries that sit heavily in those top government offices, make news and have their influence on national policy.

Then it inevitably falls into the hands of the press, sometimes dramatically magnified. In one of these periodic office shifts of senior diplomats, Gideon Rafael was nominated Ambassador to the United Kingdom in January 1974.

23

The Yom Kippur War and its repercussions

It was the spring of 1973. The Independence Day military parade was once more scheduled to be in Jerusalem. Our tickets indicated that we would sit in the official grandstand together with the President, the Prime Minister Golda Meir, other members of the cabinet, the Chief of Staff and high-ranking officers. The Supreme Court justices, dignitaries from the various religions, Knesset Members and members of the Diplomatic Corps also filled the stand. It was the style, even in the official section to look "picnicky". Men came with open shirts; some opted for a white handkerchief flattened on their head – tied with a little knot in each corner. It was a touch of local colour taken from Arab folklore, absorbed in good heart and spirit. The women wore scarves as a protection from the mid-day sun, sensible shoes with flat heels, and cotton dresses.

As we were entitled to take two guests to the parade, I had invited the sculptor George Segal and his wife Helen: he had been creating the "Sacrifice of Isaac" for the Tel Aviv Foundation for the Arts. The neat soldiers aligned to perfection along Jaffa Road kept their martial pace amidst the rhythmic applause of the crowd. The Holy City was one ribbon of music and fluttering flags. The military units – army, air force, navy, and the women's corps – marched by to the rolling sound of clapping. The clatter of tank chains on the road gave rise to even more demonstrative emotion. Because the parade took place in Jerusalem, it was not accompanied by the usual fly-past. Afterwards, numerous empty "gazoz" (fizzy drink) bottles, by then as hot as the earth, had to be kicked aside in order to get through the crowds. We returned to our Jerusalem home, faces puffy and flushed from hours in the sun.

This was to be the last Independence Day military parade; they were discontinued after the Yom Kippur War which was to have a profound and traumatic effect on the entire nation. Some years later I reflected sadly on how we all missed the buoyancy and pride of those years between 1967 and 1973, with the army band almost totally capturing the national mood.

The key to understanding the impact of that war is the fact that it caught Israel unawares. Despite clear signs on both the Egyptian and Syrian fronts that something was afoot, the intelligence services and political echelon were labouring under several fixed concepts: they were sure the Syrians would not go to war without the Egyptians, and no less certain that the latter would hold off an attack until the Russians had supplied them with upgraded fighter planes and offensive missiles. So strongly entrenched were these assumptions that no evidence on the ground could budge the assessment of the head of Military Intelligence – and the Defence Minister – that Israel would not be attacked, even hours before the war was launched.

So, at the source lies the fact that the political leadership and the people were misled by analyses from both the American and Israeli intelligence agencies that failed to draw the proper conclusions, even though they picked up repeated signs of a build-up on both the Egyptian and Syrian fronts. Israeli intelligence advisers in the army, Mossad and the Foreign Ministry had stated that there would be no threat of war for at least the next five years! There had been several false alarms defined as enemy "manoeuvres" but nothing serious ever emerged from them.

Israel knew the US would not tolerate a pre-emptive attack on Israel's part, in addition to its inability to properly read the movements on the other side because of the "konseptzia" – the belief that after the Six Day War, Arab states would never attack. Egypt's President, Anwar Sadat, had given clear signs that he would go to war to regain lost territory, and Jordan's King Hussein had explicitly warned Golda Meir of the coming Syrian attack. Dado, the Chief of Staff, asked for permission for a pre-emptive strike, and was turned down but given the OK only for a partial call-up of reserves.

The country was preparing itself for Yom Kippur, the Day of Atonement, the holiest of holy days in Judaism. This is the only day in Israel when the country completely shuts down, with even radio stations going off the air, and the streets – at least in Jewish towns and neighbourhoods – completely emptying of any traffic. At two o'clock in the afternoon of 6 October, the Day of Atonement, to everybody's surprise the air-raid sirens – the war alarm – were sounded throughout the whole, immobile country. People rushed out of their synagogues in the middle of prayer and hurried home. There was an emergency national call-up of all units and even those not called up rushed to their bases to volunteer.

At that time Abba, as Foreign Minister, and I were in New York for the opening of the UN General Assembly for which we had set out in mid-September. Henry Kissinger, who on 22 September had just been appointed Secretary of State after serving as President Richard Nixon's National Security Adviser, had talked to Abba before Yom Kippur to check the information each one had had from their own Intelligence about the northern frontier of Israel and the Suez Canal zone. Neither had received anything threatening about the situation and this seemed reassuring for the coming day of prayer and contemplation.

A few days before, we had been invited to an elegant party given by Henry Kissinger's friends at New York's Metropolitan Museum in honour of his recent appointment. Henry had asked Abba to sit with his parents which was not a diplomatic choice but an emotional one. Little did we realize then that Abba and Henry would so soon be spending many days and nights consulting on the fearful emergencies of the Yom Kippur War, called the October War by the Arabs. Abba would later describe 1973 in his autobiography as the "Year of Wrath". Indeed the latter part of that year would be packed with immediate dangers at every military and political turn.

On the Day of Atonement we were on our feet very early as Eytan Bentsur, Abba's political adviser, had already woken us up at 5 a.m. New York time with the alarming news. We were shocked and anxious as hell! The sudden outbreak of war and the initial terrible losses we sustained had the country in shock. Mount Hermon was covered in snow and freezing cold at night, the battle for the Mount was sheer confusion and all efforts proved hopeless. There had been no general call-up, no command was operating, and the result was a massive slaughter of Israeli soldiers. Mount Hermon's peak is known by Israelis as "the eyes of our country" because of its exceptional strategic value but to this day the incredible human cost in putting the national flag on that peak is remembered: that single act was carried out by a lone fisherman.

Nearly a week into the war, President Nixon gave the authorization and Kissinger began to apply pressure on a Pentagon that was in no hurry to help. Massive American military aid was flown into Israel, we soon regained the upper hand on both fronts and the tables were turned. Israel pushed the Syrians, who had come close to over-running the border of the Golan Heights, back out of the Heights, and on the southern front, Israel recrossed the Suez Canal under Ariel Sharon's command and entered Egypt proper.

At that point, Henry Kissinger was called urgently to Moscow by Premier Kosygin, on behalf of the Egyptians, for talks meant to bring about a cease-fire. The Egyptians were now the hard-pressed party. Golda Meir and Abba were both surprised and offended when they learnt that Henry Kissinger had rushed to Moscow at Kosygin's request. For his own reasons Kissinger had not troubled to inform them of that move: he was not going to miss the opportunity – a Russian SOS to the supreme USA! He had moved from the Middle Eastern scene to world politics and had seized the occasion to strengthen irreversibly the fact that American power in the Middle East was *the* major power.

Abba was called home by Golda Meir for consultations. In 1967 we had obtained a cease-fire with no political conditions attached, but now, in 1973, we knew there *had* to be political conditions. We returned to a blacked-out Israel: lights in the streets were dimmed and shop windows were darkened. All windows were once more pasted in a criss-cross manner with sealing tape. No able-bodied men were to be seen anywhere: they were all at the front or at their army bases. The country, its energy limp and its soul traumatized, would take months to recuperate.

Immediately after our return, I went to visit the wounded at the Hadassah Municipal Hospital in Tel Aviv (although the name is similar to Hadassah Jerusalem, there is no connection between the two hospitals). I was taken to three departments: eyes, orthopaedic and the surgical unit, which had taken the extreme cases, especially burns. In the latter ward the boys had oily, black, cakey faces out of which stared pairs of completely red eyes. The edges of the burnt skin were raw and blood had caked in the contour of these shapes. The scene was like a frightening dream and, in my heart, I wondered what I would say to them but as I got near the bed of each one, they were willing to talk and this made me feel honoured. I made notes on my visit and here is the story of three of the young men.

Danny was a twenty-one-year-old tank operator from Ashdod. "I fasted like everybody else on Yom Kippur. At 3 p.m. I was told to go to the Canal. [In their slang, the soldiers called it "the Suez".] The Egyptians had already crossed to our side. Rockets and bazookas were flying over us like ants. My commander's tank sunk in a swamp. I went to help him and I myself was suddenly hit by a shell. The heat of it was 250 degrees. I felt I was being cooked. My crew cooked too. They could not jump out of the tank because the fire caught them. The next thing I knew I managed to jump out; I rolled around in the sand, and the sand put out the fire that was all over me. The commander and I started running. We ran four kilometres, wounded as we were, to a tank, and the commander ordered the tank to take us to a front-line hospital." Danny continued in a whisper, "We almost all died." He began to cry and then he pulled himself together and said, "We must not break down." He paused and added quietly: "It is hard to absorb what happened."

Matanya was a nineteen-year-old from Kibbutz Yavne. His name translated literally means "God's gift". He came from a religious family and I later met his father, a noble and dignified man, who was then a lecturer in education at Bar Ilan University. "We were all fasting when we were told to rush and put our equipment in our tanks. At 1.50 p.m. we were shelled. MiGs, Sukhois, everything seemed suddenly there, coming from the East. Six of my group was killed. I saw the Egyptian infantry crossing the Canal. We had two dead from our kibbutz. I am a gunner. I got flames in my face and on both legs. I could not leave till the others left – that is the rule. So I left last, then I rolled in the sand and that stopped the burning. Then I was evacuated." I asked the boy next to Matanya who was also burned over large parts of his body if Matanya ever screamed. Matanya answered: "I never screamed, I only felt terribly swollen, as if I was getting bigger all the time. Apparently this is how it is with burns. They swell terribly at first."

I asked Matanya's father, "When did you get the news of your son's injury?" He answered: "This happened on the second day of the war." His son was wounded at 4 p.m., and the telephone call came at 8.45 p.m. The father remembered the time, because it was just before the 9 o'clock news. The parents were with Matanya at 10 p.m. He mentioned the speed of contact between the families and the front. The boy was black from the fire but he was conscious. The father said: "To feel what he must have been through, just put your finger in boiling water." He had four sons, all grown up. One boy had fought in the Six Day War and survived. Three boys were then in tank units. "We are a family like that," he added. "All the boys worked on tractors in the kibbutz, which means they had a feeling for the machine – are familiar with it." The story of this family has many facets of the overall Israeli reality: the full-fledged dedication, the working of the land and the defending of the land by the same people.

In one ward I was at first very badly received by one of the wounded who was carrying on in great grumbling fits which I could hear across the room: "What do you mean! It is not visiting hours. So you let in the wife of a minister and you don't let in my girlfriend!" I did not know at first how to handle these remarks but by the time I had finished talking to everyone in the ward, he was the one who now protested loudly that I had not yet come to see him, which I was on the way to do, and we had a friendly conversation.

In Moscow, Kissinger and Kosygin had begun to negotiate a cease-fire on the Egyptian front which we didn't want to be implemented too soon, since our position had improved so much. Then, to our surprise, Kissinger closed matters with the Russians without consulting us once more. We were, to say the least, shocked at his high-handed manner towards us but soon realized that the contents of the cease-fire were better than we had thought. Israel was, in fact, occupying a territorial position beyond the limits she had held before the war. Politically, too, we had achieved what we had been seeking for many years – Arab acceptance of the principle of negotiation.

I remember vividly the issue and the encirclement of the Egyptian Third Army in the days following 19 October. There were endless private conversations throughout the nation about Israel occupying the "Land of Goshen" – the biblical name for Egypt. One felt as if we had completed a circle: from leaving slavery in Egypt 3500 years ago to returning as conquerors!

After our military situation had changed spectacularly for the better, were we to keep them encircled or not? There were many discussions in government and in homes too on the subject. The Egyptians would be defeated on this second round and would be starving. There were some in our leadership wanting to maintain the siege, which would give Israel a hundred kilometre open road to Cairo. But reason prevailed: the human cost to us was estimated at a thousand men or more and the government wisely demurred. Humiliating Egypt would not necessarily work in our favour. Besides, what would we do with masses of newly captured prisoners who would need to be fed and cared for? Israel seems always to run into these kinds of humanitarian dilemmas. She might win but that does not necessarily mean that she can dictate the terms of peace.

The Yom Kippur War lasted a total of twenty-three days. One hundred planes were lost and 800 tanks were destroyed. The cost in Israeli life was staggering: 2,701 died, 7,500 were wounded and 300 Israeli soldiers were taken prisoners of war. The country had never before seen such a massive and upsetting spectacle as our prisoners, blindfolded, with their hands tied above their head.

The political scene and the negotiations were becoming important and the referral to United Nations Security Council Resolution 242 (Territories for Peace) which had followed the Six Day War, and its reinforcement by the joint American-Soviet sponsored Resolution 338 were brought to the fore. This resolution included a cease-fire which was declared on 22 October. The trauma of the war's initial onslaught and the drama of Israel's miraculous recovery would next be followed by a peace conference in Geneva on 22 and 23 December at Foreign Minister level. Though the conference was initiated by Kissinger with Moscow's agreement to attend, it was officially held under the auspices of the United Nations.

Abba set in train the government's acceptance for the Foreign Minister to represent Israel. I was so fascinated by the thought of so many enemies coming to sit together to *try* and make peace that I could not resist joining the group. Even though we were well used to constant security measures, those facing us in Geneva were quite incredible. In our hotel room, the curtains were drawn over the windows during the day, and every couple of hours our terrace was filled with armed Swiss soldiers.

At the conference itself at the Palais des Nations, when the delegates had to take their places around the hexagonal table, the Egyptian delegate refused to sit next to Abba. Everybody was in a flap. My husband said that this was intolerable since the gathering was meant to be a peace conference, and if this absurdity was not solved, he would simply go back home. Officials scrambled frantically to and fro and tried to redo the seating arrangements. Someone from our delegation even came up to me and said facetiously, "You have been a hostess so many years, try your hand at this one!" The difficulty was resolved by placing a major power between Israel and Egypt.

The conference discussed the proposed cease-fire "in place" without going into details. The main point of contention was the disengagement agreement that was being negotiated at the military level at what was known as "Kilometre 101" on the Suez–Cairo highway. This was led on our part by Colonel Aharon Yariv, former head of Military Intelligence and at the time appointed assistant to the Chief of Staff, but it was now moving to the political level where it might have a more realistic chance.

Now that disengagement cease-fire talks had also moved to the political level, Egypt escaped the encirclement of its Third Army. Israel, co-ordinating with the USA, was against leaving a political void in the area between the war and the forthcoming Israeli elections. The conference adjourned on its second day, by pre-arrangement, and the disengagement talks went back to the military level at Kilometre 101. Diplomacy always abhors a vacuum! Abba was encouraged that things had moved on and thought those at home would have renewed spirit and help the much-criticized government of Golda Meir and the Minister of Defence, Moshe Dayan, to regain its strength.

We returned home to the restlessness of a country that was slow to pick up momentum. There continued to be much discontent about the way we were taken by surprise and were unprepared for the sudden assault by the Egyptians and Syrians. There was anger and many demonstrations in front of Golda's residence and the newspapers and television were the daily stage for voicing the hurt and resentment of the people. Motti Ashkenazi, an army officer who had survived the traumatic experience of the Egyptian attack on the Israeli bunkers lining the Suez Canal, began a silent demonstration, camping out in front of the Prime Minister's office in Jerusalem or in front of her home, holding up a poster with accusing slogans demanding her resignation. Other veterans of the war joined him in solidarity. The impact reminded me of Chinese water torture.

Golda's conscience gave her no respite although she handled the war reasonably well. She became less suspicious of Kissinger who had the ambition to transcend the regional conflict and transfer the situation in the Middle East to the auspices of the two Big Powers. To save Israel, the USA was versus the USSR in the Yom Kippur War but in Geneva the USSR and the USA coalesced to save Egypt! Golda had leaned heavily on Moshe Dayan's judgement prior to the war and was distraught that he had misadvised her, causing such a catastrophe. Moshe Dayan was, of course, also criticized for not preparing the armed forces for the contingency of war and for opposing the Chief of Staff, General Davis (Dado) Elazar's request for full mobilization. Following public demand, a Government Inquiry Commission headed by the President of the Supreme Court, Judge Shimon Agranat, was established.

Although the Commission exonerated her, Golda began to realize that she could not hold on to power anymore. She submitted to the growing domestic pressures and resigned in April 1974. Moshe Dayan was forced to resign from his post as Minister of Defence three months later. When the Prime Minister resigns the whole cabinet follows and here we had both the Prime Minister and Minister of Defence resigning – this called for an election. In Israel when a government resigns, by law it is given three months' grace and continues to operate until a new government is sworn in. For us it meant that until the outcome of the elections, Abba was still Minister of Foreign Affairs.

Golda had never made the slightest move in Abba's direction. She had openly concluded that she did not like his policy of actively seeking peace with the Arabs, for "After all," she had said once, "who are the Palestinians? There are no such people." Having decided that she would circumvent her Foreign Minister Abba's influence, the question remained: How? Her answer was that there would now be at each major Israeli embassy, two heads of information and desks, one from the Prime Minister's office and one from the Ministry of Foreign Affairs. Abba had violently opposed the idea and said that the Minister and Director-General should decide about an embassy's head of information from within the staff of the Ministry. He called Pinhas Sapir, the Finance Minister, at midnight and said he would resign the next morning if such a chaotic, insulting and incredibly costly duplication would come about. Sapir immediately called Golda saying that Abba was firm about his decision and the next morning at breakfast, she sent Abba a message: "Although I acquiesce now, it does not mean that I won't have my reckoning some time."

Now the question was who would head our party's list for the coming elections? Mapai, still the majority of the Labour Party, continued to hope for a candidate to come from within its ranks. There were people, among them Eytan Bentsur, diplomat and son of a diplomat in our Foreign Service, who wanted Abba to run. Abba's own separate group within Mapai included a young Amir Peretz, who would years later become head of Histadrut and eventually head of the Labour Party and Minister of Defence at the time of the Second Lebanese War in the summer of 2006. An able and ambitious politician himself, his assignments were not exactly Israel's finest hours.

Abba's loyalists believed he could get twenty per cent of Mapai, but Abba felt that it would not be enough to change the situation. Eytan, on the other hand, thought in terms of the main characteristic of Israeli politics, where so many small parties exercise the balance of power. He felt that Abba could have a bargaining position, but my husband did not want to play that kind of hand. Abba admitted later that he had made a mistake.

Mapai was left with two possible candidates to lead it. The Mayor of Tel Aviv, Yehoshua Rabinovitch, although an excellent mayor, was silently judged as not being sufficiently charismatic for the role. There was now only one other possibility: Pinhas Sapir.

Abba had asked the dynamic Sapir, the power in our party, several times to declare himself a candidate for Prime Minister but he always refused. Abba considered him to be such a creative force and achiever, building and implementing, indefatigable, and with no other interest besides adding to the strengthening of the infrastructure of the country. Sapir and Abba had the same view on international affairs – he knew who the Palestinians were – and Abba hoped that, as with Levi Eshkol, he would be left to pursue foreign affairs.

Everything was still uncertain, when one afternoon I met Sapir at the inauguration of the Sir Charles Clore Garden, on the hill opposite the Knesset. As we walked down the steps together, Sapir suddenly pointed and waved his index finger in a threatening manner in front of my face and said: "Tell him [Abba] not to submit his candidacy." I reported this to Abba and added my own interpretation that either Sapir thought that if he pulled Abba away, which Golda seemed to want, she might reconsider her resignation and save Mapai, or he might have thought it over and perhaps, after all, wanted to be the candidate. Abba himself was keen to continue as the Minister of Foreign Affairs, which people recognized as his forte.

Achdut Ha'Avoda and Rafi, two small independent left-wing parties, had merged with the dominant Mapai Party to form a new entity, the Israel Labour Party (ILP), in January 1968 and were now building up their power within the ILP. If I had to describe the members of Achdut Ha'Avoda, I would define them as a kind of sect, purists of the old Labour values but not averse to personal, self-prompting tactics. Our close friend, Arye Tzimuki, political journalist for *Yedioth Ahronoth*, the largest circulation Israeli newspaper, was an habitué of our home. His two daughters were Gila's great friends and they came in and out of our home even more frequently than their father. Arye, who was close to the Achdut Ha'Avoda leadership, assured Abba that he would remain Foreign Minister after the coming elections. It was not long before we found out that, for the sake of his own party loyalty – and certainly not on the basis of international policy – he had misled us.

A day or so later, at a cabinet meeting, Abba passed a note to Yigal Allon saying that he had heard a rumour that he, Allon, was the Achdut Ha'Avoda candidate for the post of Minister of Foreign Affairs. Allon firmly denied this but, notwithstanding his denial, Allon's next move was to demand to be concurrently the Foreign Minister and the Deputy Prime Minister. Abba, in a fall-back position, had asked to be the Deputy Prime Minister and was later to say to the press that Allon and Achdut Ha'Avoda "had closed" not only the door but also the window to him!

Achdut Ha'Avoda, till then a faction of the Labour Movement, became a very strong factor under the leadership of two generals – Yigal Allon and Yitzhak Rabin – as the country prepared itself for elections. Golda, who had worked all her life for Mapai, was now so embittered by past events that she decided to change camp and, on the advice of her long-term friend, Israel Galili, the leader of Achdut Ha'Avoda, she selected Yitzhak Rabin as head of the Labour Party which won the election. Rabin appointed Yigal Allon the new Foreign Minister of Israel. Abba requested to be Deputy Prime Minister – a position that would mean he would still have a place in the cabinet. Both Rabin and Allon opposed this – not on any matter of policy. It was a spectacular sell-out of the old Mapai structure and dominance. The two generals had connived to kill the goose that had laid the golden egg.

I wondered in my heart, was it jealousy? Was it sheer headiness at the approach of power? Abba and I felt he could have continued to be a valuable figure on the international scene in his – admitted by many – own irreplaceable style. I leave it all to historical interpretation and will only add that party pride and collegiality had reached murky waters. Perhaps mine is not the most gracious way of accepting defeat, and yet why should I, when speaking now for Abba who has gone from us, dismiss a gross abandonment and add a congratulatory smile to the two generals' achievement when it was not occasioned by any political failure? All the more so because they were going to play their international cards about the territories in the same spirit as the one initiated by Abba.

And how wrong I was in my interpretation of Sapir's reprimand! Little did we guess that he, Sapir, was going to sell out the Party we had all worked for together with such single-minded devotion since the founding of the State. I have often thought that if Abba had been at the Charles Clore ceremony, he might have picked an argument with Sapir. On the morning of the nomination, Sapir announced that he was going to move his support away from his own party Mapai and vote for Rabin and the smaller Labour faction of Achdut Ha'Avoda. Dov Ben-Meir, whom I knew very well from his days as Director-General of the Israel Cancer Association where he had worked with me, had left the Association to become deputy Mayor of Tel Aviv on the Mapai ticket. On election day he had taken Sapir in his car to the convention and told me later that when he'd said to Sapir, "You are abandoning your loyal supporter Eban," Sapir shrugged his shoulders and said, "I don't owe him anything!" He was fulfilling Golda's wish. Sapir, the maker and breaker of men in the Mapai Party, had sensed her opposition to Abba.

That evening there came to my mind what she had written on her tiny folded piece of paper in her angular Hebrew writing about her appointments of a second director of information in each major embassy: "Although I acquiesce now, it does not mean that I won't have my reckoning some time."

24

Ismailia revisited

On Christmas Day 1977, I was part of the first Israeli Peace Mission to Egypt – to Ismailia, where I was born. Four days before, I had no suspicion of what was to happen. On an El Al flight from London to Tel Aviv, Abba and I had travelled with the Prime Minister, Menachem Begin, who was returning home from his talks earlier that month with President Jimmy Carter. Begin and Abba were deep in political conversation when suddenly the Prime Minister turned towards me and said, "You were born in Ismailia. Wouldn't you like to see it again?" "Of course," I answered: I was to be the first Israeli woman to land on Egyptian soil.

Thirty years of disconnection from Egypt vanished overnight. The implacable inaccessibility of the land of my birth to me and in fact to *any* Israeli since the 1948 war, was over. I was stunned by my unexpected good fortune. After all, as a Labour Party Member of the Knesset, Abba belonged to Menachem Begin's opposition. Herein lay both the subtlety and the generosity of the gesture.

Four days later, I was off, one of the Peace Mission's twenty-nine members, my coat bearing an Israeli identification tag like a luggage label with my name in Hebrew lettering, detailing the journey from the airport at Lod to the Egyptian military base at Abu Suweir. Next to it I wore an Egyptian tag in Arabic to identify me at Abu Suweir, when along with the other Egyptian and Israeli mission members, I would step into one of the four Egyptian helicopters that would pick us up and carry our group

off to work together for the next day and a half: we were all
dropping the ballast of enmity from our lives. I crossed two
alphabets and two regions in the span of a takeoff and what
seemed an almost immediate landing, some forty minutes later.

As we came down, amid clouds of ochre sand churned up by
the jet's engines, I realized that I had not had adequate time aboard
the aircraft to survey the full length of the receiving line at Abu
Suweir. There were effusive handshakes and smiles from the army
brass, cabinet members, and diplomats who knew one another
through the press and television and from past polemics across the
frontier and on the world stage. When the firm asphalt of the
runway was beneath my feet, I caught sight of a female silhouette.
Above the tweed coat and the black fur collar was a woman's
smile. I recognized Aziza Hussein, my friend from the American
University in Cairo, who I had run into some ten years later in
Washington when her husband, Ahmed, was the Egyptian
Ambassador to the United States, mine his Israeli counterpart, and
our countries enemies. Now, in Ismailia, I gasped at the thoughtful
planning that had achieved, at such short notice, the nearest
possible simple human contact. Everybody was calling her Dr
Aziza.

We were driven to President Sadat's residence in Ismailia and
soon found ourselves escaping the assault of the world mass media
on the two eminent peacemakers, knowing that they would be
sitting for hours around the dark mahogany table I had glimpsed,
with its orderly row of green leather-bound memo pads crested
with the golden eagle of the Egyptian Republic and bearing a
blue repeat of the crest on every page. A young chamberlain, Rauf
Abdin, with a decoration on his lapel which turned out to be from
Togo, came to introduce himself in English and say that – among
other concerns – he was in charge of my visit. Did I have any
special wishes? In view of the security problems, I thought I had
better limit my touring to a minimum, and so my requests were
quite modest. "Yes," I said, "I would like to see the house in which

I was raised until my teenage years, and I would like twenty postcards to send to my friends, mostly in America." Obviously, I could not yet send any to Israel, though I was right across the water. I also wanted to buy some Egyptian stamps. Abdin said that he would see to everything on my return from a small rest house on Lake Timsah, a few miles along the Canal, where Aziza was taking me next.

We passed through a grove of tall eucalyptus-like trees with furry leaves that gave the light a greenish hue. I was back once more in Ismailia's Bois de Boulogne. I was reminded of a stage set: trees and huge posters of Sadat, sometimes in uniform, sometimes in civilian clothes, were placed at optically interesting angles. These extended into the deeper parts of the grove, just as sounds on the stage would have echoes. It was as if that world were all his and the next act of the play would be a monologue.

The rest house was an old hunting lodge from French-colonial days. Aziza and I sat on a flagstone terrace at the edge of the water, listening to each other and the lapping waves. I was cold in the sun so we wore our coats and were offered, alternately small glasses of guava juice and hot Turkish coffee. Only two days before, she said, she had been sitting at the Mena House Hotel, near the Pyramids, where the small Israeli Preparatory Mission for the Ismailia conference was staying. She had been told by Egyptian friends that all over Cairo everybody was talking about the Israelis. Could somebody point out the Israelis? I felt as if we were from some other planet.

And then she had been asked to come to Ismailia to meet me. There was perfect symmetry between her situation and mine in the surprise and speed of adjustment. There she was, among members of her government and ours; and we were both touching history. Although I am Jewish and she is Muslim, we had both had a convent education as our primary schooling. We compared notes about ourselves, our friends, our teachers – some now dead – our people, our countries. The orbit was becoming broader – very different from that time in Washington when she had introduced me apprehensively to her husband and I introduced her to mine, and we settled for small talk.

I asked Aziza about her title of "Doctor," and she said that as President of the Egyptian Family Planning Association in Cairo, a voluntary agency made up of many doctors, the people now called her "Doctor" as well. She found it amusing. She had done field work with volunteers in the village of Saindyoun, starting with child care and going on to mother care, at which stage one could talk to some of the women about the spacing of births. The government had 2,400 family-planning clinics. Her agency complemented them, and she worked closely with Jihan Sadat, the President's wife. The birthrate had recently come down by six per cent and if the trend could be continued, she said, they would know they were on the right track to solving Egypt's greatest problem, the population explosion.

Take Cairo, which then had a population of nine million. Unless there were both birth control and population diffusion, it would be a monstrous city of twenty-two million by the year 2000. Sadat himself had used these statistics in conversation with Begin. Aziza was also President of the Central Council of the International Planned Parenthood Federation, chosen from ninety-one countries. She told me about her work for the United Nations Commission on the Status of Women from 1962 to 1976, and I talked about my involvement with the Israel Cancer Association. We were both involved with fateful modern issues. There were moments of silence which the gentle lapping of the waves helped to ease; although we had been given an international all-clear for uninhibited talk, it seemed that Aziza and I needed to follow our own inner timing in order to recapture a true harmony. The reversal had happened too quickly, too suddenly – too much like some unbelievable caprice of the mind.

A huge, grey dredger was anchored along the east bank of the

Canal, and on the horizon I again saw the two slabs of the First World War Memorial of Djebel Mariam where my sisters and I had played. At the point where the Canal enters Lake Timsah, we noticed a ship's upper deck and black funnel gliding behind the sand dunes and as it slowly emerged into view, I found myself in a discourse from the past: "Here is the motor launch that will bring the pilot to the ship for the Canal transit from Ismailia to Suez." The workings of the Suez Canal traffic, which took two shifts of pilots over the fifteen-hour trip from Port Said to Suez, suddenly became familiar again. The headquarters of the old Canal Company – now called the Authority – had always been at Ismailia. They used to be in a one-storey building separated by a large lawn from Quai Muhammad Ali, and adorned with a band of elaborate gingerbread carving under the roof and on its supporting wooden pillars. I noticed that after all that time, half of the Suez Canal personnel's houses were still painted beige and terra-cotta as I had known them in my childhood, and the other half in a more recent pale green and white. The administration staff are housed in a modern, eleven-storey cube with a perfectly flush exterior and what seems to be a glass-cage observatory on top. The staff who used to be entirely European, mostly French, was now Egyptian. I reflected that this was the most decisive political achievement in Egypt since Nasser nationalized the Suez Canal in July 1956. The Canal must "for sure" – to use Sadat's favourite expression – have undergone substantial dredging and deepening to accommodate such great tonnages. When I was a child, a 20,000 ton ship sailing through the Canal was a big event and much talked about in the town.

So many details now seemed to come into my view, faster than memory could corroborate. I was embarrassed to ask, to compare, to be nostalgic and to talk of the time my father was the consulting engineer to the Dutch company, P. Bos, of Dordrecht, that then carried out the dredging. I knew it would seem funny if in the midst of all the political tumult I now asked to see the power station put up for the Canal by a Swiss company with which my father had been associated, or the Al-Ahram electric-bulb factory, created by the same company.

In fact, my mention of the company's name was now greeted with a blank expression. People here were concerned with politics and not with nostalgia, although I remembered the company as having been one attempt to create an indigenous Egyptian industry for Egypt's own market. In retrospect, it seems odd that before the Second World War, the British, instead of encouraging exports, persuaded the Egyptians to levy export duties on locally manufactured products (my father carried out endless experiments and one was to bring the local sand to a very high temperature in a platinum cup to check its suitability for the making of glass.) Now the Canal traffic averaged sixty ships a day, with a maximum of eighty-seven. These and other bits of local colour I learned from a bright-yellow leaflet put out by the Canal Authority.

As we talked, Aziza remarked that for security reasons the area of the Canal around Ismailia would be closed to small ships that night. The precautions taken to protect us were stringent, but I would never have thought of that, though it made perfect sense. All that would be needed was one little rocket aimed at the city from a passing ship. I was surprised at my own surprise, because I thought I knew a good deal about security rules.

At about one o'clock, Aziza and I went back to President Sadat's residence for lunch: it was not only Christmas Day, but also Sadat's birthday. There were nineteen of us, Israelis and Egyptians intermingled along the sides of a long table, while Begin and Sadat faced each other across the centre. Sadat had Vice-President Hosni Mubarak on his right and Prime Minister Mamdouh Salem on his left; the Israeli Minister of Defence, Ezer Weizman, sat next to the Vice-President. Begin, opposite, had Moshe Dayan on his right and General Muhammad Gamazzi, the Egyptian Minister of War, on his left. I sat next to Gamazzi; on my left was the outgoing Egyptian Foreign Minister, Boutros Boutros-Ghali, an erudite member of the minority group of Copts, who had become a Minister of State following his term of office as Secretary-General of the UN. Weizman was elegant down to his blue tie of soft silk, Gamazzi, in uniform, wore his medals. They had a forthright style, as befits the military. The diplomats had to be different, certainly not so direct. On the walls, framed photographs of Sadat were interspersed with ornamentally illuminated verses of the Koran. The lunch was excellent; fish, meat, stuffed vine leaves, dessert and fruit served on china crested in gold over dark green. Sadat, who ate only one meal a day, did not touch any food. The toasts were made with orange juice: first came Begin's birthday toast to Sadat, right at the start of the meal. For a few moments, we could not grasp why he should start the proceedings, but as soon as he mentioned the birthday, all became clear. The more formal toasts came towards the end of the meal, when Sadat stated that this was the happiest day of his life.

The footmen wore black suits and white gloves. When I later asked Abdin, the young chamberlain, if it was no longer the custom for those in attendance in the household to wear the white *ghallabiyehs* with the red sash and red fez, he said that it was, but that "something special" had been wanted on this occasion.

Now and then there was a silence that nobody made any effort to relieve. It was as if you heard the leaders' minds ticking on either side of the table, each in brief solitary thought, using the meal hour to the utmost in order to put his thinking in better focus – each no doubt groping for some extra measure of inspiration, inventiveness or strategy to make his policy or interests acceptable to the other side, and also to his own colleagues and his own people. The rest of us gave the floor to the two central figures and made our conversations light and at times fragmented, so as not to miss anything that might take place at the centre. For small talk, Mordechai Hod, who had been Chief of the Israeli Air Force during the Six Day War, praised the use of Boeings for overnight cargo flights to Europe. Four Boeings had left Lod the previous night, he said, entirely filled with flowers for sale in the Christmas trade in Europe the next morning. At one point, President Carter was scheduled to call from Georgia to extend peace wishes on that Christmas Day. The two leaders went to the phone like twins to be greeted together, but spent despairing minutes shouting "*Allo!*" into an unresponsive instrument. Dayan mentioned the sound failure during the candidates' debate in the American presidential campaign of 1977 adding, "Imagine what would have been said if that had happened in Israel." It was a gallant apology for both Israeli and Egyptian telephones. Each of us had a printed menu, as is customary on state occasions. Its glossy cover was printed in delicate red and green arabesques, and when we got up from the table I took mine with me, because of the date and place printed on it. I even stooped to the level of a souvenir hunter and asked my ministerial neighbours to autograph their place cards, written in large, lush Arabic calligraphy.

After lunch, Aziza and I sat on the front lawn in wicker armchairs, and as we sipped more Turkish coffee, Abdin re-appeared. It turned out that he was one of eight chamberlains who made up the presidential cabinet. I spotted the "great chamberlain", head of them all, referred to now as Mr Teymour since the title of "pasha" had been abolished. His father had been chamberlain to King Farouk's father, Fuad, and he himself had served briefly under Farouk. Now, naturally, he was serving under President Sadat; he was dapper, grey-haired and courteous in his French phraseology.

Abdin said that a car was waiting to take me to my childhood home on the Place Champollion – its identity unknown to any officials until my arrival. They were all from Cairo, and I seemed to be more familiar with Ismailia than they were. Abdin kindly produced a sheet of one-piastre stamps with one hundred grey pictures of Ramses, like mini-Warhol duplications. That was all he could find for me, because the post office was not open. Nor were there any postcards to be had.

I had rehearsed to myself how I would ask the people living in the house to let me see the rooms that had belonged to each member of my family. I would look through the row of windows on to the garden, stand in front of the fireplace in the main sitting room, and stroll through the two kitchens (my mother kept a kosher household, and we'd had both a meat and a dairy kitchen). I would tell the people in the house not to worry if it was not at its tidiest. Would they reject my plea to enter? I doubted it. The Middle East takes pride in hospitality. How would I handle it all?

Accompanied by three security cars, I was driven to Place Champollion. A watchman was sitting on a stool near the front door of my old house. I saw that the key was in my security man's hands, and thought this a strange omen of ownership. I stepped in. Suddenly, a visual pallor blanked out my colourful expectations. Sandy rubble, flaking paint, floorless rooms, stones lying chaotically around − it was a place deprived of any human content. I wanted to gaze at the garden again from the upper floor, but I could not make any headway. Every inch of parquet was gone. A muted light suffused this scene of destruction. I was about to stand on tiptoe in order to see beyond the balustrade of the upper veranda, but there was no time for the mental command to pass from brain to toes. A grey brick house was now facing me across the gaping space. Where were the mango trees and the papayas? It was as if an unkind soul had projected some slides on those yellowed walls as a private illustration, to rub it in for me: confronting me was the damage of time and three wars. I remembered Proust's soaking of his madeleine in his herb tea and the unfolding to him, by association, of the world of his childhood and the memories of a secluded, intimate, genteel age. That experience was quite unlike this. Here my world was exposed, open, public. Soon, those who accompanied me became impatient and bored by the dilapidated walls. I walked out, and felt a dissolution of tenderness. I was no longer nostalgic; this new reality had superseded old memories.

It was 3.30 p.m. when we returned to the President's mansion. Reporters were gathered in the adjoining courtyard, as they had been all through the morning, photographing us through their zoom lenses, and looking like an international army of expectant fathers hoping to be able to give away cigars: they were naively waiting for peace to emerge. Aziza was leaving for Cairo. She, like me, had originally been told that the Israeli Mission would go back home the same evening, but it turned out that we would be in for a long day and night session.

The press took buses to Cairo to glimpse its night life and its souks, open now to Israelis for the first time in thirty years. Only the official party and two journalists stayed behind in the government guesthouse, which was once called La Résidence, and was the home of officials of the Compagnie Universelle du Canal Maritime de Suez – the company that had owned my childhood home. Comte de Serionne, *Agent Supérieur,* and two presidents of the Company, Marquis de Vogüe and M. François Charles-Roux, stayed only in the winter and spring, steering clear of hot weather. Now, red, white and black Egyptian flags coupled with navy-blue flags bearing the white emblem of the Suez Canal Authority, decorated the iron front gates.

At the corner of the building, we passed a wooden arch painted light blue and festooned with ropes of electric bulbs, one of many bedecking the city to hail the October victory in 1973 and the opening of the Canal by Sadat. Trumpeting victory minutes away from where we were staying seemed an anachronism, not to mention an odd form of hospitality; but counteracting it were big cutouts of white doves opposite the presidential residence, which were the first welcome signs we saw when we arrived. Across the street from the heavily guarded gates was the embankment of the Sweet Water Canal, running the length of the city and supplying drinking water to a population of perhaps a quarter of a million – a place I had known as a small town of fifteen thousand. Later, beyond the suspension bridge over this Canal, we discovered with great delight some arches bearing quotations in Hebrew under their Arabic text.

The Israeli leaders were no longer in sight. The legal people sat nearby, waiting for their hour. Every now and then one of the senior Israeli officers accompanying Begin would pass through the corridor with a rolled map in his hand. I remember sitting for what seemed an endless time in one or the other of two drawing rooms. They were extremely high-ceilinged, but cold if you were immobile, and contained oriental rugs, good but well worn, and marble-topped Louis XVI chests scattered about. There were parquet floors and walls panelled with plaster mouldings; ropes of crystal sparkled from a chandelier lit at the centre. In fact, it was mini-France except for a mashrabiya screen (a mashrabiya is a type of projecting oriel window enclosed in wooden lattice work) behind curved curtains separating the two drawing rooms. Pictures of Sadat were everywhere.

On the same side of the house as the two drawing rooms was a study with a small library containing nothing but French books, all of them about Egypt or the Canal. One book was immensely big, almost a metre square, lying flat. Moshe Dayan spotted it the next morning before we all left. He and I leafed through it together, with an Egyptian in attendance. It was dated 1818, and spelled Cairo in French, with a K: *le Kaire*. One of the obelisks was named "Cleopatra's Needle". A Colonel Jacobin, cartographer of Napoleon's Engineer Corps, had put the book together.

Among drawings of the Karnak and Memphis Pyramids were some bas-reliefs with processions of stylized figures, the central female figure presenting a mirror held up in front of her. The only telephone was in the study, and during the evening, in the middle of an electricity failure, the editor of *The Jerusalem Post* occupied himself by shouting to his correspondent at the Mena House, trying to overcome a bad connection. He was incensed at being the only newspaperman who had stayed in Ismailia – just in case. The power had gone off while I was looking at Ferdinand de

Lesseps' room – he was the nineteenth-century French diplomat who was responsible for the construction of the Suez Canal. Now maintained as a tiny museum behind the study, the room contained a steel bed with thick netting so dusty from age that it was brownish, dropping from a rectangular steel frame above and reminding me of my childhood and how we used to sleep under such mosquito nets.

In another small room were memorabilia of Europe: a needlepoint embroidery under glass on the wall, a white marble clock with Roman numerals, topped by a bronze bust of a woman with her head turned romantically sideways, perhaps a subconscious association with ancient Egyptian art in which faces were usually drawn in flat profile. There was a pair of decanters, card games based on Egyptian antiquities, knick-knacks and a Bible with both Old and New Testaments. De Lesseps' carriage was rather eerily displayed in a glass case on an elevation in the front garden.

The torch that had taken me through this bout of sightseeing was now dwindling, so I went back to the drawing room, hugging my coat in the dark, and feeling tired. Yet none of us who were waiting in the Antechamber of Peace permitted ourselves to leave the room. Our Egyptian guides were going to and fro, bringing in a portable Lux lamp and candlesticks. A little later, a young chamberlain appeared with gift-wrapped offerings to commemorate the state visit. He handed me a navy-blue velvet box with a card from Jihan Sadat. In it was a beautiful hand mirror. The back was silver *repoussé* in a lovely floral design, and the handle was a little silver peacock, like the knob of a lid. I knew I would treasure it forever.

It was 10.30 when the Prime Minister returned. All the members of Menachem Begin's official party were going to dine together. He was his courteous self in spite of a day's hard work and turning to me, he said "Madame," and offered his arm to escort me into the dining room. He went at such a brisk pace that

I thought for a moment I was being asked to dance a gavotte or a minuet. It pleased him to know that I was enjoying the experience and had been to my old home. At midnight he said he felt rather tired, and went to his room. We all dispersed: twenty-nine of us were accommodated in twenty-four rooms in La Résidence and in an adjoining guesthouse, with baths in which big, old fashioned tubs stood on squat, curved legs. The next morning we all filed through the front doors of our guest houses and thanked the staff, who had exerted themselves with great efficiency and speed within the short time between dinner and the distribution of rooms, co-operating with our security men in putting the name of each one of us on the appropriate door.

Our car procession was now moving in an order demanded by protocol towards our host for informal talks and farewells. When my turn came, President Sadat said, "Tell him [Abba] that from this minute he is invited to Egypt. You should both come to Upper Egypt." When I told him that Abba and I had been to Upper Egypt on our honeymoon, he said: "Well, it is time for a second one." I answered that if it did come about, it would be a honeymoon politically and personally. He laughed and wrote a dedication in Arabic on one of the green leather memo pads with the eagle crest that had been on the conference table.

Aziza and I went to the final press conference, in a Suez Canal Authority building. It took place in a huge room that contained magnificent oriental draperies with quilted geometrical designs of many colours on a red background. Inside were rows of oriental rugs, roses in their centre, and hundreds of chairs made from light wood. Above us, billowed long strips of red, blue and white material. Beside a table covered with green felt, stood the Egyptian flag and – for the first time – the Israeli flag. All the dignitaries of both sides sat in a row on the stage behind the two leaders: Begin, the author of *The Revolt*, and Sadat, the author of *Revolt on the Nile*, neither of them looking now like the revolutionary of his autobiography. The room was packed with over a thousand journalists, broadcasters, commentators and editors. I found it strange to recognize, among all the unfamiliar faces, the very familiar ones of Israeli newsmen whom I had seen at all the Israeli dramas – the wars, the Jarring missions, the Kissinger shuttles. Now they were here on Egyptian soil. They all filed by, doing obeisance to the microphones. Sadat exuded equanimity behind clouds of pipe smoke, and Begin glided over one of the questions like a seal. Some of the questions seemed designed more to provoke war than to accelerate peace and I made a mental record of what was said to tell my husband and friends back home. The last moments of the journey were devoted to a jaunt over the Pyramids – a hospitable farewell. When I landed at Ben-Gurion airport, fifty minutes later, I found that they had heard everything. Nevertheless, Menachem Begin had to be put through a second, almost identical press conference, and I wondered why – until I concluded that the way of saying it for domestic consumption was now in demand.

As I went home from the airport, I realized that my passport could not be used as a memento of my visit to Ismailia. It had been inspected but not stamped. Since there were no embassies then, there is no official record of my ever having arrived in Egypt or having left.

25

Anatomy of an election

The political events in our Labour Party on 15 June 1988 brought us into a new era. It was the first internal party election that adopted the new system of primaries, although the full primary system was not adopted until 1992. Some said it was the end of the idealistic period in the Labour Party's political tradition. The Party's aims were to "democratize" the process and to bring in new blood. Likewise, they also wanted to keep some known figures with both national and international experience. The new style was rough and impatient; young political candidates, unknown in Israel or in the world, sought to replace the experienced and renowned, before proving themselves. There was a taste of *Clockwork Orange* in the market place.

Abandoned by his colleagues to the rank and file of the 1,200 Central Committee members who had pushed for the new system for Israeli Party elections, Abba could not, surprisingly, make even the second round of ten candidates for the new Knesset list.

In a way, this brought full-circle the rejection of Abba Eban by the Party leadership that had begun in June 1974, when he was offered the junior post of Minister of Information in Yitzhak Rabin's first cabinet. After having been Foreign Minister for over eight years, Abba thought that this kind of appointment would be degrading and felt compelled to turn it down. As he aptly described it: "The function of becoming a spokesman for policies fashioned by others was a humiliation."

I wrote to my children and a few close friends on 22 June 1988 that, "even if I opted for using a facetious style, I would still be sad – and I am." Perhaps *The Jerusalem Post* best echoed the feelings of thousands that day:

> Abba Eban's crude ouster from Labor's [sic] Knesset list is perhaps just another macabre sign of the times. Israel, at a moment of grave crisis, has spurned the man who was its voice and its pride at its most exalted moments. And the Party which at last is confronting the dangers of deadlock, and adopting pragmatic policies of peace, has cast out the statesman who consistently warned of those dangers and urged (perhaps too meekly) those policies for long, unheeded years. But Abba Eban is not a moshav secretary, nor a hawk, nor a Sephardi. He is merely the most renowned Israeli alive. So for Peres he was expendable.

The power game and party alignments had given way to the new supremacy of individual ambition; the public display of inner ambitions was no longer contained as when the selection was less within public view. Abba vacillated because the terms of the new system were not those he had chosen when answering the call of service to his people. They now consisted of a new set of rules. Though at first defined as "exploratory", after three such elections and surprising corruption in "the system", today there is a tendency in both leading parties to revert to selection committees that would uphold a better balance between new and experienced candidates. But in 1988 the new political creation, called "the change of the electoral system", aroused hopes, opposition and fascination with political trendiness, and drove politicians, some willingly and others unwillingly, to take a chance. The new system had been offered to our party by its Constitution Forum. Everybody was most curious about what the power brokers would magically bring on. For the public, it was a firework thrown into our Party's own political firmament, and like all fireworks, it was due to extinguish and fall until some new firework would rocket into the sky.

The weeks and months that preceded the dramatic night of the party primaries at the Ramat Efal Kibbutz Conference Centre were replete for us with contradictory thoughts and soul searching. In April, Abba knew he had to decide if he was going to be involved with the next election to the Knesset or back out.

We discussed it back and forth and the subject tormented us endlessly till the elections. Abba had always been so eager to participate in the top political strategies of the country. He had become accustomed to his record speaking for itself but now he seemed hesitant, and this was new to me. It was a very big decision to take; he was still leading Labour conceptually, writing and commenting in the media, and in the polls on the selection of Foreign Minister, he was still the most popular choice. To wilfully retire would seem as if he was inflicting upon himself his own political demise. Our discussions were close and frank, but I felt I had no right to influence him one way or another. How could I say "leave", when the next day a new constellation might open up. So we decided Abba would not make a bid for a ministerial post, for which there were limited possibilities with the government tied to a coalition. He would just run for Knesset as a listening post and framework for action.

There was a "sacred list" of seven that the leadership had "awarded" itself calling it "The List of the Exempted". However, this list did not include Abba, although in the last three national elections he had always been amongst the top candidates. Abba was left to fend for himself, unprotected, and at the mercy of the 1,200 Central Committee members of our party, which left him no time to stage a proper campaign.

At this point we were in New York and the Party sent an SOS that Abba had not registered and must do so right away. We returned home and he started mailing the Central Committee members, and meeting candidates. He now had to explain who he was – the "new boys" in the party had to be told.

Our fatal mistake was in not asking the question: "If the 'Seven Knights' are protected by their considered value to the Party, what is the value of Abba Eban?" Yet I think Abba was worried that temperamentally he would be unable to work with Rabin. He never said anything of the sort to me, but in retrospect I knew this was part of his hesitation.

The Rabin group was obviously working against Abba in order to dominate the Labour Party. There was a history: when Rabin was Defence Minister Abba had once questioned some of his "bone-breaking" policies against Palestinians during the first intifada. Abba, then Chairman of the Knesset Foreign Affairs and Defence Committee – he served in this capacity from 1984–8 – had also expressed reservations regarding Rabin's decision to go ahead with an incursion far into Lebanon, without consulting beforehand even the Prime Minister, Yitzhak Shamir, let alone the Foreign Minister, Shimon Peres. There was also Abba's startled reaction when Rabin mentioned his plan to bomb deep into Egypt at the Washington State Department and that the officials he had met "did not fall from their seats". There seemed to be some kind of diplomatic procedural incompatibility between Abba and Rabin, although in the waiting period before the Six Day War they had been united in their identical views.

Nevertheless, in the light of the much-proclaimed principle of "democratization", it seemed to Abba wrong to exclude himself from the process dictated to the rest of the candidates and place himself in an "exclusive" list. So we stayed as we were, hoping that Abba's well-proven abilities would work in his favour, as would the claims by leading members that the Party needed him. But we were soon to see how their praises wafted into thin air and the chicanery in party processes took over. Throughout all the years this had been Abba's personal drama within his Party. He was exploited much more than supported. Jealousy was always rampant, as it is in all politics, but it had been repressed when Israel's international position was in jeopardy and the country needed the force of his diplomacy, his projection of the nation's issues and his reverberating "voice". But now the Party meant to buttress Shimon Peres, Leader of the Labour Alignment Party.

The candidates to be graded were grouped into four lists of ten each. We had decided at home that if Abba was not elected with the first ten, he would leave the grading phase and not proceed further in running for the Knesset. But when, on that fateful night, he did not make the first round on account of political deals, the disbelief was such that the editor of the largest circulation afternoon paper *Yedioth Ahronoth*, Dov Judkovsky, sitting close by, whispered to me in a French idiom, lest those nearby understood: "You have been through a bad quarter of an hour. Abba *must* run again in the second round."

At that point we were beset by the world's media. People pushed against us ruthlessly, whilst I really wanted to ask the caring editor "*Pourquoi?*" He pre-empted me and said in an astounded tone: "They made such a gaffe, they will feel guilty and will vote for him now. He *must* run!"

There was only half an hour between the result of the vote of the first ten – and running again. The head of the Haifa Trade Unions, accompanied by his Mayor Arie Gurel, was standing by, and begged and pleaded that Abba continue in the race. They promised the backing of the whole Haifa contingent who were on the premises. When I questioned, "How can you do it technically – time is so short?" he answered, "Leave it to us, our group will be under instructions." Instructions come from ministers and from the heads of the party in the major districts. The head of the Party's Jerusalem branch was led by a hawk, Immanuel Zissman, who was running for the first time and who had, in deference to Abba's prestige, promised that Jerusalem would back him.

Unknown people around us shouted: "Abba run. Abba run – please run! Nobody has dropped out, you must continue." We were dazed. Abba wanted to consult Aharon Harel, an ex-M.K., a supposed friend, the head of our supporters, and director of the Bet-Berl College of which Abba was the chairman.

The college was founded in 1949 initially for training Mapai cadres. It aspired to be a "Kibbutz university" and in 1987 it gained full recognition as a higher academic institution. Harel had not been seen on the premises all morning or, more vitally for us, in the afternoon before the vote. We kept asking for him but to no avail. Two days earlier he had been appointed head of the Broadcasting Authority where, we were told, he was organising a reshuffle of the radio staff and was threatened by a strike. He was very pleased with himself and with the telephone in his car (the new status symbol in Israel). Perhaps the telephone in our car should have co-ordinated votes with the telephone in his car! Harel, the head of our campaign, never delegated the responsibility of our campaign strategy to anyone, or sent a message; he just defaulted.

The kibbutz movement, once the epitome of democracy, acted openly in advocating "deals". They were frank and shameless about it, stating that expediency *must* come first. There was no democratic voting and we were suddenly alone in the crowd.

Ex-Chief of Staff General Chaim Bar Lev was also in great danger of not being elected, but Ezer Weizman's number two, Eliezer Ben-Eliezer, known as Fouad, took command and bulldozed the Party to vote for Bar Lev. It only illustrates that had the Party willed it, the same could have been done for Abba.

Among the assistants and advisers in our campaign there was no great enthusiasm for Abba to risk running for the second ten. Abba himself figured out that with all those who dropped from the list of the first ten to the second, it was going to be an even greater struggle. He was still reluctant, but the people around us continued to holler "run, run, run".

I could hardly breathe. Abba and I consulted each other… there were only a few minutes left. Between our faces there were only inches, but it felt as if thousands were crowding there. Neither Shimon Peres nor the secretary of our Party, Uzi Baram, (who was laid up with lumbago) appeared to advise us. In spite of Peres's later statements that he had supposedly given instructions to help Abba we never saw any indication that this was so. In fact, Peres was working for five other candidates – suddenly it was realized that there were not enough Moroccans on the list and Peres went around pushing their names in front of the Party members, coaxing them to vote for his protégés.

Abba and I were suddenly so much on our own. I remembered what Dov Judkovsky had said: "You have been through a bad quarter of an hour." Now, only seconds were left for the final decision. We turned to each other again for the right answer. Could there be a *right* answer at such a point, or just an answer? I realized in a flash that the gamble of success, or the risk of failure, were so contiguous to the terrible preceding moments. Why not go along with the supplications and shouts around us? I sensed that we were coming to a fatal conclusion yet, oddly, I thought we should risk trying again; in retrospect I wonder from what political or sub-conscious instinct did that decision derive, when all in all I just wanted to have it all behind us.

My feeling was that if the whole episode was a political loss it was also a moral triumph. Had Abba not run for the second round, every Party member would have made us feel responsible for the way things turned out. Besides the disappointed hundreds who had begged him to run, there would have been hundreds more who would have called or written to say "You spoiled it for yourself, you were not a sport, who cares if you were in the first or second ten. The main thing was to get in. *We* would have got you in, all of us, and at the top of the list too."

I can hear it so clearly, even in their intonation and style. The leadership failed us in showing the minimal solidarity expected for longstanding colleagues. Our public understood it and felt a great revulsion. There was a vast expression of shock across Israel and the world, but a few hundred Party members decided the issue otherwise. Abba would comment later: "I don't regret that I went for the second round, otherwise people would have said that because of prestige or pride I missed the opportunity. This way I am more at peace."

After he was relegated to eighteenth place in the voting of the second group of ten and decided to quit the Party, Shimon Peres paid some lip-service to Abba's defeat so it not be said that he shed crocodile tears. In a much publicized statement, he stated: "I terribly regret Abba Eban's defeat. He is a unique person with special talents. It is difficult for me to explain why he was not elected. The movement needs him and I am certain that we shall find a way to avail ourselves of his talents."

Immediately after the second "killer-vote" Abba decided we should leave the hall and go home for a while. There he wrote a letter to Shimon Peres.

Dear Shimon

I have been part of the Labour movement for many decades, through all its campaigns and struggles. During the course of a whole generation I have carried its banner and voiced its message throughout the Land and in the world and many took notice of what I said.

It is evident that I am incapable of carrying this banner the way I did in the past for the simple reason that the Party's leadership bodies have taken away this power from me and decided that others will bear this responsibility from now on, and according to the democratic rules their wish should be respected.

I congratulate with all my heart all those upon whom has been entrusted this responsibility and I wish them success in their words and deeds. As one who supported you in all the phases of leadership of the Labour Party, I hereby wish you special success in the days of the big challenges expected ahead – in the coming weeks.

Yours
Abba Eban

Of course the line that mattered most in this letter was the reminder, in the last paragraph, "As one who supported you in all phases of leadership of the Labour Party…"

We came back later, once at 11.30 p.m. for the third round of votes and then at 2.00 a.m. for the fourth and last vote, to support the candidates of each group who had been our supporters. They first stared at us in disbelief and then all looked down in shame.

The next day Teddy Kollek, the Mayor of Jerusalem, not mincing his words, pronounced with typical frankness:

> What was done to Eban is a historical mistake. I really cry.
> A Party that does not understand what a treasure it has and shows such disregard this way, has a problem. It is also a grave mistake in relation to the Jewish people in the world. The Labour Party will still pay dearly for it. It is too great a luxury to give up a man like Abba Eban.

The following words from one of Israel's leading poets, Chaim Guri, who was close to Rabin from the days of the War of Independence and who always belonged to a different political camp from Abba, still touch me very deeply as I re-read them today, years after the traumatic event in our life:

> The expression on Abba Eban's face when he learnt the outcome of the vote. His wife's expression. Their sadness – they, who have stepped down from their greatness. Their alienation within a different public, in a different era.
> What a sense of "it's a pity" in the air, as they are now

confronted by the public's abandonment of him as they by-passed him. Such anger at the injured dignity of the man to whom we are so deeply indebted. And the public bewilderment at the erroneous considerations of the mass that judged and voted.

The voice of Teddy Kollek, "his elder brother" – of the same generation, in the morning radio commentary, his cry of astonishment that Eban had continued to stand for the Party nomination, although he was not included in the first elected ten. He, Teddy, would not have done this.

Yet, years later, although Teddy Kollek was advised not to run a seventh time for Mayor of Jerusalem, he still decided to run and lost.

I so understand Eban's heart that still wants "that", the belonging, the activity and the highly rated mission. And then, the misleading feeling that you are still wanted and that your "Scroll of Merits" will be a guarantee in the face of a threatening risk. Yes, I feel for him.

Eban now leaves the stage, accompanied by a storm of ovations. A great actor who has done his part and has been replaced. His parting letter is a masterpiece, but it does not conceal the pain and the bitterness.

I remember him in the summer of 1942, in his British officer's uniform, when he came from Cairo to the Palmach Camp in the Mishmar Ha'Emek forest. Aubrey Eban then .... The days are before El Alamein – the period of temporary co-operation between the Haganah and British Intelligence in the East. The days of plans for parachuting our people in to occupied Europe, and for activity behind enemy lines in the Middle East.

I saw in front of my eyes a whole life entirely in the service of the nation. I was filled with sadness that this stormy and revolutionary "Central Committee" that reflects now such a different reality, was not wise enough to understand that this man would be an asset to any party list.

The brilliant advocate, defending our people against the pressures of world opinion. The oratorical genius and the literary craftsman. A man of the spirit at its best. And perhaps, who knows, in the collective subconscious, his investigating and condemning stand in the Pollard Affair* was not forgiven.

An aristocrat. Even after so many years, he was sometimes considered an outsider. Different in his culture and his tongue. Somewhat out of place in the landscape. He once told me that had he been born in Degania or Kfar Tabor, his situation would have been different. But one can't say that he was discriminated against all his life. No, he is a true success story. Our Sages in their teachings to us have said that, "No person leaves this world with half his ambitions fulfilled." All the more so, when it relates to public activity and to politics.

It is a pity that we don't have a House of Lords. He would have found his honoured place there next to Yitzhak Ben-Aharon, Ya'acov Chazan and the other "giants". There he would have been able to continue making his orations that have graded him amongst the "First Ten" of the World's greatest orators in our generation. Millions would have placed him there. Abba Eban don't relent! Continue. Your admirers and your rivals accompany you with feelings of gratitude.

---

* Jonathan Pollard, a US citizen, was sentenced to life imprisonment in 1987 on a charge of selling military information to Israel. Abba's frank stance over what he dubbed "an anthology of blunders", and his naming of senior Labour Party Members, may explain why his name was relegated in the 1988 primaries.

The country was stunned. Countless people, friends and strangers alike, couldn't overcome a sense of hurt and disappointment at the humiliation inflicted on Abba by these shabby proceedings which soon became world news. Telephone calls were recieved at home from Canada, Australia, France, Germany, Switzerland, Norway and from friends in the USA and family in England. How did so many strangers suddenly have our private phone number? Cartoons repeated the theme of "Gulliver and the Lilliputians" or illustrated "the Exempted" in their tanks and Abba jettisoned in the sands – and more. Telegrams came from all over the world. A fellow from a remote village in Galilee walked two kilometres just to cry to me on the phone.

Abba saw himself as a political educator. He felt he had absorbed more systematized ways of decision-making, and was eager to impart his knowledge. In the aftermath, he was left with a deep yearning to be in a position where he would be allowed once again to turn things around in public opinion as he often did in moments of danger and great drama for Israel. Stripped of the world stage he became an individual too powerful conceptually to be re-absorbed willingly by the Labour establishment.

After years in which he was assigned vital tasks for Israel by our Party and nation he perhaps assumed that this might be so once again. But now it was a free-for-all. It was a different system and a different political culture – and although criticized, is still valid to this day. Abba had neither the Party ranks behind him nor the feel for a "personal" campaign. He thought he was still the product of the original system. He did not sit enough in smoke-filled rooms and then go out from there to make "deals".

26

The private years

In our life after politics, Abba and I travelled everywhere together, eager to enjoy each other's companionship and attention. Freedom enabled him to influence a much wider audience. He lectured, and wrote and made both the unique nine-part TV documentary series *Civilization and the Jews* and its follow-on *Personal Witness* about the peace process.

It took five years as the producer, Mark Segal, and other colleagues insisted that the documentary be filmed on site, with all text memorized and no prompter! The most difficult episode to film was the one on top of Mount Sinai (2,285m) where we landed on the helicopter pad of the Greek Orthodox Monastery of St Catherine's. The monks have lived there in isolation for centuries with provisions sent up in a basket at the end of a rope. As we, the descendants of the first custodians of the Jewish legacy, stood upon the site where Moses had received the Ten Commandments, I was strongly aware of the way in which we had been transported up the mountain from Tel Aviv a city of recent history, by modern technology – the hiatus in time.

I personally benefitted from the filming of this series as it was for me a lesson in Jewish history, from ancient times with a portrayal of its personalities and sights, to the beginnings of modern history with its figures, issues, achievements, and of course horrors, not that our history lacked grim episodes before our time, but nothing was even remotely comparable to the Holocaust.

While still a Member of Knesset and Chairman of its Foreign

Affairs and Defence Committee, Abba was invited to Cairo by Boutros Boutros-Ghali and his wife as part of a delegation of leaders from the Israeli Labour Party and I travelled with him. Mrs Ghali's hospitality was impeccable but she was cautious and restrained. Boutros-Ghali later came on an official visit to Israel as the guest of Moshe Dayan, then Foreign Minister. We had dinner at the Dayans' home with just Dayan's second wife Rachel, Yigael Yadin and Boutros Boutros-Ghali. Dayan gave us a detailed tour of the extraordinary antiquities he had dug out with the assistance of borrowed heavy military equipment. Within earshot, Yadin, in a kind of military directness, took us all by surprise by commenting, "That is why he lost the Yom Kippur War!"

His was a unique collection: if Ben-Gurion had had the taste of a passionate bibliophile, Dayan was a great self-made archeologist. He would patiently and lovingly restore broken shards to their original form, almost as if his affinity for ancient history was in itself some unique gene in his constitution. It was impressive to find an amateur with such expertise, fortunate in his discoveries, and successful in bringing them carefully up from the sands with the help of only a couple of Bedouins. What a moment it must have been, every time!

The ordinary citizens did not always approve of the process of search and discovery when the army was used for Dayan's own pursuits. Teddy Kollek understood the danger of a personal stigma and intervened on behalf of "his" beloved Israel Museum created in the 1950s. The result was that the collection was bought by the late Larry Tisch, a renowned financial figure, benefactor and CEO of CBS television, and donated to the Israel Museum. It is a fabulous asset not only for the museum but for the country and the world.

After the peace treaty with Jordan was signed on 26 October 1994, King Hussein and Queen Noor invited us to Amman for a private lunch. This informal invitation was very unlike the seven or eight secret meetings which the King and Abba had held at sea off the port of Aqaba, directly across from Eilat; or in a dentist's clinic in London. For some of these meetings, Abba was accompanied by the Director of Prime Minister Ben-Gurion's office, Yaacov Herzog (brother of Chaim Herzog, the eighth President of Israel between 1983-93). Yaacov Herzog, a Jewish scholar with a Rabbinical degree, felt more at home on the diplomatic scene. He was an impeccably loyal civil servant, a very able diplomat, and was extremely close to Ben-Gurion. During later encounters with the King, Abba went with other specially assigned intelligence officials. Our visit to Amman was a bridge over three wars between Israel and Jordan and over the secret diplomatic discussions where King Hussein, really eager for a peace agreement, had first said to Abba that since he was not the most powerful of all the Arab states he could not be the first to lead a peace process. But now, in Amman, they were moving openly on the chessboard of Israeli-Jordanion relations, not with a perspective on the past but in the spirit of a new way of thinking about the future. The Israeli journalist who accompanied us had been admitted to the court garden and was outside waiting to take photographs. The diplomatic "underground" years were not even talked about. The European butler was in the room, and I remember wondering whether the other staff in attendance were intelligence or security. Everyone was very relaxed, yet each one of us was using the time as best they could for their national interests.

A political talk between the King and Abba preceded the lunch. The Queen, who was pregnant, had sat with me separately and told me about her interest in creating a cancer hospital on the frontier area between our two countries.

Lunch at the round dining table was surprisingly served in the very characteristic Jerusalem pottery, which is so decorative and colourful and was cleverly put together, just like the Russian wooden babushka who, once opened, keeps producing ever-smaller replicas of herself in differently coloured designs: as every course was cleared, the serving plates kept getting larger. It was all rather charming and almost game-like. Although obviously specially ordered, this kind of crockery has been produced since the Balians, an Armenian family, founded their pottery in the Old City of Jerusalem. This delightfully informal visit centred on two pioneers who had dared seek a peace accommodation for their two nations way before the Peace Treaty.

We were invited to Jordan again, but this time to the grander "official" palace, and in a different guise. Abba came to interview the King for his TV series about the peace process. This time I was merely part of the team but it was the waiting that was so interesting. The King was preoccupied that morning by some health problem in the family and kept being delayed. We were brought into the main boardroom where the King held State consultations. A vast table and well-cushioned chairs occupied the whole length of the room, while the walls were covered with an equally lengthy row of elegant portraits of royal (male) ancestors. All the portraits were the same size, the black robes worn by their subjects were identical and each one had an *agal* and *kefieh* on his head. In an adjoining room there was a portrait of King Hussein's grandfather, Emir (later King) Abdullah, who had been assassinated at the Dome of the Rock on 20 July 1951.

The presence of these portraits seemed to me to reflect an Anglicized Arabism. The Circassian guards standing at specific spots in the adjoining room were dressed in Circassian uniforms of a subtly iridescent midnight-blue silk with gold braid on the cuffs and at the waistline, with the traditional scimitars handy at their waists. The little cups of coffee passed around ever so frequently throughout the morning had a marvellous fragrance, as if the bean had just been ground. We stayed for several hours, fortified by delicious sandwiches and other snacks and later went to the most frequented café in Amman (empty because of security) to eat oriental pastries. I left for home with two huge bottles of rose water. Abba followed soon after, returning to Israel by the same route.

I recall another wonderful memory: Abba and I took a cruise along the Mediterranean coast of which the greatest experience was passing through the Bosphorus Straits towards exotic Istanbul, and the port of Constanza in Ceausescu's Romania. There the food in an old royal palace-turned-hotel was too terrible for words and at every step in the street moneylenders pestered us to change dollars. In Istanbul I was plunged back into the old exotic Middle East so familiar to me from my childhood and adolescence. The Sultan's Palace was dazzling and I was quite taken by the fact that the women outside were all dressed in European fashions while we inside were being shown the location of the harem.

In 1995, while living in New York during the academic year, we set out twice a week for George Washington University in Washington, DC where Abba gave a series of twenty-six lectures to postgraduates of the Elliot School of International Affairs. The President of the University, Stephen Joel Trachtenberg, made us feel most welcome and housed us in a re-decorated old red-brick house on the campus. After we left, a plaque was put up in Abba's honour and the building was named "The Abba Eban Building".

Then, gradually, after such an extraordinary life together, things became hard for us. Abba fell off a platform in California after delivering a speech to an overflow audience and broke his thighbone. He had to be operated on that very same night. I was in New York at the time, preparing for our trip to Aberdeen University where he was to receive an honorary doctorate but when the orthopaedic surgeon, who happened to be in the audience at the time of the accident, called me with the news, I flew out to San Francisco on the first available flight. Abba recovered but various ailments soon started invading his life. He felt he had accomplished all he could abroad and asked that we return home to Herzlia, to the house we had built in 1961, which we loved for its spaciousness, its individual character and its garden, which had a lawn in the front and flowers in the back.

Both Eli and Gila helped with winding things up at the apartment we had rented for the last several years as a New York base. Located inside the Delmonico Hotel on Park Avenue and 59th Street next to the old Christie's auction house it had a combination sitting room/dining room, a master bedroom and an office for Abba. The landlady, Sara Korein, an incredibly able businesswoman, was the owner of several buildings in Manhattan. She was welcoming, very loyal and considerate, and kept a caring and watchful eye over us.

Abba's mind remained clear for quite a while and he kept his hair to the end, even though it turned completely white, but he gradually lost his power of speech. He was aware of this and was in great anguish about what was for him the ultimate irony of his life. Occasionally, I would invite friends to come and lunch with us which he liked at first, but later, as he became more impaired, he always asked me to cancel these arrangements. In the spring of 2002, he was hospitalized with pneumonia and the press fell upon the hospital, thinking he was going to die. I was allowed to stay in his room overnight so as to protect his privacy, which was a great help for both of us. Despite the press's dire prognostications, Abba recovered within a week and we returned home to our beloved Herzlia.

Once home, I made a point every afternoon after lunch to take a rest with Abba in his bedroom – which we had converted from his study – and I read to him. Every morning after breakfast somebody would read the daily newspapers to him so that he would be continually informed of political events. He looked forward to these sessions eagerly. Within a few months, he again came down with pneumonia. He was hospitalized, and this time the doctors were less optimistic. Eli came from Indiana to be with me when we knew the end was close. He arrived in time for his father to register his presence; Abba tried to lift his hands to hug Eli but he couldn't fully raise his arms.

The following scene has remained engraved in my mind: on Thursday, 17 November 2002, Abba gave two big sighs and returned his soul to his creator. His wonderful doctor, Professor Garty, and the director of the hospital, Professor Oppenheimer, co-ordinated to give us time to get home in order to avoid the press and protect our privacy. Professor Oppenheimer then made an announcement to the press on our behalf.

As is customary in Jewish tradition, the funeral had to be held the next day, Friday, because of the coming Shabbat. There was an official ceremony at the Herzlia War Memorial (Beit Yad LaBanim) attended by the President, Members of Knesset, ministers, members of the Diplomatic Corps, the Mayor of Herzlia and many other dignitaries, family and friends. The President Moshe Katsav, Shimon Peres, Isaac Herzog (my nephew), the Dean of the Diplomatic Corps and the Mayor of Herzlia Mrs Yael German delivered eulogies. At the burial site in Kfar Shmaryahu, the Ashkenazi Chief Rabbi, Meyer Lau, spoke most movingly about Abba, the politician and the man.

I returned home to widowhood and to life alone in the house Abba had loved – yet how much more had he loved the world of political thinking and knowledge, our small and precious country, his original dream that brought us together, the dream of the European Community and the growing movement of globalization. The great challenges of the modern world were paramount in his life. He had lived within his own code of ethics, expecting the same in others, which in politics had not served him well. Nevertheless, he left an impressive legacy and is often mentioned as the "Legendary Abba Eban". This relates to his unique formulations, his languages, his force in debate, his irony, sarcasm, and humour.

As I look back, the years divide themselves for me into two phases of our history. I have given them a prominent place in my life and have relived much of those years through my writing. I have tried in the first part to portray how we started with an ideology which was a very clear belief in classical, historical Zionism. Its basis was a sense of moral justice, doubly strong after the revelations of the Holocaust, and of total dedication, hard physical work and the right to a Jewish State in this ancestral home. This view was the central core of Abba's life and mine: many other possibilities may have comfortably absorbed us but Zionism surpassed them. We paid a heavy price for this total merging into this political reality.

In the second period of my life, I found, sadly, that our classical Zionism was viewed with a question mark by both Israelis and the world. In this time of post-Zionism, ethical, moral and material values have changed so drastically. The departure from the old values and from constant anxieties, uncertainties and loss of life have brought about a desire for ideological revision. But these ideologies seem to have nowhere to go as Israel accelerates towards modern western mentalities, values and a breathless pace of development, without a partner. From a socialist, quite homogeneous state, yet one in which pluralism was the dominant social factor, a strong polarization between right and left now grips us and remains entrenched in the various social entities that make up Israel. We are strongly united by the Israeli experience of togetherness as shown by the exemplary civil population during the Second Lebanese War in 2006 (albeit with a deficient emergency infra-structure), and at the same time we find ourselves again and again divided as to how to deal with three levels of Arab proximity: the Israeli Arabs, those of the neighbouring territories, and those who wish to see the region in a single monolithic way (though not Arab, Iran is a major player in the Middle East). I dare not count how many factions we have today in our Knesset, but at least we have a democratic system.

I feel sad and disappointed that Israel still does not have proper frontiers, nor will she have them for a while in spite of the tremendous diplomatic successes reached with Egypt and Jordan. It is clear to me that Abba's story and mine, which took place over a span of forty years, is already history. Our story is definitely a chapter in the annals of the State of Israel, perhaps one of the cornerstones of Israel's existence. I have immersed myself in this historical epic all my life and have felt the need to tell it now from my individual perspective. For better or for worse, this was Abba's and my reality as I saw it. This is how we handled our life from within the profound belief we had in the path we chose.

Abba and I chose to live in Israel. We continued in our intense identification with Israel's every step and in keeping our inner spiritual affinity with our people. Abba mentioned in one of his writings that our people, throughout the centuries, have had this dual necessity of, on the one hand returning to their roots, and on the other immersing themselves in the trends of the wide world. And yet we as a family have remained with our strong early beliefs, our attachments and our unceasing concern for our country. Ideals and ideas that one has fought for have a continuity of their own. One goes on living with them and caring no less about them, as life moves us from one historical period to the next.

After Abba died, memorials followed over the years. I place each of them in my heart as I often remember them. The Ministry of Foreign Affairs had been for many years our second home, and Tzipi Livni, the Minister at the time of writing, acknowledged that Abba had played a special role in establishing the foundation of Israeli diplomacy on which today's diplomacy is still based. The occasions had a special depth, by which one felt that Abba Eban's legacy is very much alive today, "within the walls of the Ministry" as Tzipi Livni formulated it. Abba endowed the Israeli nation with the foundations on which to continue its mission both at home and in a newly globalized world.

I continue to have spells of wonderment – and also anxieties – about Israel's inborn fragility, powerful as she may be. We remain the few among the many. Like individuals, countries too have their specific characteristics. It will always feel special to me to have lived and played my part in Israel's story. I still cast a loving eye on her green and modern allure, her deserts and rocks, her touchingly narrow rivers, and the vastly consoling Mediterranean giving the country breadth, depth and a sense of space. I am ambitious for Israel. I keep hope for her wisdom and liberties and trust she can keep a careful balance in a vast, fast-moving world.